The Power of
Gender in Religion

The Power of
Gender in Religion

Edited by

Georgie Ann Weatherby
Gonzaga University

Susan A. Farrell
Kingsborough Community College

The McGraw-Hill Companies, Inc.
College Custom Series

New York St. Louis San Francisco Auckland Bogotá
Caracas Lisbon London Madrid Mexico Milan Montreal
New Delhi Paris San Juan Singapore Sydney Tokyo Toronto

McGraw-Hill's **College Custom Series** consists of products that are produced from camera-ready copy. Peer review, class testing, and accuracy are primarily the responsibility of the author(s).

McGraw·Hill

A Division of The McGraw·Hill Companies

THE POWER OF GENDER IN RELIGION

3 4 5 6 7 8 9 NET/NET 09 08 07 06 05

ISBN 0-07-021768-8

Editor: M.A. Hollander
Cover Design: Lauren K. Adair
Printer/Binder: HAMCO/NETPUB Corporation

TABLE OF CONTENTS

INTRODUCTION

Understandings, definitions, and interpretations of gender are an integrated part of most religious traditions. Creation stories, rituals, spirituality, and ethics reflect each religious tradition's view of how women and men relate to each, to their faith, and to their God (Atkinson, Buchanan and Miles 1985; Bynum, Harrell and Richman 1986; Erickson 1993; Ruether 1974; Ruether and McLaughlin 1979; Sanday [1981], 1987; Sharma 1994). This interplay between gender and religion has been examined periodically in recent years from a variety of perspectives. However, the fresh, diverse sociological approach provided by the following set of papers deserves special attention. Most of the papers were originally presented at the 1995 Annual Meeting of the Society for the Scientific Study of Religion. Organized in sessions put together by Georgie Ann Weatherby, these essays, as well as tow additional papers by Karpathakis and Lummis, help to chronicle the progress made in our understanding of the power (both latent and manifest) of gender in religion.

Gender can be a powerful agent for change even as it has been used to maintain traditional gender roles in society and religion. The socio-historical approach in some of the papers included in this reader clarifies how much understandings of gender changed and continue to change in religious traditions. Mirroring changes in the larger culture, religious traditions respond in various ways to the transformed roles of women and men in society. We can see how religious traditions responded to challenges to traditional gender roles and how far each tradition changed or accommodated challenges to their structure, rituals, and ethics. Papers detailing contemporary struggles and challenges to patriarchal religious authorities illustrate how far we still are from egalitarian institutions, religious practices, spirituality, and ethics.

Although not every religious tradition is included, the essays in this reader provide excellent examples of various research methods. These methods and research designs can be used for understanding gender and power in any religious tradition. Many of the essays use some comparative data and refer to a variety of religious traditions even as they focus on one particular religious group or organization. From surveys and questionnaires to content analysis and application of feminist theoretical paradigms, the researchers give us the tools with which to understand the importance of the power of gender in religion. Thoughtful analyses of and reflection on gender issues and the way power is used or misused in religion create fruitful areas for exploration. We hope that these essays provide new insights into the interplay of gender, religious beliefs, practices, and ethics as well as inspiring continued research in the field.

Georgie Ann Weatherby
Gonzaga University
Spokane, Washington

Susan A. Farrell
Kingsborough Community College
City University of New York

References

Atkinson, Clarissa W., Constance H. Buchanan, and Margaret R. Miles, eds. 1985. *Immaculate & Powerful: The Female in Sacred Image and Social Reality*. Boston: Beacon.

Bynum, Caroline, Stevan Harrell, and Paula Richman, eds. 1986. *Gender and Religion: On the Complexity of Symbols*. Boston: Beacon.

Erickson, Victoria Lee. 1993. *Where Silence Speaks: Feminism Social Theory and Religion*. Minneapolis, MN: Fortress Press.

Ruether, Rosemary Radford, ed. 1974. *Religion and Sexism: Images of Woman in the Jewish and Christian Traditions*. New York: Simon & Schuster.

Ruether, Rosemary Radford and Eleanor McLaughlin, eds. 1979. *Women of Spirit: Female Leadership in the Jewish and Christian Traditions*. New York: Simon & Schuster.

Sanday, Peggy Reeves. [1981], 1987. *Female Power and Male Dominance: On the Origins of Sexual Inequality*. New York: Cambridge University Press.

Sharma, Arvind, ed. 1994. *Today's Woman in World Religions*. Albany, NY: State University of New York Press.

The editors of this volume would like to thank Margaret Hollander and Rose Arlia and the McGraw-Hill production team whose enthusiastic support made this book possible.

EQUALITY AND THE GENDER ISSUE IN TRADITIONAL AND MODERN JUDAISM

Régine Azria

Centre d'Etudes Interdisciplinaires des Faits Religious
EHESS-CNRS (Paris)

Abstract

In spite of the diversity of its approaches, the Jewish tradition is basically to be considered as a source of inequality between men and women. In her paper, the author analyses issues related to gender and equality in traditional and contemporary Judaism, as seen from both sides, Judaism and women.

Firstly, she shows the variety of women's representations one finds in Jewish Scriptures and traditions (biblical, mystical, demonological, talmudic-rabbinical); then, she lists the diverse, yet complementary, attitudes to women of the main-line rabbinical tradition. Thirdly, she identifies and analyzes four types of Jewish women's attitudes to Jewish tradition and to modernity : the secular attitude; the modern reformed attitude; the feminist orthodox attitude and the non-feminist orthodox attitude. She concludes that even though most contemporary Jewish women are deeply attached to it, equality is not necessarily a taken for granted positive value for all of them.

The questions I would like to raise in this paper are as follows :

1. Firstly, is Jewish tradition to be considered as a source of inequality between men and women? Why and to what extent?

2. Secondly and most important for us here whatever the answer to the previous question, to what extent is this issue relevant today to women spontaneously committing themselves to traditional Judaism?

One may take for granted that discourses, representations and the very functioning of Jewish tradition did and still do constitute in some cases, an obstacle to the full achievement of sexual equality at least according to Western standards of equality. But such a brief statement is inadequate. It has no demonstrative significance and it does not focus on the main point, that is to say on the ways Jewish women have articulated their Jewishness together with their claims to equality.

To be demonstrative one has to start from the grass-roots and consider the very sources of Jewish tradition. One notices then that traditional Jewish views on men and women have been highly differentiated from the start and rest on basically non-egalitarian grounds. This differential treatment is as old as Judaism. It goes back to the times when gender relations were associated with a patriarcal system.

Actually traditional Jewish scholars have always been concerned with gender issues, especially with purity and sexual issues. They considered them as central to religious and social life. This is why rabbis kept on elaborating them during the whole talmudic period and more. To illustrate this constant attention, let's mention the Talmud itself which devotes a whole treaty to these matters, the treaty called *nashim*, "women".

And what about equality? Of course, women themselves were never requested to give their own opinion at the time, nor were they ever invited to participate in rabbinical discussions. The whole system then rested exclusively on the sole male point of view. As a matter of fact and on the whole, gender equality was not yet a relevant issue in pre-modern times. It didn't mean anything to people.

Nowadays, this issue is relevant in so far as this traditional way of putting things is still operative, even in democratic modern societies where it interferes with the everyday life of individuals, whether they like it or not. In Israel for instance and as far as Jews are concerned, marriage, divorce and related matters are regulated according to talmudic law.

As far as I know, all or most religious traditions were concerned with men and women's rights and duties. All of them selected the tasks and responsibilities respectively assigned to men and women. The central issue at stake here is precisely that modernity (whatever the ambiguities of the notion and the critical approach one may have to it) hardly accepts or takes for granted these traditionally assigned rights and duties. It considers them as archaic and unfair to women. It sees them as an impediment to women's self-realisation, to their access to freedom and autonomy of action and expression. Hence, potential conflict may arise between Jewish tradition and modernity. But on the other hand, some Jewish women are very critical about modernity and choose to turn back to tradition, as we shall see.

These first statements need further development. Those of you who already know about Jewish tradition, please bear in mind that the functioning of its law-system, the *halakhah*, is more flexible and potentially open-minded than one might expect at first sight. In spite of its claim for a transcendent origin, to which it owes its legitimacy, the Law of the Torah is neither homogenous nor invariable. Since its very beginnings it has permanently been reshaped according to the spirit and needs of the time.

Moreover, if one agrees that pragmatism takes its part, side by side with principles, in the functioning of any legal system, one may assume, without drifting into functionalism, that one of the primary functions of Jewish Law was to find the appropriate answers which would conciliate the spirit of the revealed tradition with newcoming questions. In other words, as divine and unchanging as it may be, the Torah law ought to develop and adapt during the course of history.

The task of Jewish lawyers was to help people to live with and according to the Torah rather than to compel them to strive against it. They had to know how to best articulate, without compromising nor denying themselves, the constraints due to the observance of religious prescriptions on the one hand and those due to the requirements of everyday life on the other. Most often, they would find a pragmatic solution.

Today, the adaptability and flexibility of Jewish Law is still unaffected. As an example, let's consider the attitude of religious authorities with regard to scientific and technological advances in fields such as genetics or medically aided procreation. Their openness and case-by-case capacity to adjust and legislate is quite remarkable. In most cases, the solution depends mainly on the religious orientation of the lawyer and on his readiness to interpret the law in a more progressive and adaptative direction or in a more conservative one.

Besides, in spite of the rigorousness of its juridical apparatus, Jewish tradition did not generate a society and a way of life oppressive to women. No Jewish law compels Jewish women to hide behind a veil or a scarf; no Jewish law keeps them in confinement or dooms them to silence and passivity. Jewish women didn't wait for their civil emancipation to go out of their homes, work outdoors and participate in economic. cultural and social life.

Actually, women are very present on the scene of Jewish life. But one has to carefully observe the kind of a presence it is. So, let's have a closer look and see firstly what Jewish tradition says. Then, we shall consider the ways Jewish women reacted to it, how they accepted or refused their own image as drawn by Jewish tradition. In a last part, I'll suggest an ideal-typical range of Jewish women's attitudes towards Jewish tradition on the one hand and towards modernity and secularized societies on the other.

I. Representations of Women in Jewish Scriptures and Traditions

Jewish religious scholars may be compared to their Christian counterparts, those theologians who, while refering to Jesus's life, stress the fact that Jesus chose his apostles exclusively among men in order to legitimize their own conservative positions with regard to gender issues. Having a similar purpose in mind, one may assume that, similarly, rabbis selected among legendary traditions in order to choose authoritative references. Thus, selected referential images of men and women progressively emerged from these age-old memories and traditions until they finally became the very norm. Up to now, Jewish tradition still functions according to these normative references.[1]

Hence, going back to the Scriptures seems unavoidable. In spite of the fact that the gender issue is, by its very nature, a modern issue related to a modern set of values and problematics, it is impossible to consider it without turning back to scriptural traditions. This is necessary to us as social scientists not so much due to the contents of the scriptures themselves as due to the social effects of their multi-levelled readings on Jewish individuals and groups. Moreover, we should not forget once again that up to now, the legitimacy of certain attitudes and behaviors is still referred to their compatibility with these authoritative norms.

Now, if we take a closer look we cannot but be amazed by the ambivalence and ambiguities of women's representations both in the Bible (written tradition) and in the Talmud (oral tradition), both in the midrash (homiletic tradition) and in the kabbalah (mystical esoteric tradition), both in their normative (halakhah) and in their legendary (hagadah) aspects. Traditional views on women are certainly not as coherent as one would have expected. Thus, one has to keep in mind that beyond the dominant view, other opinions do also exist and have their importance.

A. There is no need to be a biblical expert to know that Genesis narratives of the Creation are far from presenting a coherent description of the first human couple.

As you know, two rather contradictory narratives are proposed to the Bible reader. Which raises numerous questions, not only to theologians but also to social scientists concerned with their socio-cultural impact. According to the first narrative the first human couple is described as an androgynous couple, or to put it another way, as a male/female false-twin couple.

"So God created man in his *own* image, in the image of God created he him; male and female created he them". (Gen. I, 27, Authorized King James version)

From this description one could logically conclude an egalitarian conception as no one takes precedence over the other.

But a second narrative follows immediately in chapter II and blurs the whole picture. It gives a different scenario where man is created first.

"And the Lord God formed man *of* the dust of the ground, and breathed into his nostrils the breath of life; and man became a living soul." (Gen. II, 7)

And woman comes second, after quite a while, shaped out of the rib of her fellow-man :

"And the Lord God caused a deep sleep to fall upon Adam, and he slept : and he took one of his ribs, and closed up the flesh instead thereof;"

"And the rib which the Lord God had taken from man, made he a woman, and brought her unto the man."

"And Adam said, This *is* now bone of my bones, and flesh of my flesh : she shall be called Woman, because she was taken out of Man." (Gen. II, 21-23)

According to this version the female creature is no longer equal to the male creature for at least three immediate reasons: 1) she comes chronologically second; 2) She is not godly oriented: she is not brought to life through a godly "breath of life". There is no mention either of her being inhabited with a living soul; 3) By her very nature, she is dependent on man.

B. Mystical tradition is ambivalent too in this regard. Despite its fondness for romantic images of a bride/groom couple where God plays the part of the groom and Israel that of the loving and beloved bride, this tradition produces also a feminine God, a loving, comforting, immanent God, the *shekhinah*, the "Presence", a God staying close to its suffering people in its worldwide wanderings. This representation of God contrasts sharply with the transcendent, authoritarian, masculine other God.

C. Jewish demonology is far less ambivalent, when giving the myth of Lilith a central place. Lilith, the First Eve, is a central figure in the Jewish pantheon of evil creatures. With Lilith, woman, generally speaking, is placed on the dark side. She evokes transgression, temptation, seduction, corruption, death, instinct, evil inclinations; in other words nature opposed to culture, the latter being assumed by man.

Why such a disgrace? Legendary narratives explain it and take us back to our starting point: the equality issue. According to some legendary traditions, our primordial female ancestor Lilith wanted to be on equal terms with Adam. She let him know it by refusing to lie under him during their sexual intercourse. In doing so, she was actually expressing something more: she expressed her refusal to submit to what was supposed to be the "natural order of the world." Therewith she was introducing confusion into the world.

Lilith's myth has most probably been used as a dissuasive example addressed to women likely to question their own rank and status. For Lilith was severely punished: on the one hand, she was expelled from main-line tradition, she is hardly mentioned in the Bible and has to be satisfied with the sulphurous margins of tradition; on the other hand, she was expelled from Adam's bed also and doomed to haunt the darkest areas of the world, doomed to spread terror and death around her, doomed to shed endless tears over her ever dying new offsprings, doomed to be permanently deprived of a legitimate lineage.

It is worth mentioning that a well-known Jewish contemporary feminist American movement chose the name of Lilith as its label, as a symbol of its struggle for sexual equality within traditional Judaism.

D. Main-line rabbinical-talmudic tradition does not display much kindness either with regard to women. I'll save you the trouble of listening to the list of the nice things it addresses them. But here again, things are not that clearcut and simple. Male representatives of Jewish mainline tradition are inclined to honor, to magnify, to protect women, while being at the same time inclined to be afraid of them, to keep them at a distance, to confine them, to marginalize them, even to exclude them.

Speaking of equality is quite non-relevant here. Let's see briefly then what constitutes the role and place of women within this traditionally male-shaped world.

II. Role and Place of Women in Traditional Jewish Society

1. *Honored.*

Women are honored as spouses and mothers, as family caretakers, as guarantors of the transmission of lineage and tradition.

This conception corresponds to a most stereotyped traditional approach. Yet, if one takes into account the central place of family in Jewish society as well as the fact that a large number of religious prescriptions and rituals are to be observed within the domestic sphere and that women are in charge of most of these prescriptions and rituals, especially those related to conjugal purity and to food, one bears witness to the honour and consideration owed to women.

In order to award greater prestige to this role, tradition invokes feminine biblical models. As an example let's bring to mind the vibrant praise addressed to the *eshet 'hail*, the "virtuous woman" of the Proverbs' Book (Prov. 31, 10-31). It praises the woman rising early in the morning, when it is still night, and taking no rest. Not only is this woman who devotes her whole life to her family a perfect family caretaker but she is also a well-advised business-woman. She is physically strong, brave and modest; she is a source of pride and wisdom to her husband, she fears God and is a model to her children.

Now, what does the Talmud say about women? When asked: "How do women become excellent?" it answers, "When they send their children to the synagogue to learn the Torah and their husband to the rabbis' schools to improve their knowledge" (Ber. 17a).

In her essay called *les Matriarches*,[2] French philosopher Catherine Chalier gives a convergent interpretation of the Bible conception of women's role. She suggests that the biblical mythological figures who stand as the archetypes of a humankind divided between right and wrong ought to be considered as ethical models for the present time. According to Chalier, these spouses and mothers are living and consenting instruments within God's hands, permanently aimed at the achievement of an ethical ideal.

2. *Magnified*

Jewish liturgy and religious symbolism magnify women through the channel of sexual metaphors: from the Mystical Bride of the Sabbath to the black Shulamite spouse of Solomon's Song, they are shown as beautiful, strong and ardent. As human Lovers, these emblematic women physically embody the spiritual violence of Israel's love to God. On the other hand, when incarnating the *shekhinah*, the "Holy Presence", which is traditionally featured as a female person, women assume a mystical dimension as well as their specific part in the mystery of God. Moreover, women are also part of God's mystery when being sexually "known" by their husbands. Actually, Jewish tradition magnifies sexuality. It compares it to the Covenant between God and his Chosen People. In this regard, Jewish tradition does not claim austerity within marriage. On the contrary, women may claim their right to physical pleasure. As soon as they get married, men are bound to provide their wives with pleasure by contract.

3. *Protected*

Jewish law protects women. But the problem is that the way it understands their protection is not the same as the way modern jurisdictions do. The principles at the source of this law system were fixed about two thousand years ago. Even though they have undergone some adjustments since then, they basically haven't changed. According to this law, women rank at the same level as children and slaves: none of them are legally autonomous.

Therefore one should not be astonished when considering the laws on marriage or divorce, widowhood or levirate. Considering them as proof of Jewish tradition s willingness to keep women in an inferior position, hence the necessity for protecting them as children, or as proof of its reluctance to acknowledge women s claims and rights to equality, is completely misleading as one ought not to forget that these legal dispositions were fixed according to criteria which are no longer ours.

The problem is that orthodox authorities are mostly reluctant to adjust. From the start, most of them reacted negatively to modernity. They considered it as a threat to tradition, which actually happened to be real. As a result, they reinforced their social and legal barriers to preserve themselves from the influence of the outside world. Their capacity to adapt was not lacking. On the contrary, they displayed a capacity to resist, which is another way of adjusting one's attitude. What was lacking was rather the willingness to adjust positively to modernity.

As a result Jewish law, which had developed over the centuries in order to help people into the ways of the Torah, proved to be ineffectual for at least three reasons: it lost its authority among the people and is no longer observed except by a few; instead of being regarded with respect as it ought to, it appears offensive to women because of its anachronisms and archaisms; finally it does not give appropriate answers to some of the most critical problems raised by modernity and secularization (intermarriage, conversion, women's ordination, divorce). In addition, this unfitness gives birth to internal tensions.

Yet, when elaborated, these laws introduced significant positive changes in women's lives. They fixed a legal framework within which non-autonomous individuals, as they were, could not be totally dispossessed of their own persons and be deprived of some of their most basic rights as human beings. Even though not equal, Jewish women could at least benefit from a legal protection against an otherwise non-limited male rule. As such, this legal protection revealed itself to be a considerable improvement on women's condition at the time. However, as their condition has radically changed these laws no longer seem adequate today.

As already suggested, women are also to be feared, to be kept at a distance, marginalized, excluded and confined. What does it mean?

I already mentioned some of the anti-feminist preconceptions of the rabbinic circles. Just to give a further illustration, the Talmud charges women with four major features: "They are greedy, they are eavesdroppers, they are idle and jealous. Moreover they are talkative and fond of wrangling" (Gen. R., 18. 2). More seriously, they are affected with other severe failings: they are superstitious and fond of forbidden practices.

Transcending its ambivalence this tradition favours negative terms to picture women. Women are primarily agents of transgression, sin-carriers and at the source of some of the worst threats hanging over humankind. Therefore one ought to protect oneself against them, against their influence as well as against their physical contact. One should keep them at a distance, which has been scrupulously effected.

On the grounds that they are frivolous, licentious, weakminded or inconstant, women are systematically kept at a distance from the sectors traditionally held as essential, i.e. the "sphere of the sacred" (*koddesh*): public prayer and study. Therefore and until now orthodox women have not been given a chance to become rabbis. In the synagogue, they are not counted as members of the quorum of ten, the *minyan*, requested for the public prayer. They are not allowed to conduct the service, nor to read the Torah publicly. Their voices should not even be heard by men. For similar reasons, women are not admitted to the study-houses; they are neither allowed to become judges nor to witness at a rabbinical court.

Owing to their domestic duties that keep them busy all day long, women are freed from some religious prescriptions, especially those related to time: the three daily prayers, the public reading of the Torah.

Contrary to an opinion often taken for granted, I am not quite convinced that originally purity motives were the sole or main reason for the religious marginalisation of women, since men were as concerned as women with purity prescriptions. Actually, the Bible, and later on the Talmud, make a distinction between three sources of impurity : 1) being in contact with a corpse; 2) leprosy; 3) outflows of sexual origin. Now each of them may concern indistinctively men or women. In order to put an end to the state of impurity generated by any of these agents, a series of purification measures had been listed: quarantine, purification by immersion or by washing, and sacrifice. However, as the Temple was destroyed and as sacrifices do not exist any longer, most of these rituals have become obsolete. Therefore and since then men and women are considered as being in a permanent and equal state of impurity that can't be helped for lack of appropriate ritual means. Nowadays, immersion remains the last and unique available purification ritual: women practice it for the first time before getting married, then before the revival of conjugal intercourse when their monthly period is over, and after each delivery. As for men, only ultra-orthodox men still practice immersion rituals, on the eve of shabbath.

Actually, if sexual intercourse is naturally forbidden during their monthly period, women are nevertheless allowed to participate and take their part in other spheres of the sacred : they may attend a synagogue service, prepare meals or light the Sabbath-candles.

It remains that, traditionally, women used to attend services without participating actively. Their active implication in public religious activity, in liturgy and study is quite recent and limited to progressive trends of religious Judaism.

However, their long-lasting banishment from public religious activities never released women from their duty towards the Law. Moreover, they are bound to three specific commandments directly aimed at them: 1) *'halah*, the tithe on the dough; 2) *niddah*, the purity laws concerning married women; 3) *hadlakat hanerot*, the lighting of the Sabbath candles. If put together, these specific duties indicate quite clearly the limits of the role and function allotted to women by Jewish tradition. Home and family are supposed to be the landmarks on their social horizon.

This traditional normative approach draws the general outlines of a mythical ideal Jewish woman. So we have to ask ourselves now: "what about reality?"

On the whole, Jewish women fulfilled their home and family duties. But many of them did not confine themselves to that part of their role. Incidentally social and historical circumstances pushed them ahead. As no room was left for them in the public management of the sacred they would involve themselves in other fields of action, all the more so as many were bound to be breadwinners. Therefore Jewish women were pushed to play their part in Jewish affairs and more particularly in the economic field.

Women contributed also to the secularization of Jewish culture through the channel of language and education. As they had no access to Hebrew, the sacred language of prayer-books and study, the only available languages were the secular languages, Jewish or local, that they were currently speaking at home or in the marketplace. These were the links to secular culture and education. Most educated girls who went to school were taught in vernacular languages. There they learned a lot about the outside world, whereas their brothers were still having a traditional hebrew/yiddish type teaching, focused on religious topics.

So the new ideas and practices of the outside world entered Jewish homes in as much by way of girls and mothers as through the ex-talmudic-school students' young revolutionaries breaking with tradition.

I would like to suggest that these new opportunities partly compensated for the unequal status and condition women had to cope with within their traditional environment. Their capacity to adjust to modernity was a valorizing agent in their own opinion and in their social environment's opinion too.

Migrations, mainly from central and eastern Europe and then from the Mediterranean area, contributed also to alter the social status and position of Jewish women within their communities, since the collapse of the traditional structures of power and authority provided them with new opportunities for promotion.

However one still has to ask whether their successful breaking through in many other fields helped Jewish women to improve significantly their position within the core of Jewish life, i.e. the field of Jewish law. To suggest an answer let's see what the situation is like at the moment

It is quite impossible to give a clearcut answer to this crucial question for there is no common assent among Jewish religious authorities over the issue. The best way to evaluate the situation then is to try the other side and observe directly the attitudes of women themselves towards the norms of traditional Judaism. Four main types of attitudes then appear: a secular attitude, a modern-reformed attitude, a feminist-orthodox attitude, a non-feminist orthodox attitude.

III. Jewish Women's Attitudes to Tradition and Modernity

This hypothetical ideal-typical range of attitudes was mainly elaborated from a French field of observation.

1. *The secular attitude*
This attitude is the most common one. It is the attitude of Jewish women who do not feel concerned with Jewish tradition and practices. Their withdrawal doesn't necessarily mean that they feel unconcerned with Jewish affairs. It merely indicates that their Jewish landmarks are in the secular side. They may be deeply integrated and very active in the Jewish establishment, in education, culture, politics, social work and so on without having anything to do with religious or ritual norms and practices. There is nothing particular to add about these secularized Jewish women except that in France, some of them may be radical "laïques" anti-religious militants.

2. *The modern reformed attitude*
This label applies to women who identify with the theological liberal or reformed Jewish movement. Those who join this movement praise its successful association of tradition and modernity, Revelation and Rationality, for the benefit of women. The adjustment of religious law to the ethical and humanist values promoted by the Enlightenment appears to them as legitimate, loyal to the spirit of tradition and as having a positive hold on history and on the world at the same time.

Reformed Jews consider Jewish law as a law that ought to change with the course of history without its betraying the spirit of tradition. It considers that a sexist approach to tradition can be accepted only in so far as it corresponds to a historically grounded view. But it ought to be transcended when the mores and customs have changed. In such conditions, it seems quite legitimate and even advisable to liberal and reformed Jews to relieve Jewish tradition of its anti-feminine preconceptions and to come back to an expurgated reading and interpretation of the traditional sources.

3. *The feminist orthodox attitude*

This attitude appeared in the wake of the American feminist movement of the late 60's - early 70's. It expresses a search for identity as well as a will to accede to religious authoritativeness. This attitude is as radical as the previous one, and even more so, in as much as it advocates a sort of a socio-cultural and hermeneutical revolution within the orthodox tradition itself, the theological grounds of which are not basically disputed.

Actually feminist orthodox women are no longer concerned with claims for women's right to read and study the Torah. This stage is over now. They rather question the inner logics of traditional hermeneutics which through a methodologically one-sided approach prevented women from full-share fellowship in torah-study and law decision-making. Feminist orthodox Jews want to put an end to this state of things by imposing their own hermeneutical approach.[3]

Their analysis articulates theological knowledge with religious authority. Their ultimate aim is with being acknowledged as authoritative scholars and decision-makers. According to their view this condition is necessary to their intellectual and spiritual realization as women, as Jews and as orthodox Jews. This way is also challenging because it represents a means of gaining power and authority in community leadership.

As a matter of fact even before the feminist movement emerged, women had already improved their position within their communities quite significantly. As students, their Jewish curriculum had been improved and as graduates they were admitted as teachers in most Jewish religious educational institutions, except for ultra-orthodox talmudic academies. In other words, women have succeeded in commanding respect; their seriousness and skill are no longer contested.

Still, did they achieve equality with regard to Jewish law? This is far from ascertainable. Orthodox authorities have not notably changed their positions until now and no aggiornamento is to be expected in the near future.

Why should they, by the way, at the very time when orthodox currents appear attractive to many newcomers?

4. *The nonfeminist orthodox attitude*

Until now, the attitudes just described agreed at least on one point: the three of them considered "equality" as a positive value, whatever their path to it. The fourth type, the nonfeminist attitude, contrasts with the previous ones as far as it fundamentally disagrees on this point. Non-feminist orthodox women accept and take for granted the traditional rabbinical position on women's status.

This position is to be met in ultra-orthodox and neo-orthodox circles. It expresses their rejection of modernity, of modern values and social standards. As far as ultra-orthodox women are concerned their rejection of modernity is deep-rooted in the education and in the way of life they were handed down from their mothers and grandmothers. These women embody and perpetuate the continuity of tradition, even though this tradition is far from being totally immune to changes and external influences, in particular with regards to women. For instance, Israeli anthropologist Tamar El-Or (Hebrew University, Jerusalem) shows that, while representing a great change in the everyday life of ultra-orthodox women, the introduction of study has been an efficient means to withhold social change. As it is totally controlled by the men of their community, adult women's education is far from being a way to individual emancipation. On the contrary it is aimed at the reinforcement of the traditional social order. Let me cite Tamar El-Or's own quotations:

> "Our school education will be considered a success when the girls reach the level of their grandmothers who never attended school"
> —Rabbi Wolff
> *(headmaster and founder of*
> *a large Jewish girl's school)*

> "If you teach a woman to read so she may know her place, she may learn that she deserves you"
> —C. Kaestle, 1985.[4]

Now, as far as neo-orthodox women are concerned the situation is quite different as most of these returnees come from secular backgrounds and have had a secular education. Basically, their rejection of modernity is founded on their own experiences of modernity, which they have experienced personally from inside. As shown by Lynn Davidman or Debra Renee Kaufman in their illuminating surveys and conclusions,[5] to some of these women, so-called women's liberation has been lived through as a frustrating experience if not a traumatic one. Rather than a liberation they see it as the modern most sophisticated form of women's alienation.

In committing themselves to the most radical form of the Jewish traditional normative system they intend to fill the vacancy of modern life while settling their own identity. Their search is for a moral community, for social landmarks, for norms and values. But, above all, they look for a reliable authority in which they may put their faith. Their rejection of modernity is their way of rejecting their own autonomy and responsibility: they don't want to make their life-decisions by themselves any longer. On the contrary, their rejection of modernity expresses their acceptance without limitation of Torah-Law authority.

As they are newcomers to tradition these women do not want tradition to change. They freely accept all of its requirements and among them their position within it as women. Just as most of them are not curious any more about the outside world and have no mundane dreams, they enjoy the form of gender segregation their new style of life prescribes them. In a way it makes them feel free from men's attention, which they resent as heavy and alienating.

By contrast, as they wish to reconquer their dignity as women as well as a positive identity, they manage to valorize the sectors of Jewish life where their role is central: home, family life, social and educational work. They primarily focus their attention and energy on being virtuous spouses, mothers (having large families) and educators. But they go further and do their best to profit from their previously acquired skills and know-how.

I would suggest that neo-orthodox women are modern as far as they deliberately choose to be non-modern. In this respect, their choice is individual and autonomous. But they are fundamentally anti-modern in their value choices and in the choice of their standards of life. Equality does not mean much to them. They see it as a delusion and not as a positive value. They are not ready to fight for it.

Conclusion

I will conclude by suggesting that equality remained a non relevant personal value for Jews as long as Jewish society was ruled according to traditional inequalitarian values. This remark is true for other pre-modern societies also. How could it be possible to think about equality and how could it be possible to have it operate while individuals and groups all over the world were hierarchically linked to each other and equally submitted to a transcendent overwhelming order? For sure, women were socially not equal to men. But all men and all groups of men were not equal to each other either.

Only when society as a whole became receptive to the notion of equality, only when equality started becoming a positive and a desirable value, a value open to all, only then could Jews allow themselves to feel concerned about it. As a first step equality was to be a collective political claim for them: they got it through civil and political emancipation. As Jews, they were becoming equal to their non-Jewish fellow human beings. Then, only after a while and as secularization was making progress in western societies, could Jewish women in their turn allow themselves to feel concerned about equality, no longer as Jews but as women.

Yet, as I just tried to show, socio-cultural emancipation did not naturally go hand in hand with religious emancipation. In this regard, Jewish women have remained subordinate to men's religious law.

As they failed to be acknowledged as legally equal to men according to the Jewish law, most Jewish women were pushed to find their way outside tradition. Thus, their personal emancipation gave them opportunities to confront men. The Book of Proverbs's "virtuous women" were turned into workers, militants, trade-unionists, professionals, intellectuals, artists while still being Jews.

Most Jewish women have given up the idea of fighting for equality within traditional Judaism. They just do not feel concerned with this issue. Those who still feel concerned have two possibilities : they can turn to more progressive Jewish religious currents: Liberal or Reformed. There, they are given better chances and opportunities for religious promotion. Or they may fight from within in order to break open the gates of orthodox tradition. Owing to the age-old resistance of these gates, they are likely to become engaged in a long lasting struggle. Finally, some young returnees are even more radical in their demands and attitudes. While considering the gender issue as fundamentally non-relevant, they question modernity itself and turn their backs on it.

Notes

1. Brenner, Athalya. *The Israelite Woman. Social Role and Literary Type in Biblical Narrative.* Sheffield, JSOT Press, 1985.; Biale, Rachel. *Women and Jewish Law. An Exploration of Women's Issues in Halakhic Sources.* New York, Schoken Books, 1984 .
2. Chalier, Catherine. *Les Matriarches: Sarah, Rébecca, Rachel et Léa.* Paris, éd. du Cerf, 1985 (préf. Emmanuel Lévinas).
3. Storper-Perez, Danièle. "Femmes juives et étude des textes de la tradition", *Traces*, 9/10, sd.
4. El-Or, Tamar. "Are They Like Their Grandmothers? A Paradox of Literacy in the Life of Ultraorthodox Jewish Women". *Anthropology and Education Quarterly*, 24(1), 61-81, 1993.
5. Davidman, Lynn. *Tradition in a Rootless World. Women Turn to Orthodox Judaism.* Berkeley, Los Angeles, Oxford, University of California Press, 1991; Kaufman, Debra Renée, *Rachel's Daughters. Newly Orthodox Jewish Women.* New Brunswick and London, Rutgers University Press, 1991. For a more general approach of Jewish returnees to traditional Judaism, see Danzger, M. Herbert. *Returning to Tradition. The Contemporary Revival of Orthodox Judaism.* New Haven, Conn., Yale University Press, 1989.

BIBLICAL SEXISM AND THE GENDER IDENTITY OF CHILDREN

Stuart Z. Charmé

Department of Religion
Rutgers University

There is a common narrative structure to women's accounts of how the dawning of feminist consciousness has impacted their religious identities. Most often, the two identities are inversely related. As their feminist consciousness becomes heightened, they experience progressive disillusionment with the sexism they encounter in religious ritual, narratives, and doctrine. For women who wish to affirm both a feminist gender identity and a religious identity, there is a disturbing tension to be negotiated. This tension is particularly difficult if, as Valerie Saiving suggested in 1960, the perspective of much of Western theological tradition is rooted in specific concerns and dilemmas that arise in male gender identity development.[1]

As both psychologists and anthropologists have long observed, human beings arrive at their identities as women and men by profoundly different paths. A variety of psychological theories from figures like Nancy Chodorow and Carol Gilligan have focused on the different attitudes toward relationship that emerge as boys' and girls' identities develop. The gender identity of boys, for example, seems to require a suppression of relatedness, stemming from boys' realization that they are separate and different from their mothers. Girls' gender identities include a greater sense of self-in-relation, since they experience their mothers as fundamentally like themselves. Girls do not need to distance themselves from men and maleness to understand their female identities, whereas boys' sense of male selfhood remains linked to a strict differentiation of themselves from femininity and a progressive perception of woman as other.[2]

Of course, the process by which gender identity emerges involves much more than the psychodynamics of the parent-child relationship. Sandra Bem has described the complex, intersecting forces that combine to produce gender identity. This includes not only psychodynamic processes of identification and dis-identification, but also cultural forces of socialization, cognitive development, and more.

The insight of socialization theories is that the adult woman or man is, in part, the product of the child's encounter with the culture. The insight of

15

psychodynamic theories is that because the process of socialization necessarily regulates the child's natural impulses, the adult psyche inevitably
contains repressed desires and psychic conflicts. The insight of identity-
construction theories is that even a child is never merely the passive object
of cultural forces; both children and adults are active makers of meaning,
including the meaning of their own being. And finally, the insight of social-
structural theories is that at least some portion of who people are, even as
adults, is not what they have become inside but what either current level of
status and power requires or enables them to be. [3]

All these psycho-social forces inevitably contribute to the process of how children understand the place of religion in their lives, and they suggest reasons why
girls and boys may respond to various religious ideas and stories in significantly
different ways. Just as the disparate responses to the recent O. J. Simpson verdict
awakened people to possible racial differences in how black and white Americans
perceive reality, evaluate evidence, and assign moral responsibility, gender differences may also be crucial in how various situations and moral dilemmas are evalu-
ated. It has become increasingly clear, moreover, that the experience and interpretation of religion is likewise influenced by one's gender identity.

As Valerie Saiving points out, since a boy's path to male identity requires specific acts of self-differentiation and individual achievement, the psychological and
theological danger for men is an excessive development of this tendency to "magnify their own power, righteousness, or knowledge."[4] The Biblical doctrine of sin,
which discourages over-involvement with the self and its achievements and pos-
sessions, can thus be seen as a response to this particular male dilemma, as well as
to a generic human one. Religious exhortation to selflessness and love of others, elements which encourage and nurture relationship, is especially appropriate if male
identity development has made relationship a source of ambivalence. In contrast,
since a girl's sense of self becomes defined to a greater extent out of relationship
than from self-differentiation, the danger girls (and women) need to guard against
is not the over-assertion of the individual self, but rather "underdevelopment or
negation of self."[5]

Cultural myths like the story of Adam and Eve reveal a great deal about a particular culture's collective assumptions regarding gender identity and the values
ascribed to male and female. Given the different paths of gender identity development and the different pitfalls on boys' and girls' paths, it would not be surprising
to find that males and females react differently to this story. After all, the dramatic
action of the story focuses on broken relationships that result from the overexten-
sion of a self, a self that challenges supreme authority and strives for greater power.
Such a story might serve as a useful cautionary tale particularly suited to the type
of temptation confronting men, were it not for the fact that much of the male
authors' fear or anxiety about this problem seems to have been displaced onto a
female character. The story thereby becomes an example of the exact problem about

which it warns, namely of distorted efforts to protect the individual male self from harm or blame, even when it involves sacrificing solidarity and relationship with one's own partner.

The second and third chapters of Genesis have traditionally been cited as a proof text for the subordination of women. For many people, their message has been that men must be protected from women's demonstrated weakness in the face of temptation, their challenge to divine (male) authority, and their inferior intellectual development. Contemporary feminists have largely dismissed this Biblical story as a hopelessly sexist projection of patriarchal arrogance, envy, insecurity, and misogyny. Yet other Biblical scholars, many also marching under a feminist banner, have embarked on a revisionist attempt to reclaim the "real" meaning of these stories. Phyllis Trible's brilliantly intriguing exegesis has inspired a host of such readings.[6] Trible called herself part of an emergent "biblical hermeneutics of feminism"[7] that has rediscovered equality, harmony and balance in the relationship of Adam and Eve.[8] One recent book on women in the Bible claims that "no character has been more misunderstood or more maligned" than Eve. The hermeneutics of rehabilitation of authors like this attempts to dismantle claims that the Biblical account of woman's creation implies ontological inferiority or that her role in the Fall implies moral inferiority. It dismisses efforts to "belittle, malign, or condemn" Eve as a result of faulty translations and exegesis.[9] Revisionists contest the claim that patriarchal hierarchy is a natural part of the text. Rather they see it as an add-on that has to be read into the story. Their overall effort is most often motivated by a desire to accommodate both a claim of equality for women and also respect for the Biblical account. In the past, the Jewish and Christian traditions have generally been more than willing to sacrifice the idea of women's equality on the altar of scriptural sacrality. Hermeneutical rehabilitation has the advantage of displacing sexism from the sacred text and locating the sexist elements in later dispensable traditions of interpretation within the church and synagogue. In this way, the Bible's sacredness and authority can be preserved, and sensitive readers can be spared the spectacle of a sexist God.

Yet if the text is not sexist, where did its sexist associations come from? For some Christians scholars, one unfortunate strategy has been to deflect responsibility for sexism onto the Jews. This implies an unsullied, reclaimable meaning of the Bible distinct from its Jewish cultural roots. These roots can then be held accountable for any misuses that result in the subordination of women. Paul Jewett writes, for example, that reading subordination into Genesis 2 is a result of "the patriarchal relationship between the sexes which was an historical fact in Israel rather than the necessary meaning of the text itself. So far as Genesis 2 is concerned, sexual hierarchy must be read into the text; it is not required by the text."[10] Thus, it is the historical accident of Jewish patriarchy, not the ahistorical or revealed divine word which is responsible for the subordination of women. Even Paul's sexist use of the Adam and Eve story in notorious passages like 1 Timothy 2: 9-15 have sometimes been attributed to Paul's Jewish roots rather than his Christian faith. Such views are ironic in light of Jewett's further observation that by blaming Eve and all women for humanity's woes, the early Church Fathers were merely reenacting Adam's blaming of Eve. Certainly, Jewett's kind of position re-enacts ancient Christian tendencies to blame Jews for having distorted the truth of sacred scripture and Christian teachings.

The major problem with the hermeneutics of rehabilitation is that it requires massive reeducation away from elements that seem to be deeply embedded in the structure of the story itself. It is not my purpose, however, to judge whether or not these alternate interpretations are historically or theologically valid. Transforming or "reinventing" a "new" Eve who is a heroic figure, an independent woman, or a Goddess worshipper is certainly appealing for a variety of reasons and may be more consonant with contemporary sensibilities. My question, rather, concerns how girls and boys without any significant hermeneutical or theological background make sense of this story. Although it would clearly be absurd to think that even fairly young children are engaged in an ahistorical, neutral reading of the story itself from which all other cultural associations had been pruned, their responses still can give us valuable insight into how this story is initially being absorbed and incorporated without the more complicated theological overlay.

As a result of many individual interviews with grade school children, several conclusions emerge. First, as long as this story is retold to children, even without comment or judgment, it is likely to elicit and reinforce interpretations in many children that presuppose the inferiority and subordination of women. Not only does the Bible itself provide little other support for what Gerda Lerner has called the revisionists' "optimistically feminist interpretations,"[11] but children's spontaneous responses to the story offer little evidence that such interpretations are intuitively obvious from the text itself. Quite the contrary, conversations with children reveal that sexism does not need to be "read into" the text. Nor does this seem to be true simply because children have already been exposed to and internalized societal sexism, which must, of course, be accepted as a baseline. For many children, sexist conclusions flow naturally from the text. As Pamela Milne has argued, there may be something troubling in the structure of the story itself that cannot be hermeneutically corrected.[12] Nor can children's responses be explained solely as a consequence of unenlightened religious training, since reactions from children with no religious training or background who hear about Adam and Eve for the first time are not much different from those of children with religious training.

Second, despite a considerable overlap in the response of boys and girls to the story, there is still evidence of significant differences of perspective that is tied to children's gender identity. If Saiving is right that "the individual's sense of being male or female, which plays such an important part in the young child's struggle for self-definition, can never be finally separated from his total orientation to life,"[13] it may be useful to observe this interaction between gender and world-view at its early stages.

To find out the extent to which grade school children's emerging gender role identities color their understandings of the stories of Adam and Eve, approximately sixty grade school children (aged seven to ten) from a variety of religious backgrounds, were interviewed. To a certain extent, the story was used as a projective screen for the children's ideas about gender, as well as a means to examine their understanding of a well-known Biblical story. Although the children had a wide range of prior religious education, most had at least some familiarity with the stories of the creation of Adam and Eve and their expulsion from Eden. In order to refresh the memories of those children who had already heard the story and to inform those children who never had heard it, all interviews began with a short paraphrase of the story to serve as our common reference.

Among the most common complaints about the Adam and Eve story is the obvious hierarchical ordering of humans from the moment of their creation. The story emphasizes the creation of the man as the central narrative focus and the creation of woman as a secondary derivative event. In middle childhood, children develop their senses of being boys and girls in part through identification with same sex parents, teachers and other adults. It is natural to assume most children would identify most with the same sex character in a story like that of Adam and Eve. The cognitive, developmental theories of gender identity of Piaget and Kohlberg indicate that after children establish their identity as either girls or boys they prefer, value, and identify with things/persons that they see as similar to themselves. Their thinking is, says Kohlberg, I am a boy, so I like boy things. Boys identify with their fathers and girls want to be like their mothers.

At the same time, it is reasonable to expect that some girls may be attracted to Adam became of his more prominent role in the story. Girls' identifications do not preclude identification with their fathers as well. Girls do not have the same resistance to identification with males and masculinity. At one level, male merely means large and powerful, qualities which may appeal not only to boys but also to some girls.

The evaluation of any human interaction that one witnesses or hears about depends a great deal on which side or character one most identifies with. This is a crucial factor that is much manipulated by political propaganda in election campaigns, social policy debates and wars. The "science" of juror evaluation and selection in the judicial system acknowledges that levels of identification with victims, defendants, prosecutors and lawyers, will deeply influence moral considerations of guilt and innocence, appropriate punishments, etc. Accordingly, children's patterns of identification with the characters in the Adam and Eve story is a good place to begin.

When children were asked which character in the story he or she would most like to be, the overwhelming majority, as expected, identified with the character of the same sex as themselves, for the simple reason that "she's a girl" or "he's a boy." However, unlike the boys, who almost never wanted to be Eve, there was a significant number of "gender defectors" among girls, a third of whom preferred a male character such as Adam or God. This choice among girls may reflect either the less appealing depiction of the female character available, or more likely, the special appeal of Adam and God as characters of greater importance and power. Girls who chose Adam liked that he had been there first and got to play with the animals, whereas those who chose God were drawn to God's freedom (God can do whatever God wants to) and power (God makes everything).

Psychodynamic theories have emphasized that male identity is to a great degree dependent upon separation from and denial of any identification with the primary female figure, the mother, and by extension, with things and behaviors considered female. From an early age, boys are socialized to differentiate themselves from females and femininity. Consistent with this idea, over a third of the boys who were attracted to Adam because of his maleness, also included some explicit rejection of the possibility of identifying with a female character. Most expressed some variation of the idea: "I wouldn't want to be a girl." When boys did not mention Adam's gender, their reasons for choosing him were related to Adam's role and position. They consider him more impressive than Eve because he is first, he is more powerful, and he gets to name the animals.

Children's explanations of why God chose to create Adam first reveal the powerful force of traditional views of God's gender and traditional gender roles for men and women that are legitimized by God. About half the children thought that Adam was created first for two reasons: 1) God himself is male (or a man) and therefore prefers men;[14] and 2) men are stronger and better than women. However, if creation had been left up to children, the process may have been somewhat different. Less than a third of girls and boys would have created their own sex first. Half of the children did not think it mattered which sex was created first; they were open to the possibility of an alternative sequence of creation, or the simultaneous creation of the first woman and man (as is found in Genesis 1). For most children, the question of who gets to go first is a common childhood dilemma that evokes issues of selfishness versus fairness. This dilemma is frequently solved by taking turns, or acting together in concert, and such experience may influence how children think about the sequence of creation.

In the second part of the Adam and Eve story, the responses of boys and girls became more divergent, especially when explaining the motivation behind Adam and Eve's behavior. The story of the Fall is the traditionally more troubling part of the story, especially for girls/women, since Eve has often been seen to bear greater responsibility for the fall of mankind. Identification with the same sex character drops off considerably among both boys and girls. While nearly nine in ten boys identified with Adam in Genesis 2; only a half do so in Genesis 3. Similarly, girls' identification with Eve was halved, from two-thirds to one third. Unlike the story of creation in Genesis 2, the story of the Fall in Genesis 3 raises particularly sensitive moral questions for children related to the charged issues of disobedience and punishment. A central issue in the story is resistance to temptation, which is an especially difficult area for children. It is not surprising that identification with disobedient characters who are caught and punished by God became less appealing to them.

Eve and Adam each exemplify at least one typical childhood weakness. On the one hand, one might say that in the face of temptation, Eve demonstrates excessive curiosity, poor impulse control and disrespect for authority. On the other hand, in accepting without protest or question what his wife gives him to eat, Adam offers a possible representation of the power of peer pressure to overcome obedience to rules. Understandably, children do not like to identify with a morally culpable character and certainly not with one who gets caught and punished. Their tendency is to exonerate or mitigate responsibility in characters with whom they identify.

In this story, it is clear that gender has a great impact on how children interpret and evaluate the behavior of Adam and Eve. The minority of girls who still identified with Eve mostly ignored her act of disobedience (the eating of the fruit) when they explained their choice. The other two thirds of the girls now chose from among the three male characters in the story: Adam, the snake [presumed to be male], and God. In each case, their choices seem to minimize any experience of wrong-doing in regard to the fall. The most popular choice for girls, aside from Eve, was God. Nearly one in three girls say they are attracted to the character of God the most, both because God is powerful, and also God, unlike Adam or Eve, doesn't get punished for anything. One in five girls preferred Adam, noting that he hadn't done anything wrong, or at least what he did was less wrong than what Eve did. The snake was appealing to an even smaller number, because it was tricky, yet did not seem to get in as much trouble.

Although girls' high level of identification with the character of God might confirm some doctrines of the Church Fathers regarding women's perpetual reenactment of Eve's sin, the desire to be like God, it is surely preferable to see this pattern of response as a form of resistance to the subordinate role of women in the story. For some girls, God is an attractive, empowering fantasy, one which seems to reflect a healthy self-image rather than the kind of arrogant self-assertion condemned by the Bible.

The smoother identification of boys with Adam and power may make explicitly identifying with God less necessary. The figure of God may also be a source of more ambivalence to boys than to girls, since God contains the projected feelings that are produced by the oedipal stage. God is admired yet feared. The figure of Adam himself shows this ambivalence. He perceives himself as more obedient than Eve, getting into trouble only because of the woman. But he can no more resist the temptation to violate God's prohibition and to seek knowledge than Eve can. This ambivalence is reenacted in a number of boys who see Adam as innocent or only mildly guilty compared to Eve, yet simultaneously feel attracted to the figure of the snake (the most popular choice of boys after Adam), who appeals to them because the snake is tricky and successful in his deception. The projection of gullibility and untrustworthiness onto a female insulates them from their own temptations, which comes out indirectly in their attraction to the snake.

An important element in children's perception of morality is their identification of the intentions of agents. Piaget has noted that consideration of intention becomes more salient around the age of eight. Prior to that he found that children's sense of the appropriateness of punishment is connected to the quantity of damage done, not the intention. In the case of the Fall, the quantity of damage done is arguably equal, since Adam and Eve both ate the fruit and experienced its effects. For most children, the critical factors that differentiate the moral gravity of Adam and Eve's actions are: a) the sequence of their acts of disobedience and b) their intentions. Understandably, the relevance of the issue of sequence of violations is more persuasive to boys, since it places Adam, the favorite male choice, in a more positive light. Girls and boys interpret Adam and Eve's intentions quite differently, each being more accepting and understanding of the same sex character than the character of the opposite sex.

In Eve's case, the Biblical story itself provides two reasonable answers to the question of intention or motivation. The first explanation involves Eve's appreciation of the qualities of the fruit. The story says that Eve saw that the fruit looked good and tasty, and that she wanted to obtain knowledge. Kim Chernin and Phyllis Trible both present Eve's choice of the fruit as evidence that Eve is a wonderful role model for women—courageous, intelligent, sensitive, and decisive. Trible writes, "If the woman is intelligent, sensitive, and ingenious, the man is passive, brutish, and inept."[15] While most girls did not go nearly as far as revisionist feminists, they were as a whole more likely than boys to find extenuating circumstances for Eve's decision. The most common motives that girls mentioned were ones that placed Eve's actions in a more positive light. These are references to the fact that Eve thought the fruit looked good and tasty and she wanted knowledge. Other remaining responses, e.g., that she was hungry, it was the only fruit left, etc., also make her action at least understandable, if not justified.

The second textual explanation of Eve's reasons for taking the fruit produces a very different image of Eve. When she is caught and accused by God, Eve excuses herself by claiming that she had been deceived by the snake. There is a dramatic difference in how girls and boys responded to these two explanations of Eve's motives. While fewer than one in five girls mentioned the snake's deception as the main reason for Eve taking the fruit, the majority of boys (59%) cited this. This explanation finds Eve's action far more blameworthy, a reflection of character weakness, stupidity and gullibility.

In the case of Adam's behavior, the terseness of the text lends itself to a variety of possible interpretations. In this case, the suggestion that he was tricked or talked into disobeying God's rule by Eve is not so much a source of blame and weakness as it is an exculpatory defense. Not surprisingly, three-fourths of all the boys claimed that Adam's action was a result of having listened to Eve. They offered this interpretation as evidence that Adam was a victim of deception and entrapment by someone he trusted. In other words, for Eve, listening to the snake is a sign of moral weakness, while for Adam, listening to Eve is an indication of marital loyalty. Many boys thought that Adam became implicated in a sinful rebellion because of his desire to maintain relationship and his willingness to share his partner's mistake. Furthermore, once the moral violation occurred, boys saw Adam's participation as adding little to the seriousness of the crime. In a sense, he was only following orders. Why Adam listened to Eve was a matter of interpretation for these boys, but most suggestions mitigate his guilt in some way. Some young boys also considered other extenuating possibilities such as that Eve had forced Adam to eat, that he had trusted her and merely wanted to make her happy, or that he had not known where the fruit came from when Eve gave it to him.

The parallels between the responses of these young boys and the traditional interpretations from Jewish and Christian sources is perhaps more than coincidental. They give support to the idea that both the text and its traditional interpretation resonate with issues and dynamics that are already present in the early stages of male identity. One Jewish legend, for example, tells that after Eve ate the fruit she saw the angel of death approaching.

> Expecting her end to come immediately, she resolved to make Adam eat of the forbidden fruit, too, lest he espouse another wife after her death. It required tears and lamentations on her part to prevail upon Adam to take the baleful step. Not yet satisfied, she gave of the fruit to all other living beings, that they, too, might be subject to death.[16]

According to this legend, too, Adam does not realize what he has eaten until it is too late and he has experienced the effects of the fruit. Eve is actively involved in corrupting him. Most boys, likewise, see Adam as a victim who suffers because he loved and trusted his wife. They are very much in agreement with the medieval theologians like Aquinas for whom "Adam's loyalty to Eve diminishes the gravity of his sin."[17] Whereas Eve sins by an envious desire to be like God, Adam only sins out of faithfulness to his wife. Surely, a woman's assertive effort at self-deification and a man's humble acquiescence to his wife's desires certainly would not seem to be the kinds of "sins" that are produced by normal gender identity development. Indeed, Saiving's analysis of the different male and female paths to identity suggested that excessive self-aggrandizement is the basis for sinful distortions of self for men in most cases, while excessive self-effacement is a potentially sinful pitfall primarily for women, whose sense of self may lack adequate self-definition to begin with. In the same way that the Genesis account of the creation of woman out of the body of man is a reversal of biological reality, the fall story is structured on a reversal of the psychological reality of sin in men and women. This male appropriation of female creativity and disavowal of traditional male self-assertion presents boys with a far more attractive and comforting scenario than it does for girls.

Hermeneutical consistency between centuries of western theology and young boys of today probably indicates not that the boys interviewed were theologically precocious, but rather that traditional interpreters were very much boys at heart. Apparently, most Biblical interpreters and theologians have identified with Adam and used the same reasoning as boys today to bolster Adam's alibi and displace blame onto Eve and women in general. In a child's worldview, it is better to be first when it comes to something good, and worse to be first when it comes to being caught doing something bad. Paul uses precisely this thinking when it comes to justifying the subordination of women to male authority in the church: "For Adam was formed first, then Eve; and Adam was not deceived, but the woman was deceived and became a transgressor." (1 Timothy 2:13-14)

While nearly half the girls followed the thinking that Adam ate because Eve told him to, even more girls noted a variety of other possibilities: Adam was hungry, Adam himself was tricked by the snake, Adam also thought that the fruit looked good and tasty. Unlike the boys, however, girls rarely reported that Adam acted innocently, without knowledge of where the fruit came from. On the contrary, girls tend to see both Adam and Eve as sharing equally in the act and its consequences.

It is difficult to judge conclusively whether girls and boys are following a different moral compass in the case of Adam and Eve. On the one hand, boys' responses appear to be more individualistic. Their need to distinguish themselves from girls may involve an effort to separate Adam's moral responsibility from Eve's. Girls' emphasis on shared responsibility may reflect their more relational view of the situation. On the other hand, it may also be true that boys and girls each analyze situations in ways that maximize the moral standing of the characters they most identify with. Identifying more with Adam to begin with, some boys raised the issue of Adam's knowledge of the source of the fruit in order to establish "reasonable doubt" about his guilt. If Adam did not know where the fruit had come from, boys reasoned, he was less accountable. While they saw no good reasons why Eve ate the fruit, they saw mitigating factors in the case of Adam. Girls do not blame Adam for the Fall; rather, their strategy is twofold. They can identify more easily with Eve if they can find other motives for her action than mere disobedience or gullibility and if they see Adam and Eve's moral responsibility as comparable. Failing that, they are more likely than boys to find a different character to identify with.

The gender differential in understanding Adam and Eve's motives carries over to children's views of God's reaction to the first couple's infraction. Most of the children (somewhat more boys than girls) agree that God was more angry at Eve than Adam. The primary reason has to do with her timing; she disobeyed God first. Beyond the consideration of intention in evaluating guilt, children treat temporal sequence as central. The first person who does something wrong bears more responsibility than someone who is following another person's lead. Of course, this reasoning is Adam's own defense in the story. If God was more angry at Adam, as a few boys reasoned, it was because of his superior position to start with. He was older and smarter than Eve and should have known better.[18] But four times as many girls (40% vs. 10%) thought that God was equally angry at both Adam and Eve. They reasoned that Adam and Eve both were equally culpable before God, since they both had broken the rule. The story's structure clearly predisposes many children, both male and female, to hold Eve more accountable than Adam. When children do succeed in transcending the structural bias, they most often are female.

The final aspect of the Fall story is the imposition of punishments. Children's suggestions of appropriate punishments for Adam and Eve reveal a great deal about the meaning of crime and punishment for them. For many children, the sin of Adam and Eve is conceived fairly concretely as the actual eating of a fruit, rather than the act of disobedience against God. As a result, forcing Adam and Eve to forego food for some period of time was a frequent suggestion. Related to this idea were suggestions that would undo the sinful act or make its repetition unlikely. For example, God could make Eve throw up or choke on the apple, or do something to prevent her teeth from biting the fruit again. In addition, children draw on their own experiences of punishment to offer other alternatives. What must be a child's version of expulsion, e.g., sending Adam and Eve to their rooms or giving them a "time-out," were common answers.

Since boys judge Eve's responsibility more harshly, it is not surprising that their punishments for her tend to be more punitive and violent. Their suggestions include a variety of ways of obliterating Eve: one boy said Eve should be turned back into a rib; another boy applied the *lex talionis* on behalf of the apple; Eve should be turned into a worm and stuck inside an apple where she could worry about being bitten. Other boys thought Eve's sin warranted summary capital punishment.

In relation to Adam's punishment, many boys and girls suggested similar punishments. The primary gender difference was the significant number of boys (around 1 in 5) who supported Adam's acquittal. They insisted that Adam should not have been punished at all. Consistent with boys' view of Adam's diminished responsibility, they felt that what happened was not his fault. Either he did not realize what he was doing, or he was only doing what Eve told him to do it. In contrast, the only excuse offered by a girl for not punishing Adam was that Adam was probably sorry for what he had done, not that he wasn't deserving of punishment.

One element of the Fall story that was not discussed with children was the immediate effects that eating the fruit had on Adam and Eve. Among other things, new knowledge was first manifest in their shame over their nakedness. Perhaps this first moment when Adam and Eve look down and at each other and become aware of their genital difference ought to be interpreted as the confirmation of their different gender identities. It is obvious that children's awareness of their own gender difference has tremendous impact on their responses to this story. Kim Chernin quotes an old Jewish folk saying: "Adam's last will and testament read: "Don't believe Eve's version." Unfortunately, it is only Adam's version that the text preserves. And yet, by listening to the imagination of children, we may begin to hear the echoes of what Eve's version might have been as well.

NOTES

1. Valerie Saiving, "The Human Situation: A Feminine View," in *Womanspirit Rising*, edited by Judith Plaskow and Carol Christ, New York: Harper and Row, 1992, p. 25.
2. See Nancy Chodorow, *The Reproduction of Mothering*, Berkeley, CA: The University of California Press, 1978, and Carol Gilligan, *In a Different Voice*, Cambridge, MA: Harvard University Press.
3. Sandra Bem, *The Lenses of Gender*, New Haven: Yale, 1993, p. 137.
4. Saiving, *op. cit.*, p. 26.
5. *ibid.*, p. 37.
6. *God and the Rhetoric of Sexuality*, Philadelphia: Fortress Press, 1978.
7. *ibid.*, p. 7.
8. Trevor Dennis, *Sarah Laughed: Women's Voices in the Old Testament*, Nashville, Tenn.: Abingdon Press, 1994, p. 8.
9. *ibid.*, p. 10.
10. Paul K. Jewett, *Man as Male and Female*, Grand Rapids, William B. Eerdmans Pub Co., 1975, p. 125.
11. Gerda Lerner, *The Creation of Patriarchy*, Oxford, 1986, p. 184.
12. "The Patriarchal Stamp of Scripture: The Implications of Structural Analyses for Feminist Hermeneutics," *Journal of Feminist Studies in Religion*, vol. 5, no. 1 (Spring 1989): 17-34.
13. *ibid.*, 34.
14. In the paraphrase of the story, God was always referred to by name and never by gendered pronoun.
15. *God and the Rhetoric of Sexuality*, p. 113.
16. Louis Ginzberg, *The Legends of the Jews*, Phila, Jewish Publication Society, 1968, p. 74.
17. Eleanor McLaughlin, "Equality of Souls, Inequality of Sexes: Women in Medieval Theology" in Ruether, *op. cit.*, p. 218.
18. In Jewish legend, God is angered by Adam's blaming Eve, not only because she was a gift, but also because as "the head", he should have known not to obey her. Ginzberg, *op. cit.*, p. 77.

INCONGRUENT STRUCTURE AND IDEOLOGY BETWEEN WOMEN'S SPIRITUALITY GROUPS, INCLUDING WOMANCHURCH, AND THE CHURCHES THEY CHALLENGE

Teresa Donati

Department of Sociology
Fairleigh Dickinson University

Introduction

This paper explores the "fit" between two organizational forms: (1) the organization of women's groups seeking equality/ordination in their churches, and their ideologies of legitimacy in challenging current church rules and practices; and (2) the organization of those churches, and the ideologies supporting their structures and rules.

Do women's organizations and ideologies dovetail with or fit into the institutions and ideologies of the churches? In other words, would the strata in established churches simply grow deeper or wider with the integration of the women's presence/demands, or would there be a shift or major modification in the organization, necessitated by changed locations of status, power, and authority? Presumably, a dovetailing or fit would be "easier" to incorporate or absorb; organizational restructuring, particularly where power and authority are at stake, are perceived of, and are, revolutionary, wherein the reactionary position is that of the "loyalist."

What amount of congruence or lack of it, then, exists between women's groups including WomanChurch, and the established churches? I am proposing to show here that the lack of congruence or "fit" between the two is greatest when the women's groups are youngest or newest, and that over time, organizational necessity produces a mirroring by women's groups of other formal organizations, including churches. At that point, greater congruence makes it "easier" for churches to set up formal meetings and explore interfaces with women's group.

Parenthetically, regarding the terminology here: at first it seemed that the word "disarticulation" rather than "incongruence" would be more suitable to describe what I see as disjunctures between women's groups and churches. But I rejected "(dis)articulation" for several reasons: first, it is a very "academic" term, e.g. reminding us of "articulation agreements" between schools; second, I came to realize that the most apt word to describe the "rub," and "lack of fit" among the various entities (women's groups, churches), was incongruence, because the word itself implies qualitative differences in the parts that do not match up; and finally, incongruence bespeaks the kind of confusion or puzzle ("incongruity") or lack of harmony that leads people to speak past each other, because their premises are so different at the start.

I believe the absence of that deep structural congruence is the reason for many of the frustrations experienced by women who are attempting to gain full sacramental equality in their churches. To the extent that male religionists actually believe the exclusion of women is "self evident," and amply justified by theology and especially by tradition, they too are experiencing the frustrations of incongruence. I must say at the outset, though, that I have no personal appreciation of exclusionary traditions, and that things which are declared to be "self evident" nonetheless tend to require protracted "proof," explanation, and elaboration.

This paper makes frequent use of the Roman Catholic example of incongruence; its hierarchical structure, though, has parallels elsewhere, e.g., in Mormonism; and the explicit male biases of its interpreted message is exactly that, an interpretation, whether in the case of Roman Catholics, or Mormons, or for that matter, Muslims.

Women's Groups, WomanChurch[1] : Primary Structures (For a While)

One of the major realities of women's groups and caucuses in larger (hierarchical) religious and academic bodies, is the claim to living out, and thereby legitimating and reinforcing, "another way," "women's way," of thinking about religious issues. The absence of initial hierarchies in most of the women's groups means that the quality of interpersonal relations is not governed by status, but by shared membership and presumably, shared ideals. These are connected, in that (1) the affiliativeness and inclusiveness of women's groups creates primary bonds—i.e., friendship—rather than contractual or secondary bonds—i.e., statuses and formal rights and duties attached to those statuses; and (2) a woman's "right" to interpret, to present alternatives, to be heard at all, is part of being present in the group rather than being "something" in terms of status. Ruether describes the process for "religious academe:"

> Women doing feminist studies in theological education often find the openings at established institutions too restrictive. They feel a need for fuller exploration of feminist consciousness and research in an atmosphere where it is normative, not marginal. So feminist scholars have reached out to form networks among themselves. (1994, p. 282)

She goes on to say that women's sections and caucuses in various professional societies such as the American Academy of Religion, have provided the networks and intellectual exchanges women need.

Behaviors in such a context are, however, already patterned hierarchically. Churchly and discipline-based organizations, with their acknowledged efficiency of clear lines of responsibility and answerability, become the organizational model whereupon elections and hierarchies of office do start to occur.

As groups grow larger, inclusiveness is harder to maintain. In an effort to maintain at least a sense of primary connection, intra-group coalitions may form; these can be based on specific areas of interest, on race, on class orientation, or on any number of other dimensions including geographical proximity. The professional groups begin looking more and more like the male structures the women challenged and thought they could replace. Much verbal homage is paid by leaders and high ranking members to the primary, "personal" ideal of the group's early existence. Lines of hierarchical achievement and reward, though, are typically more material and greater than can be earned in the "marginal" women's groups. In a parallel example: the Women's Breakfast at the Society for the Scientific Study of Religion has grown ever larger each year since its inception. I watch with interest as, when the breakfast concludes, women find each other and exchange information based on professional advantage, much as the men have always done. While it is a fine thing that women are finding the ability to advance through each other's resources, the organizational shift must be understood as a departure from "women's ways of relating." Even where women consciously work to preserve their original inclusiveness and equal access to each other, the paradoxical "success story" is that the women's meetings become a showcase of inclusiveness, but once the meetings/breakfasts/receptions are done, friendships are governed as always by shared interests and statuses. This is NOT a condemnation of women's groups; it is simply an attempt to consider the unanticipated consequences of success. Since the academic disciplines are still overwhelmingly male, success in one's discipline means finding one's way in the hierarchical structure, albeit strengthened first by the women's groups' support and mentoring. Perhaps "revivals" or "missions" or "evangelizing" of one's roots are necessary, as Sociologists for Women in Society (SWS) did several years ago, listening to the "Founding Mothers" and their age cohorts tell the tales, sometimes tearfully, of a time when in the professoriate, women were part of the perks of the job.

These developments in the academic disciplines are somewhat paralleled by the absorption into existing structure (with relatively little modification) of women in churches where they HAVE been ordained. The Episcopal priesthood's women bring gifts of women's insights, undoubtedly; yet these women, including the two women bishops, are part of the traditional structure. The Methodists have had women bishops as well as ministers; ordination of women has also occurred, e.g., in the United Church of Chirst, Lutheran, Congregational, Baptist, Presbyterian churches, and Reform and Conservative (though not Orthodox) Judaism.

It must be understood that women in "ordained" ranks typically feel called to do what traditionally, only men could do. The "fears" of traditionalists are that women want to do something "different," untraditional, unsanctioned. But a perfect example of how women want to be part of a continuity, far more than part of any departure, is offered by the work of Dr. Pat Robinson, an M.D. married to a rabbi: Dr. Robinson is one of the few women who do ritual circumcision (mohel, or as a female circumciser, mohelet) (Padawer 1995). None of this infers a negative judgment of the female circumciser. But I believe it helps us to clarify our understandings of the boundaries of women's challenges to established faiths. Their claim is to lead people toward a better understanding and more complete human existence and spiritual life; they do not want to lead people away from faith.

Finally, whatever the changes in clerical gender, all of these faiths still ask the questions of outreach, service, justice, and salvation, that have always been asked. Some of the answers may be enriched through inclusiveness, but the old structures, and the problems they cause or perpetuate or (cannot) deal with, are still for the most part there. In that sense, then, if we are to use history as a tool to gain better and happier lives, the history of social movements and organizational development should serve as a continuous cautionary tale. The first caution should be: what do women preserve by becoming part of an organization? (We shall return to this question in the discussion of legitimacy, below.) And once women are absorbed into the organization, what channels of power, under what conditions, actually exist for them?

How the Challenger "Fits" the Challenged.

Ironically, as those who have been part of women's challenge movements surely notice, the high morale and deep commitment of women to their reformist groups are at their highest when the group is least hierarchical. The very fluidity which creates a kind of "inspired confusion", also creates the excitement and sense of possibilities that build loyalty, commitment, and love, among the group members, making them a "movement". An example of this process is offered by Farrell:

> The Women-Church Convergence . . . is composed of elected and self-selected representatives of all the member groups . . . However, the diverse goals and agendas of all the groups also adds to the organizational problems . . . (1994, p. 9, emphasis added)

Farrell is very positive, on balance, about the effect and efficacy of WomanChurch for its members and for the institutional (Roman Catholic) church.

The diffuse, intrinsically-valuing, face-to-face, intimate, long-lived group with shared goals, is the primary group setting in which most of the major religions also seem to have begun. The egalitarianism of the primary setting transcended both class and sex. Judith, Ruth, Deborah and Esther, are examples of women who gained fame and sanctity by serving Judaism in its pre-Rabbinic days (i.e., before the codifications that took place after the fall of Masada and the Roman decision to scatter the Jews). Similarly, the presence of women around Jesus, however redacted the stories about them, are incontrovertible. Women—especially wealthy widows—provided much of the financing of Christian conversionary and missionary efforts in the first several hundred years of the Common Era. Stark (1995) elaborates on the reasons for this; one important reason was the low sex ratios among the early Christians (i.e., high numbers of women), and as ratios came into balance, the decline of women's importance and status. While Jesus lived, though, women flocked to him—and indeed, rich women and noble women later flocked to Mohammed, running from Mecca to join him in Medina after the hegira (Mernissi 1991).

The charismatic leader's egalitarian message frequently did not prevail against the patriarchal cultural context. Men were able to claim superordinate positions, and reduce the salience and importance of women to the point of subordinating women to men as a theological and "traditional" given.

Thanks to Weber (1947), we have powerful conceptual tools to analyze this transformation of a charismatic leader's followers into a "church," a "priesthood," and hierarchy distinguished by having occupied a special, close position with the charismatic leader, and who become gatekeepers for the line of successors who will come after them. Once the charismatic leader is gone (having died, or ascended, or disappeared in some way), there is the drive to insure the permanence of the "special relationship," and therefore the tendency to create "rules and rituals" for admission to the now-sacred ranks. Weber sums up the process conceptually as: the routinization of charisma. This is not a phenomenon confined to male leaders of major or minor religions; it refers also to the "charismatic aura" of early challenge-and-reform groups such as WomanChurch, with its openness of actions, emotions, revelations, joy, sorrow, community, producing a collective exhilaration and sense of adventure and holiness among the challengers.

To sum up: women challenge their traditional faiths through networks, associations, organizations such as caucuses and WomanChurch. In the beginning these groups emphasize "primary group" qualities, more like families or friendship networks than formal associations. Over time, as numbers grow, simply keeping track of everyone, and notifying members of developments, requires the specialization of function and status separations that create proto-secondary groups. (Secondary groups are larger, impersonal, based on contractual relations, extrinsically valuing of members.) Neither the primary nor proto-secondary group process is "pure," i.e., there are always ways in which women's groups depart from "primary" characteristics, even at their inception, and ways that they remain primary, even after specialization (a secondary group quality) has begun. One of the necessary changes for such groups is the establishment of control of overt emotions. All religious groups must attempt to control religious zeal, since the rationalized order of a hierarchy cannot accommodate the intense personalism of zealotry. So, WHEN do leaders and healers e.g., take up snakes, or be taken or moved by the Spirit, or vent their tears and joy at the tops of their voices? No religion sustains the "indiscriminate" expression of zeal. Even the Roman Catholic Church, which continues to canonize based on attested miracles, looks askance on credulity or uncritical acceptance of "supernatural" occurrences. (Cf. Miller 1995 for another treatment of religious zeal.)

Now there is the capacity for congruence between the hierarchies of church organizations, and the women's groups challengers, because "leaders" can talk together and negotiate. Proposals can be mailed to women's group membership, for approval or disapproval; press releases can be issued in the name of the women's group, typically by an executive committee or steering committee formed to do the day-to-day tasks required for large group survival.

It is extremely unlikely that church officials will walk among WomanChurch ranks, or into the "disorganized" setting of a newer women's caucus. The "confusion," i.e., the lack of hierarchy and externally imposed order, is so easy to see as a "deficit" in women's logic and behavior. With increased size and formal rankings, however, there can be "invitations" to "representatives" of a group; the meeting grounds tend to be the church's. Women are "invited in" when their numbers have swelled to a point requiring the "rationalization" of collective action through more formal organization. "Leaders" thus become identifiable. And dealing with one leader's difference of opinion is much easier than the unpredictable democracy of speaking to a very large group of equals who each has her own opinion.

Success of these women's groups, then, creates the likelihood of organizational evolution toward a better "fit" with the formal/hierarchical structure of the church(es) challenged.

Legitimacy, Exclusion, Ordination, and Teaching Authority.

In wanting to enter all ranks, including sacramental ones ("Holy Orders") in churches that exclude them, women continually point to the fact of their current nurturant and faithful spiritualities and ministries. (See, e.g., the publications of the Women's Ordination Conference [WOC], or issues of "Conscience," the publication of Catholics For a Free Choice [CFFC]).

Here is where several questions must be asked about how the call for sacramental equality supports the system of inequality. First: in the case of Roman Catholics, and also in other Christian churches, the teaching authority (magisterium) is legitimated by claiming to be heirs to the work of Jesus through the Apostles, and to the traditions of Jesus' time and the early Church. That authority combines with papal rule over the modern church, together with the idea of apostolic succession, i.e., that the bishops and priests trace their spiritual origins to the Apostles. Finally, the Roman Catholic church claims, citing Jesus' statement that what is bound on earth is bound in heaven, that it can make laws based in tradition and power from Jesus, to define priesthood, succession, and dogmatic certitude.

If, examining alternatives of interpretation, the traditions that come down to us are selective, how legitimate is the authority drawn from them? It is said, for example, that no women were at the last supper. Who cooked the dinner? And where were the women who were almost always with Jesus? They certainly were around with Mary, Jesus' mother, going to the visit the grave with her. (This does not even begin to address the question of how Mary did NOT become divine herself, after giving birth to God.) And the Pope, who in earlier centuries was the Successor to Peter, and who is now Successor to Christ, is believed to derive power from Jesus's praise for Peter's faith: "Thou art Peter (Rock), and upon this Rock I will build my church. . . ." That play on words could as easily have meant that the Christian church would be built on the Rock of faith, and not on a single person who showed that kind of faith. There is much evidence, moreover, that Peter was hardly a "papal" figure until, perhaps shamed by Paul's activities, he renewed his own ministry. James, not Peter, headed the church in Jerusalem. So where does the modern Pope originate? In very human history, and very slanted patriarchal interpretations of who Peter was.

Even more importantly, the belief that "what is bound on earth is bound in heaven" does not mean that one person only (the Pope) is empowered to do that binding; the church as the collective, the sense of the faithful, rather than the top-down declarations of a religious hierarchy, seem equally valid as a force to bind on earth and in heaven.

The first question, then, is whether the authority that debars a person for reasons of sex rather than spiritual unfitness, is a valid authority. It goes without saying in the present day, that exclusionary clubs which bar membership to those of other races, cannot be reconciled with a religious conscience. And, one after another, the once-exclusive school domains of male-only academies have had female students. If these exclusions violate conscience in the secular world, why are they justified in the sacred realm, where the great monotheisms believe that God transcends all limitations of sex?

If we join a group that is exclusionary, do we not grant it legitimacy by our willing membership? How, then, are women able to accept Communion from the hands of a priest in an exclusionary (male-only) priesthood?

It should be said here that elaborate justifications have been put forth, to separate the "man" from the "priest." Thus, even the "sinful" man can do valid sacramental things. No matter how sinful, in fact, the ordained priest is always a priest, whether or not canonical. If such separation exists, then there is no reason to think of "priesthood" as bound to one sex in the first place. Yet no matter how holy the woman, she cannot "earn" or "merit" priesthood. Thus St. Therese of Lisieux was glad to die young, before the age at which, had she been a man, she could have been ordained. And sympathetic biographers like Furlong point out the effectiveness of such saints even under repressive conditions:

> It is easy to underestimate how considerable her achievement was, simply because we may resent her collusion with a Church which oppressed women. In a period in which women have begun to claim their birthrights we may resent the acquiescence of Christian women in forms of life which suppressed, silenced and destroyed them. Yet pity and understanding of their plight helps us to interpret the kind of battle they were surreptitiously waging. (1987, p. 134)

The point is that today, the battles need not be surreptitious, and in fact are overt. Yet one major quality stops women cold: ordination and its role in Eucharistic celebration.

Since, in Christianity, the individual is baptized into priesthood, and since Jesus said that in the gathering of two or three in his name, he would be among them, why is Eucharist not a routine of daily life in the Christian family, friendship group, or neighborhood? The explanation routinely given is that the bread and wine at the Last Supper were given to Apostles, who then chose their own successors, and only they could consecrate the bread and wine (i.e., duplicate the last supper.) To have the power to consecrate, one must be ordained in the Apostolic succession. This means that the bishop who ordains can trace his own ordination back to the Apostles.

Understanding this, the first women to be ordained in the Episcopal Church were (and are) called "The Illegals," though their priesthood has long since been validated, and female ordination approved. They were priests, undoubtedly —because they got bishops to ordain them who were in the apostolic succession. (Just as one never loses the priestly "mark" or "power," so bishops also keep their own special powers, including that of ordination.) Episcopal bishops are in the same Apostolic succession as Roman Catholic bishops; theoretically, an Episcopal bishop can confer ordination on a Roman Catholic woman, and she would be able to consecrate a "valid," though "illicit" Eucharist for people of all faiths, if she wished. That, however, is a model of a far more open structure than currently exists in the hierarchical, women-barring priesthoods. In fact, a non-Catholic must not share in Eucharist consecrated by a Catholic priest; only baptized Catholics who are not "excommunicated" can take Communion.

Does the Women's Ordination Conference or a similar WomanChurch group really want to be part of that? The answer seems to be that they want to be a part of the "true" Church, the People of God, and that the misogynists cannot drive them out of their own church. In fact, however, by consenting to remain unordained, and remaining in the church, it is not their church; the church belongs to those who control its directions, who have a monopoly of legitimate ordination power, who can say "yes" or "no" to any given change. By remaining unordained, the church's power to deny ordination is consented to and legitimated. If a woman can pass all the same seminary tests, the psychological tests, the internships in parishes, the character examination for worthiness and appropriateness of candidacy—why not try for an alternate route to ordination? The answer is that the women themselves believe that ordination is conferred—and by exactly those same men who dare not challenge the Pope, lest they lose their own bishoprics.

Is The Unsuccessful Protest a Women-Only Phenomenon?

We must wonder whether women's groups are unsuccessful mainly because they are women, or mainly because they question a church's claimed absolute authority. I believe that it is the FORM that women's groups take, and the democratic/pluralistic nature of those groups, that are at least as threatening as all those women looking for ordination.

Evidence for this conclusion comes from news reports out of Austria, where that country's traditional Catholicism can no longer be complacent about its membership or authority. The Austrian church has witnessed mass petitions and protests over Vatican doctrines (priestly celibacy, women's ordination), sex abuse scandals in the highest ranks of the church, and a resulting distrust of the church which is only smaller than the distrust of politicians (Cowell 1995). Despite protests by more than 50,000 people of both sexes against a bishop named by Rome (where they tried to block the bishop's path to the cathedral!), and protest petitions signed by more than 50,000, the Vatican has persisted in ignoring the Austrian church's (i.e., the people's) demands and concerns. While the ultimate result for Catholicism in Austria is unknown, as of the decade ending in June 1995, more than 350,000 Catholics have left the church. When asked about the concerns of these Catholics of both sexes, the leading Austrian bishop (Schonborn) declared the movement to be "marginal," and said that the danger in such petitions was "to raise false expectations that cannot be fulfilled" (Cowell 1995, p.4.)

This is further confirmation, then, that non-hierarchical form is difficult for or repugnant to, hierarchical response. It also demonstrates that even when appointments and church rules are protested by very large numbers, the only way to challenge the conviction of legitimacy is to "vote with one's feet," i.e., exit the church. But some response does occur, within the ongoing framework of asserted legitimacy, e.g., the appointment of a coadjutor to a diocese where the bishop has been quietly summoned away after sex scandals have been revealed.

Heroic Dissent As Women's Religious Protest and Dissent: The Christian Case

In the Christian churches, Jesus' dissent from legalism in favor of love is the model that modern dissenters use; and there is I believe, implicitly at least, in the sense of "we-feeling" generated, a concomitant feeling that one is holier, and that this greater holiness of PURPOSE should be recognized as such. The claim to have the true insights of love, justice, equality, etc., can only imply or declare openly that those who oppose them are wrong, or lacking that spirituality that makes for holiness. To illustrate, contrast the reactions to the sign "The Holy Father Is Neither," where the protesters see it as humor and irony, while more traditional religionists see it as vituperative and willfully disruptive/schismatic.

One major position, then, is: "My dissent is holy; your condemnation of it makes me more like Jesus, who also was condemned." Such dissent is perceived not only as heroic, but also as touching chords of faith and renewal in the great mass of the church. But dissent is never "popular" in that latter sense, since by definition it is the thought and action of a minority, of whom the majority can say, "They are not the Church." The minority in this case is claiming that the apparent majority has lost sight of what the true church is. Both sides are claiming the same legitimacy. In fact, heroic dissent is only popular in retrospect. They did, after all, kill Socrates. No matter how great we think him now, or how filled with hubris for that matter, he did die. They killed Jesus. And innumerable modern day figures who took new directions of action and thought, have been killed. It must be remembered that the same Dr. King who is lionized by today's world, found bricks and bottles being hurled at him when he drove through Watts after the riots there in the Sixties.

If dissenting opinion becomes majority opinion, it becomes "standard," and life goes on with its insistent usualness. This is an enormous blessing, as any war-torn place can attest. But the solidarity of opposition is very different from having majority numbers, or even having majority sentiment strong enough to act on it against the established churches. No matter how solidary an opposition, there is no guarantee of acceptance into the majority fold, nor even of creating a majority "fold" by victory.

Unanticipated Consequences of Success.

When Truman Capote was asked in a television interview why he called his book ANSWERED PRAYERS, he said he took the phrase from St. Teresa (of Avila), who said that more tears are shed over answered prayers than over unanswered prayers. "Getting Into the Churches," in a full sacramental parity, has its own problems for women's consciousness and spirituality. To use denominations that have long ordained women as examples, the absence of vital, women-led and women-centered movements within the churches shows what happens when "praxis" is accomplished. The first Episcopal women priests, and the cohort right after them, were filled with zeal and the heady success of achieving justice and validation. But the woman priest is decreasingly interesting as a "phenomenon," and that is the case in other denominations as well. It seems that the "first wave" (to borrow the terminology of the women's movement) is so tenacious and committed because it encompasses all those who, until then, were denied sacramental status parity. That is what sustains the post-ordination years as well. Yet, parish work, while it can be exciting and of great service to congregation and community, has the highs and lows of any professional calling, and the special demands that are made of clergy and doctors.

Several years ago, I did a study which I turned into a paper presented at the Society for the Scientific Study of Religion entitled "Hiding the Priest...." (1990). In the interviews I did with noncanonical priests' wives, I found especially among the highly educated women, a disillusion with Rome's continuing refusal to change the celibacy rule. Many women had simply stopped going to church, or thinking that the church could give them true spiritual sustenance. And even more interesting: the wives of those priests whom I called "scholar-activist priests," who had been involved in the post-Vatican II excitement and protest against old church ways, had expected to be in the vanguard of a revolution. Instead, they became ordinary, and despite the defiance of noncanonical priests who continue to lead Eucharistic and other worship services, Rome has not budged. And one reason for the relatively weak alliance between, e.g., Corpus and WOC (though they say much about supporting each other), is that the issues are deeply divergent: the men want to go back as married men; the women want to get past the front gate, to ordination itself. Any ordained priest who would renounce his wife, would have relatively little problem in being reinstated. Any woman who promised celibacy still could not even be a deacon.

All of this serves as another cautionary note, then: that the identities, solidarity, excitement, zeal, dedication, and vibrant spiritual challenge, offered by women's groups, are in danger of success, of losing the commonality of adversity; they are susceptible to a blurring of the sharp issues, a loss of identity to the extent that the various women see their quest as action for justice. In short, the power of the group dynamic has been fueled by a common "enemy" (disparate sacramental status by sex), confronting common problems (asserting fidelity and while attempting to get dialogue with the hierarchy), and finding wide social connections in this shared quest.

In one sense, though sadly, there is probably little to "fear" in the prospect of women's success. Only one mind must change—the Pope's—and any bishop who tried to present or represent them would know papal wrath first hand. To have success without being folded into the existing institutional church, women would have to be ready to be "church" with each other, calling out their own priests, and conferring ordination through that call. Unless and until that proto-schism is dared, Roman Catholics, the various Orthodox churches, Mormons, Orthodox Judaism, still-resistant Christian denominations, and orthodox Islam, will continue to be relatively unresponsive. There is no profit for these orthodoxies to "cave in" to the women's demands; refusal only seems to fire commitment and belief, and these faiths hold "unshakable" beliefs in their "traditional" and "charismatic" legitimacy.

Notes

This paper was originally titled *The Consequences of Incongruent Organization Between Women's Spirituality Groups, Including WomanChurch, and the Churches They Challenge*, and was prepared for presentation at the Annual Meeting of the Society for the Scientific Study of Religion, St. Louis, Mo., October 26-28, 1995.

1. The definition of "WomanChurch" is inchoate at this point. I am referring to the typically large spiritual gatherings of women who share worship and inspirational experiences, friendship, meals, discussions, self revelation, self assertion as empowered spiritual beings. The Women's Ordination Conference (WOC) annual meetings are classic "WomanChurch." The final definition, however, is a "work in progress" (see essay by Susan A. Farrell in this volume for further analysis).

2. The proto-organization shows the same qualities described by Michels ([1915] 1959);

time and specialized skills developed over time lead to the inevitable rule by the few, i.e., his "Iron Law of Oligarchy." Coteries, rather than an oligarchic elite, may provide the leadership over the first decade, perhaps, of the more organized women's challenge group.

References

Cowell, Alan. 1995. "A National Church Faces a Challenge From Within." *The New York Times*, June 24: p. L4.

Farrell, Susan A. 1994. "A Community of Equality and Justice: Women-Church Challenges The Institutional Roman Catholic Church." Paper presented at Annual Meeting of SSSR, Albuquerque, New Mexico.

Furlong, Monica. 1987. *Therese of Lisieux*. New York: Virago\Pantheon.

Mernissi, Fatima. 1991. *The Veil and the Male Elite: A Feminist Interpretation of a Woman's Rights in Islam*. Trans. ed. Mary Jo Lakeland. New York: Addison-Wesley.

Michels, Roberto. [1915] 1959. *Political Parties*. New York: Dover.

Padawer, Ruth. 1995. "New keeper of an old covenant." *The Record* (New Jersey). May 29, pp. A1, A8.

Ruether, Rosemary Radford. 1994. "Christianity and Women in the Modern World." In A. Sharma, ed. *Today's Woman in World Religions*. Albany, NY: State University of New York Press, pp. 267-301.

Stark, Rodney. 1995. "Reconstructing the Rise of Christianity: The Role of Women." *Sociology of Religion* 56:3, pp. 229-244.

Weber, Max. 1947. *The Theory of Social and Economic Organization*. Trans. Talcott Parsons. New York: The Free Press of Glencoe.

WOMEN-CHURCH AND EGALITARIANISM: REVISIONING "IN CHRIST THERE ARE NO MORE DISTINCTIONS BETWEEN MALE AND FEMALE"

Susan A. Farrell

Department of Behavioral Sciences and Human Services
Kingsborough Community College

Introduction

Roman Catholic women are creating a community within the institutional church called Women-Church. They are creating an organization using feminist perspectives and feminist organizational principles. Examination of the origins, ideology, organization, and strategies for change of Women-Church allows the following questions to be asked and analyzed from a feminist perspective: Is Women-Church a feminist organization? If so, how well are they succeeding? Through interviews and analysis of Women-Church documents and the writings and speeches of individual Women-Church members, I examine their claims and the actualization of their egalitarian ideology in their organizational structure. I also analyze the extent to which Women-Church may or may not realize their vision of a community of equality and justice as part of a social movement for transformation of the Roman Catholic Church.

As a practicing Roman Catholic woman involved in various groups that make up Women-Church, I am what Merton calls an "insider." As a sociologist engaged in participant-observer research on feminist ethicists in the Roman Catholic church and their contribution to the Women-Church movement as well as their impact on church ideology and sexual ethics, I am an "outsider" as well (Merton 1972). This stance allows for an in-depth illustration of a particular case study that may "have a wide range of application" (Oberschall 1973, p. x), and contribute in a meaningful way to the study of the feminist movement and feminist organizations.

My particular focus in this paper is to analyze Women-Church as a feminist organization based on Patricia Y. Martin's analysis in her article "Rethinking Feminist Organizations" (1990). According to Martin:

an organization is feminist if it meets any one of the following criteria: (a) has a feminist ideology; (b) has feminist guiding values; (c) has feminist goals; (d) produces feminist outcomes; (e) was founded during the women's movement as part of the women's movement (including one or more of its submovements, e.g., the feminist self-help health movement, the violence against women movement. (1990, p. 185)

Both from the perspective of Women-Church members themselves and the hierarchy of the Roman Catholic church, these characteristics put the two groups at odds. These feminist Roman Catholic women understand themselves to be the "loyal opposition" or, as many of them refer to their role, "prophetic voices" in the church. In Elisabeth Schussler Fiorenza's words, Women-Church or the ekklesia of women is a

> new model of church . . . lived in prophetic commitment, compassionate solidarity, consistent resistance, affirmative celebration. and in grassroots organizations . . . a counter term to patriarchy. (1983, p. 349)[1]

Another way of analyzing feminist organizations is presented by Mary Fainsod Katzenstein in her work, "Discursive Politics and Feminist Activism in the Catholic Church" (1995). Katzenstein argues that Women-Church is engaged in the politics of "meaning-making." Women-Church members "seek to reinterpret, reformulate, rethink, and rewrite the norms and practices" of the institutional church (1995, p. 35). She also notes that since discursive politics rely primarily, although not exclusively, on language, the "linguistic construction" of the term "Women-Church" is particularly significant (p. 41). However, as Foucault rightly insists, language is not merely words, they are political acts as well. The production of discourse especially oppositional discourses reveal institutional practices as well as ideologies (Foucault 1972, 1973, 1980a, 1981). This is a notion very much in accord with the feminist concept that "the personal is the political." Women-Church is no mere linguistic construct but also an organization and a social movement (Farrell 1992).

A recent issue of *Conscience*, the official publication of Catholics for a Free Choice (CFFC), an organizational member of Women-Church, stated that Women-Church "is feminist in commitment and global in outreach (1995, p. 3), underscoring the organization's diversity as well as its feminism. The editorial staff of *Conscience* summarized Women-Church's feminist ideology in an article entitled "Equal is as Equal Does." In a section subtitled "A New Vision of Catholic Social Justice," the writers laid out several principles outlined briefly here:
1. a feminist anthropology rests on the radical equality of women and men in community
2. diversity of creation implies differences and the task of a "discipleship of equals" is to hold all of this difference in common, encouraging it and making the world a welcoming place for it.

3. women are multifaceted. Reproduction is important but only one of women's functions. Because it has been used as a basis for discrimination against women, special priority must be given to women's health needs.
4. community rather than family is our programmatic focus.
5. we strive to dismantle hierarchical structures and end discrimination . . . we encourage change in attitudes, behaviors, and laws to secure our common well-being. Our reverence is for all earth, as well as for all its peoples.

Based on this statement, Women-Church's ideology includes the global vision of the larger feminist movement. I think that the writings of Women-Church theologians have reflected this global vision for some time (see the Hunt and Kissling interviews in Milhaven 1987, Stan's interview of Kissling in Ms, 1995; Ruether 1975, 1986, 1992; Weaver 1985). The organizing aspects of Women-Church such as the Women's Ordination Conference (WOC), Women's Alliance of Theology, Ethics and Ritual (WATER), and CFFC have reached out to Europe and the developing nations to help develop Women-Church groups that reflect the needs of women around the world (see "WATER in Europe," 1995, p. 6 for one recent example). As described below, Women-Church had a strong presence at the United Nations Conference on Women in Beijing as well.

WOMEN-CHURCH HISTORY AND ORGANIZATION

Not simply one organization, Women-Church is actually a coalition of a variety of feminist groups and liberationist movements in the Roman Catholic church and tradition that are currently challenging the institutional church. Feminist women in the church want equality and a church that is nonhierarchical and nonbureaucratic, mirroring the community described in the Acts of the Apostles, based on the baptismal formula found in Paul's Letter to the Galatians, and Jesus' own exhortation to "call no man father" (Fiorenza 1979). "The task that these women see for themselves is radical reform from within, without being coopted or so marginalized that they have no impact on the institution" (Farrell 1991, p. 338). Women-Church is both a social movement seeking to change church ideology and presents an alternative model for being church as it challenges the present institutional arrangements which exclude women as well as laymen from positions of authority. Women-Church is simultaneously challenging the structure and the ideology that upholds the structure. Both the development of an explicit feminist ideological dimension as well the goals of the organization fulfill two conditions for Women-Church to be considered a feminist organization according to Martin's framework.

In order to accomplish their aims, feminist Roman Catholic women began a process of coalition building, the first of which made WOC possible. Women in religious orders had the education and material resources as well as the organizational structure to rally, publicize, and support the fledgling movement. Paralleling the secular women's movement (which fulfills another characteristic that Martin uses to define a feminist organization), the origins and continued structure of Women-Church is represented by both highly organized groups such as religious orders and numerous local grass-roots groups such as women's parish-based study groups (Freeman 1979; Martin 1990). Mary Hunt describes the Women-Church coalition as lay-led (sisters and nuns are, by canonical definition, laity not clergy), embodying a commitment to women's empowerment, autonomous from the institutional church in varying degrees, yet

> each sector distinguishes itself as church, especially as Catholic, by celebration. Sacramental life continues unabated in these circles with Eucharist (usually without an ordained celebrant) as the common bond. (1990a, p.4).

These Women-Church groups illustrate what Jo Freeman calls "a decentralized, segmented network of autonomous groups . . . held together by an often tenuous network of personal contacts and feminist publications" (1979, p. 168).

In addition, the grassroots Women-Church groups often use parish facilities for meetings. While participating in parish life, laywomen publicize their existence and purpose through parish announcements and publications. They share a Christian Catholic culture that frequently is reinforced by a life-long education in the Catholic school system as well as continued participation in local parishes. Simultaneously, they are challenging the clerical monopoly of the institutional church and transforming institutional structures at the grassroots level. Calling it unobtrusive mobilization, Mary Katzenstein concludes that even in the most authoritarian and patriarchal institutions like the military and the Roman Catholic Church "activists have strategized to recreate and sustain gender consciousness" (1990, p. 36). It is precisely this kind of social change and transformation of consciousness that Ruth Wallace sees taking place as women not only redefine ideology but begin moving into social roles in the church previously held by celibate men. Women in pastoral roles begin to breakdown the clerical monopoly constitutive of the hierocratic structure of the Roman Catholic Church (Wallace 1992).

Building on the grass-roots approach, Women-Church is the result of a process of the growing collaboration of groups on a continuum from "local feminist base communities "to highly organized religious orders with institutional resources (Hunt, 1990b, p. 2). Since they are a coalition without a formal hierarchy, they "share a common culture but are politically autonomous" (Freeman 1979, p. 169). Women-Church is actually, an umbrella organization made up of individual members and a loose confederation of Roman Catholic women's groups working for various changes in the institutional church (this is a characterization also used by Katzenstein, 1995, p. 41). These groups often formed the impetus for, and in some cases provided individuals for the informal leadership of Women-Church. Almost all the following groups have members who participate in Women-Church either as individuals or through their group's membership. For instance, the leaders of the Women's Ordination Conference (WOC), Catholics for a Free Choice (CFFC), and Women's Alliance for Theology, Ethics, and Ritual (WATER) serve on the steering committee of Women-Church. If you are a member of any of these organizations, you also participate in Women-Church.

Catholics for a Free Choice (CFFC) goes to the heart of the matter by linking freedom of conscience with sexual rights, challenging the hierarchy's interpretation on abortion, contraception, and new reproductive technologies. CFFC links all of these issues to the oppression of women and their exclusion from the hierarchy. WOC has moved even further in this direction, as indicated by my interviews with its members and leadership and my analysis of its major national conferences. They are calling for a transformed priesthood in a transformed church. The Women's Alliance for Theology, Ethics, and Ritual (WATER) provides a good example of what Women-Church is and what it is striving to become. WATER is a grassroots organization that draws together women interested in creating their own spirituality and rituals from a woman-centered perspective but in community with other women. Leaders of WATER operate primarily as consultants, preferring not to dictate a universal formula for all women to use. Theology and ethics are derived from the women's experiences with each other in their communities. Again, no preset formulas or dogmatic pronouncements are imposed on the women. WATER strives to maintain the grassroots momentum learned from the feminist and liberation theology movements.

Women-Church has made connections with Catholic social justice groups such as Call to Action (a Catholic lay group whose aim is to democratize the church), the Association for the Rights of Catholics in the Church (ARCC) and the Center for Concern and the Quixote Center (which focus on Catholic concerns over U.S. involvement in Central and South America linking religious liberation movements with political liberation). Links have also been forged with CORPUS (an organization that supports married priests). Members of DIGNITY (an organization of gay and lesbian Catholics) also participate in Women-Church. Most important, many religious orders remain active both through participation and making resources available for Women-Church. Association with *Las Hermanas* (a Catholic Hispanic women's group) extends the coalition beyond U.S. borders. Mary Hunt, co-founder and co-director of WATER as well as a Women-Church board member, notes the diversity as well as the commonality in the larger coalition: "each of these groups has come up against some form of institutional power such that coalition-building is now a necessity" (1990b, p. 3). Some of these groups work with the institutional church, while others have abandoned the association. Structure, Practices, and membership of each member group varies, depending upon their interests and place on the continuum.

The Women-Church Convergence is the actual working committee of the Women-Church movement. It is composed of elected and self-selected representatives of all the member groups. They meet several times a year for networking and conference planning. There have been three Women-Church Convergences since the first meeting in 1983 in Chicago. Women-Church itself has gotten larger since its inception at the first convergence in 1983. Fifteen hundred people attended the first gathering and twenty-five hundred went to the Albuquerque convergence in 1993. Interviews with participants of Women-Church revealed their overlapping memberships as well as their diverse agendas. These interconnections, as I have come to understand them, form one of Women-Church's greatest strengths for mobilization and growth. However, the diverse goals and agendas of all the groups also adds to the organizational problems of Women-Church. Some difficulties for mobilization also occur as it strives to find an identity as an agent for social change in the church. Yet, all seem to find a home under Women-Church as an umbrella organization that has no formal leadership and that tolerates a wide diversity of religious and spiritual practices. Creating a network of groups and individuals with similar agendas Women-Church enlarges its base of support, and brings in new constituencies such as African American women, Hispanic women and lesbians.

In all areas of church life, in all regions of the United States, and in other countries, women are bypassing and subverting the institutional church. Women-Church participants are creating and participating in their own liturgies (*National Catholic Reporter* 1981, Neu 1981). Women are celebrating the Eucharist, granting absolution to the sick and dying as well as blessing marriages and celebrating covenants for lesbian couples. Church authority is being challenged in the area of dogma as well as liturgy. As part of their feminist ideology, Women-Church members reject hierarchical pronouncements on sexuality and procreative choice (Farrell 1991). Commenting on the institutional church's attempt to control the Cairo conference on population, Frances Kissling, founder of CFFC, noted that the Vatican is a country where there are no families: no women and no children. Episcopal threats of excommunication and church interference in the American political process provide examples of institutional repression, provoking responses that can dramatize and crystallize the feminist critique of institutionalized patriarchy.

All the organizations seem to gain strength from each negative response by the official church to demands by church members for changes in the institution and the teachings of the church. We have only to look at the latest attempts by the pope and the Curia to squash any discussion on ordination or changes in the official line on issues relating to sexuality. The pope issued two recent documents *Veritatis Splendor* (1993) and *Ordinatio Sacerdotalis* (1994) attempting to reinforce the dogmatic nature of church pronouncements and include the question of women's ordination within that framework. An earlier pronouncement issued by the Sacred Congregation for the Faith in 1976 on women's ordination evidently did not close the question.[2] John Paul states in *Ordinatio Sacerdotalis* that

> in order that all doubt may be removed regarding a matter of great importance, a matter which pertains to the church's divine constitution itself, in

virtue of my ministry of confirming the brethren . . . I declare that the church has no authority whatsoever to confer priestly ordination on women and that this judgement is to be definitively held by all the church's faithful. (1994, quoted from full text printed in the *National Catholic Reporter*, 17 June, p. 7)

These documents not only did not put an end to discussion but in fact increased it. Even Senator Edward Kennedy was solicited for his view of women's ordination (he supports the ordination of women) (Niebuhr 1994). Ruth McDonough Fitzpatrick, former director of WOC, noted that after each letter or pronouncement against women's ordination, their membership increases.

Organizational Problems

However, there are drawbacks to this kind of feminist coalition. It is not yet a perfect feminist organization although that is certainly one of its goals. Inclusivity and diversity, important goals of feminist organizations, also represent the areas of most strain. The evolution of the name "Women-Church" shows evidence of the growing consciousness of the group regarding diversity. Originally called "Woman-Church," many members felt that was too-limiting. There is not one way to be woman, but many ways to be women and Women-Church. This idea mirrors the way in which feminism now speaks of feminisms rather than only one way to be feminist. Both movements strive to be as inclusive and as diverse as possible but strains and conflicts remain.

Individual Women-Church members complain of a bias toward academics when choosing leaders. Some express feelings of inferiority when feminists with academic credentials seem to "take over the steering committee meetings." Participants from the large more bureaucratically organized groups often "took over" the meeting while some asserted their authority through use of professional credentials, such as their positions as theologians or ethicists who held academic positions. This makes it difficult for women from the smaller grassroots groups without academic credentials or professional authority to assert themselves or to be heard on an equal footing. Based on her analysis of organizations striving for feminist goals, Noelie Rodriguez notes that:

inequalities in influence persist because those women who have more seniority, or who are more articulate and dependable, generally carry more weight in the group. Thus, while consensus increases the participation and formal power of individual staff members, it does not eliminate the real differences in informal power among them. (1988, p.222; see also Rothschild-Whitt 1982)

Women of color also feel "forgotten" or silenced during meetings and conferences. At the last Women-Church conference in Albuquerque, the evaluation session at the end became a forum for African American women, Latinas, and American Indian women to express their dissatisfaction with the overall conference format and with their perceived lack of input into the conference organization. I say "perceived" because the conference co-chairs were an African American sister and an Hispanic sociologist. White women who thought the conference was well-representative of racial and ethnic minorities in the church expressed dismay and confusion over the charges raised in the evaluation session.

At Albuquerque, class was an especially difficult issue — both to recognize it as an issue of equal importance with race/ethnicity and to formalize a discussion of classism within the conference. Poverty and economic problems were discussed but the specific issue of class biases, especially on the part of members of Women-Church were not given the same play as racism, sexism, and heterosexism. An extensive interview with a woman who organizes welfare mothers raised an important point regarding full participation. All people who wished to set up a table in the exhibit area were required to pay a fee. Not everyone, however, could afford the fee, especially those below the poverty level. This presented a difficult problem for the welfare mothers' organizer: How could she publicize the plight of welfare mothers when she couldn't afford the cost of a table to distribute her literature. From her perception, the organizers were singularly unsympathetic. She finally secured a table, but she stated that she was subjected to rudeness and verbal abuse from the organizers. She did speak to this problem at the evaluation session. Will this problem be addressed in the next conference? Even more important, can class differences be overcome in the grass-roots organizing? Low income women and men and nonacademics may feel intimidated by the conference-type format and fees. How can these problems be remedied by a group that aspires to encourage a "discipleship of equals" and "making the world a welcoming place" for differences and diversity?

Another question regarding inclusivity is how Women-Church addresses diverse religious practices among its members. Although most members come out of the Roman Catholic tradition, many have incorporated other religious practices into their lives. Roman Catholic feminists are incorporating rituals developed in other religious and spiritual traditions. Feminist Wiccan traditions as well as Native American rituals found a place not only in the exhibit hall but also in the Sunday morning ritual. In fact, Sunday morning was set up so that one could choose from a "plethora of sacred experiences." This included not only Wicce and various Native American rituals but Buddhist, Yoga, Tai Chi, Protestant Christian, Imani Temple Catholic worship (Rev. George Stallings' African American breakaway church), Quaker meeting, and creation (or GAIA) ceremonies as well as a feminist Eucharist. Conference participants were encouraged to attend a ceremony outside their own experience. Most attended the feminist Eucharist. In fact, the Holocaust Remembrance ceremony was canceled due to lack of participants. This raises questions of latent anti-Semitism or at the very least some insensitivity toward Judaism and Jewish women. How welcome did Jewish women feel in this convergence if there were any? What kind of outreach was done to Jewish women? Questions such as these need to be resolved if Women-Church is serious about inclusion. On the other hand the name Women-Church explicitly reflects a Christian tradition that Jewish women may not be able to come to terms with given the history between Jews and Christians. This history may be too difficult to overcome at this moment in time.

One positive interpretation expressed by some participants is that this plethora of religious rituals may be due to the search on the part of Roman Catholic women for viable alternatives to the present Catholic liturgy, which many experience as oppressive. Women-Church participants with which I've spoken, seem to either see the plurality of liturgical practices as no problem or a positive development. Liturgies created by Diann Neu for WATER appear to be rather generalized and organized around themes or important life cycle events. For example, she has created liturgies for coming out, celebration of menarche and menopause, and seasonal celebrations. These ceremonies use symbols such as water, blood, nature, aging, home, sorrow, and sexuality that exist universally but can be applied and used in personal ways respecting particular meanings in a variety of contexts. These kinds of liturgies may offer the best way to create unity with diversity. Ritual and liturgy reflect solidarity and affirm diversity as well as commitment. However, this "cafeteria-style" presentation of religious beliefs and practices does signify another tension between the Women-Church movement and the institutional church.

The Future

To date, the women in this movement do not want to, and have no intention of, leaving the church. Contrary to prior reform movements these women are asserting that they are the Church, too, and have invested much of their lives in living out what to them is the gospel message. Living and working in great tension between what the institution is, and what they envision it could and should be, Catholic feminists are searching for alternative models of church while maintaining their identity as Roman Catholics. How far can you go without losing Roman Catholic identity? Where is the line or is there one, that when crossed puts you outside the tradition? From the Vatican's perspective, Women-Church may already be over that line. Facing the same conflict as Martin Luther, Women-Church stands at the margins of the institutional church. Will Women-Church remain part of the loyal opposition, challenging from within or will it move to a feminist post-Christian stance a la Mary Daly outside the institutional church? Will this decision be based on a choice made by participants of Women-Church or will it be forced on them by some official church action?

The Pope has already urged U.S. bishops to be vigilante and fight radical feminism and goddess worship among their congregants. To what length will the official church go in its condemnations of what it perceives to be radical feminist practices infiltrating the church? Are there alternatives to the solutions of Martin Luther, Michel Levefre, or George Stallings? How long can the tension between remaining identified with Catholicism and unhappiness with the institution be sustained? However, creating a new social reality (Wallace 1988), re-imaging the church (Chinnici 1992), or re-weaving it (as in the most recent Women-Church Convergence theme) may lead some to find that it is "beyond patching (Schneiders 1991). If the Vatican continues to uphold its present position on women's ordination, ordination of married men, its conservative sexual ethics, and hierarchical organization, will women remain or leave as they perceive that the institution refuses to change? It may take larger numbers of women "defecting in place" (Winter, Lumis, and Stokes 1995) to impact on the church hierarchy or as Ratzinger has often stated, the organizational church would be happier with a mass exodus of troublesome women leaving a meaner, leaner church (Lernoux 1989). Because there is as yet little alternative to Roman Catholic identity and practice that is as satisfying to many of these women, I don't think easy exit of mass numbers will be likely (see Hirschman 1970 for a full discussion of organizational factors that may encourage or discourage exit). Reluctance to give up the more traditional Eucharistic celebration at the last Women-Church convergence and their continued participation in various levels of institutional life are evidence that most women are not yet ready to leave. Can Women-Church become an agent of transformation within the institution? Will it remain a viable feminist social movement and organization if institutional transformation does occur? The future of both church and feminism is at stake.

Update

Women-Church had a strong presence in Beijing at the United Nations' Fourth World Conference on Women. Frances Kissling, president of Catholics for a Free Choice, was an NGO delegate. Interviewed in various media, she challenged institutional church positions on women's reproductive rights, sexual orientation, family, women's employment, and their objection to the use of the term "gender" since it might endorse homosexuality and transsexuality. Kissling's engagement with Vatican discourse exemplifies the nature of discursive politics and how Women-Church engages it in hope of institutional and social transformation (Conscience 1995, pp. 3-10). The Pope's recent letter to women (1995), illustrates that Women-Church has, at least, provoked the institutional church into a response which is an acknowledgement that the issues are real and need to be addressed. The pope did recognize and apologize for passed suffering although he is not willing to bring women into the ruling hierarchy of the church through ordination. Judging from media responses and responses of some members of Women-Church, the "dialogue" is just beginning.

Notes

1. An expanded form of Schussler Fiorenza's comments on Women-Church can be found in *Women Moving Church*, ed. D. Neu and M. Riley. See also Ruether 1986 for a the "Theology and Practice of Feminist Liturgical Communities" the subtitle to her book *Women-Church*.

2. See Swidler and Swidler 1977 and Field-Bibb 1991 for extensive discussions on this earlier church document.

References

Baum, Gregory. 1988. The church and the women's movement. *The Ecumenist* 27:12-15.

Chinnici, Rosemary. 1992. *Can women re-image the Church?* New York: Paulist Press.

Distortion of the draft platform for action: How the Catholic hierarchy misrepresents the document. *Conscience* xvi (Autumn): 3-10.

Equal is as equal does. 1995. *Conscience* xvi (Spring/Summer): 3-9.

Farrell, Susan A. 1991. "It's our church, too!" Women's position in the Roman Catholic Church today. In *The social construction of gender*, ed. Lorber and S.A. Farrell. Newbury Park, CA: Sage.

_____ 1992. *Sexuality, gender, and ethics: The social construction of feminist ethics in the Roman Catholic* Church. Ann Arbor, MI: University Microfilms International.

Field-Bibb, Jacqueline. *Women towards priesthood: Ministerial politics and feminist praxis.* Cambridge, GB: Cambridge University Press.

Fiorenza, Elisabeth Schussler. 1979. "You are not to be called father": Early Christian history in a feminist perspective." *CrossCurrents* XXIX: 301-323.

_____. 1983. *In memory of her: A feminist theological reconstruction of Christian origins*. New York: Crossroad.

Foucault, Michel. 1972. *The Archaeology of Knowledge*. New York: Harper Colophon.

_____. 1973. *The Order of Things: An Archaeology of the Human Sciences*. New York: Vintage.

_____. 1980a. *The History of Sexuality*, Vol. 1: An Introduction. New York: Vintage.

_____. 1981. "The Order of Discourse." In *Untying the Text: A Post- Structuralist Reader*, ed. R. Young, 48-78. Boston: Routledge & Kegan Paul.

Freeman, Jo. 1979. Resource mobilization and strategy: A model for analyzing social movement organization actions. In *The dynamics of social movements*, ed. M.N. Zald and J.D. McCarthy. Cambridge, MA: Winthrop.

Hirschman, Albert O. 1970. *Exit, Voice, and Loyalty: Responses to Decline in Firms, Organizations, and States*. London, UK: Oxford University Press.

Hunt, Mary. 1990a. New coalitions replacing church as faith-proprietor. *National Catholic Reporter* February 16.

_____. 1990b. Defining "women-church." *Waterwheel* 3: 1-3.

John Paul II. 1988. *On the dignity and vocation of women*. Vatican Translation. Boston: St. Paul Books and Media.

_____. 1993. "Veritatis Splendor" ("The Splendor of Truth") *Origins*. Washington, DC: The Catholic News Service.

_____. 1994. "Ordinatio Sacerdotalis." *National Catholic Reporter* 17 June.

_____. 1995. *Letter of Pope John Paul II to women*. Vatican Trans. Boston: Pauline Books & Media.

Katzenstein, Mary Fainsod. 1990. Feminism within American institutions: Unobtrusive mobilization in the 1980s" *Signs* 16: 27-54.

————. 1995. Discursive politics and feminist activism in the Catholic Church. In *Feminist organizations: Harvest of the new women's movement*, ed. M.M. Ferree and P.Y. Martin. Philadelphia: Temple University Press.

Lernoux, Penny. 1989. *People of God: The Struggle for World Catholicism*. New York: Viking.

Martin, Patricia Yancey. 1990. Rethinking feminist organizations. *Gender & Society* 4: 182-206.

Merton, Robert K. 1972. Insiders and outsiders: A chapter in the sociology of knowledge. *American Journal of Sociology* 78: 9-47.

Milhaven, Annie Lally , ed. 1987. *The Inside Stories: 13 Valiant Women Challenging the Church*. Mystic, CT: Twenty-Third Publications.

National Catholic Reporter. 1981. U.S. women's liturgies too widespread to ignore. July 17.

Neu, Diann. 1981. Can the church incorporate feminist church model? *National Catholic Reporter* July 17.

Neu, Diane and Maria Riley, eds. 1982. *Women moving church*. Washington, DC: Center of Concern.

Niebuhr, Gustav. 1994. "Kennedy supports ordination of women as Catholic priests." *The New York Times*, 8 September.

Oberschall, Anthony. 1973. *Social conflicts and social movements*. Englewood Cliffs, NJ: Prentice-Hall.

Rodriguez, Noelie, Maria. 1988. Transcending bureaucracy: Feminist politics at a shelter for battered women. *Gender & Society* 2: 214-227.

Rothschild-Whitt, Joyce. 1979. The collectivist organization: An alternative to rational bureaucratic models. *American Sociological Review* 44: 509-527.

Ruether, Rosemary Radford. 1975. *New Woman New Earth*. New York: Crossroad.

————. 1986. *Women-Church: Theology & practice*. San Francisco: Harper & Row.

————. 1992. *Gaia and God: An Ecofeminist Theology of Earth Healing*. San Francisco: HarperCollins.

Schneiders, Sandra M. 1991. *Beyond patching: Faith and feminism in the Catholic Church*. New York: Paulist Press.

Stan, Adele M. 1995. "Frances Kissling: Making the Vatican Sweat." *Ms*, September/October, 40-43.

Swidler, Leonard and Arlene Swidler, eds. 1977. *Women Priests: A Catholic Commentary on the Vatican Declaration*. New York: Paulist Press.

Wallace, Ruth A. 1988. Catholic women and the creation of a new social reality. *Gender &Society* 2: 24-38.

————. 1992. *They call her pastor*. Albany, NY: State University Press of New York.

WATER in Europe. 1995. *WaterWheel* 8 (Summer): 6.

Winter, Miriam Therese, Adair Lummis, and Allison Stokes. 1995. *Defecting in Place: Women Taking Responsibility for Their Own Lives*. New York: Crossroad.

MAINTAINING "CHRISTIAN MANLINESS" AND "CHRISTIAN WOMANLINESS": CONTROLLING GENDER IN CHRISTIAN COLLEGES, 1925-1991[1]

Richard W. Flory

Sociology Department
Biola University

Abstract

This paper analyzes attempts to control changing conceptions of gender, and the changing definitions of what was considered "Christian manliness" and "Christian womanliness" in four Christian colleges in the U.S., from 1925-1991. Conservative Christian leaders of the 1920s spoke against provocative dress styles of women and their adverse moral effect on men, and debated the proper role of women in the church, the home and the workplace. Conservative Christian ideology maintains that women are to be subordinate to men, to remain in the home and child-rearing roles and are not to be in positions of authority over men, especially in the church. These themes are of primary symbolic importance for conservative Christians, and intersect other issues such as the inerrancy of scripture, the family, morality, and the influence of the larger culture. This ideology is reinforced in Christian colleges through formal means such as behavioral rules, and dating, sexual conduct and dress codes, and through informal means such as differential tracking of female and male students and faculty. Findings show that contrary to what might be expected, as these schools moved away from a more fundamentalist ideology toward a less restrictive and more inclusive ideology, mechanisms used to control gender relations, sexuality, and the female body are persistent, and in some cases, have increased.

INTRODUCTION

The growing literature that analyzes Evangelicalism[2] and gender has clearly shown that through the 1920s, women occupied often prominent public ministry and leadership positions within the movement, but that increasingly after the 1930s, and especially after World War II, women were moved out of public leadership and

51

service positions in favor of their remaining in the home as wives and mothers.[3] This move of women out of the public and into the private domestic realm was the result of the efforts of male Evangelical leaders to "re-masculinize" what had been a religious movement dominated by women. In this effort, two major themes emerged: that women had the power for good, to be godly influences in their husband and children's lives, and in the Church—or for evil, to lead men astray through their sexual wiles, and to introduce heterodoxy into the Church if allowed to be in positions of authority.[4]

Most of this research has focused on the lives of women in public ministry and within various religious organizations, and/or the public ideology of various Evangelical leaders as they preached, wrote and published about the "proper" role for Christian women, and their potential for good or ill in the Church and society. In this paper, I seek to complement this literature by focusing on Evangelical colleges as central religious organizations that have provided the institutional contexts for the training of significant numbers of Evangelical men and women. That is, I am less concerned with individual beliefs, attitudes and opportunities, than with how these institutions have adapted to changes in the larger culture, acting as socialization agents for successive generations of Evangelical young people.

In what ways, if any, have these colleges changed their conceptions of gender ideology and practice? Arguments such as that presented by Hunter,[5] would lead to the expectation that as changes took place in the larger culture through such developments as the women's movement, that these schools would increasingly accommodate their gender ideology to the norms of the larger culture. Thus we would expect there to be a decrease in the ideology that presents women as having the power for good or evil over men, church and society, and an increase in the opportunities for women within Evangelicalism, particularly as these schools move away from Fundamentalism and develop a less restrictive ideology.

THE CASES

In this paper I compare four Evangelical Christian colleges that have had extensive influence within Evangelical Christianity since the 1920s: Wheaton College in Wheaton, Illinois (founded in 1860), Moody Bible Institute of Chicago (founded in 1886), Biola University in La Mirada, California (founded in 1908), and Bob Jones University in Greenville, South Carolina (founded in 1926). These schools have produced many Evangelical leaders, and by their many and varied religious and educational programs have had an enormous impact on Evangelicalism as a whole. Moreover, since these four schools were in the 1920s, all self-identified Fundamentalist schools, but have now developed into four distinctly different approaches to conservative Christianity, they provide excellent cases for the study of the development of gender ideology and practice that has taken place within American Evangelicalism.

Areas of Analysis

Ideals of gender norms have been expressed in these schools in various ways. In this paper I will analyze three areas: 1) The development of the gender composition of each of these schools, 2) the development of student behavioral rules that regulated relations between men and women, and 3) rules that governed acceptable dress styles.

The gender composition of these schools is indicative not only of the relative predominance of men or women, but their relative position in each school, particularly in positions of authority and access to "religious authority."[6] Similarly, the behavioral and dress code rules are important not only because of the behaviors and dress styles that were both promoted and prohibited, but because they are indicators of what these schools believed to be acceptable conduct and presentation of self for both women and men.

Data

The data for this study was collected from archival sources at each school, covering the time period, 1925-1991. Behavioral rules that regulated relations between the sexes and the dress code rules were collected for each year of their publication in the student handbooks published at each school. The amount and type of these rules changed over time, but in general, these took up several pages in the handbook, and they were a core feature of student life at each school.[7]

Gender composition was collected for faculty and students, from registrar records, school catalogs, and school annuals in five year increments, from 1925-1990/91. Where possible, I relied on official registrar records for student enrollments. Where these were not available or if the school refused to allow these data to be used, the student yearbooks were used, comparing names and pictures in order to determine the gender breakdown of the students. For the faculty, both the school catalog and the school yearbooks were used to determine the number of male and female faculty members, and the areas in which they taught.

FINDINGS

Gender Composition

Analyzing the gender composition of each school serves two purposes, first it provides a picture of the gender makeup of those who taught and attended the school, and thus embodied the image the school wanted to project, and second, it serves as a measure of the growth or decline in the number of males and females within the school, and the particular patterns that such growth may take. Of particular interest is the degree to which the initial gender composition changed, as a partial indicator of the potential for change in the religious and ideological position of the school in terms of expectations and opportunities for men and women. Thus, the gender composition of each school cuts across ideological lines in terms of the proportional representation of men and women in general, and within various segments of the schools.

Wheaton. The faculty composition at Wheaton has always included fewer women than men. The percentage of the total faculty that was made up of women ranged from a high of 40 percent in 1935 to a low of 15 percent 1975. This percentage had only increased to 20 percent by 1991. For Wheaton, not only was there a decrease in the proportional representation of women in the faculty, but the real number of women faculty members declined as well—in 1945 there were forty-three women faculty out of 116 total faculty and in 1991 there were just thirty-four out of a total of 173.[8]

Within the religion faculty, as with each of the other schools in this study, no women taught in the core Bible and Theology courses.[9] Between 1931 and the mid-1970s, there were several women teaching Christian Education. This number increased from two in the 1930s to six by the mid-1940s but by the mid-1960s they had been reduced to two. After 1975 there were no longer any women teaching in Christian Education.[10]

Student enrollment at Wheaton College grew from 189 students in 1920 to over 1000 students in 1940, to over 2200 students in 1975, to its all time high enrollment of just over 2700 students in the 1980s. The enrollment in 1991 had declined by about 200, to 2548 total students enrolled. Throughout, these students were very nearly equally divided between men and women. Through the early 1930s there were between 53 and 56 percent women students, from 1950 through the early 1980s there were between 50 and 54 percent men, and from the early 1980s through 1991, there were between 50 and 53% women.[11]

Moody Bible Institute. The social composition of the faculty at Moody always included far fewer women than men. The percentage of the faculty made up of women ranged between a high of 34 percent in 1950, and low of 8 percent in 1970. In 1990, the faculty included fourteen women, which was the greatest number since 1945, although the 14 percent of the faculty that this number represents was less than one-half of that in 1950.[12]

In 1980 two women were teaching Christian Education courses in the religion faculty, and although the departmental breakdown is not available prior to 1980, it is not likely that any women taught anything other than Christian Education within the religion faculty.[13] What is important to note here is not that there weren't any women teaching something other than Christian Education in the religion faculty, but that after 1980, there were no women even teaching Christian Education.

Student enrollment at Moody grew from 410 students in 1953,[14] to over 900 by the 1960s to almost 1400 in 1990.[15] With the exception of enrollment during the 1940s, male students have generally outnumbered female students. Since the mid-1950s in fact, the percentage of male students has steadily increased from 53 percent in 1956 to 60 percent in 1990.[16]

Biola. A comparison of the gender composition of Biola's faculty and students show opposite developmental trends. Among the faculty, there were always fewer women than men, and although by 1950 that gap had narrowed from 23 percent female to 43 percent female, this was a short-lived development. By 1955 the percentage of women faculty had dropped to 27 percent, and by 1990, women made up only 22 percent of the faculty despite the fact that the entire faculty had increased by 63 percent.[17] Thus, despite doubling the actual number of women faculty members between 1950 to 1990, their proportional representation decreased because of the even larger increase in male faculty members of almost 82 percent during this same period.

Within the religion faculty,[18] there was an even lower percentage of women faculty members than in the rest of the faculty. In fact, no women taught in the core Bible and theology curriculum, and the few women that were included in the religion faculty either taught in Christian Education or in missions, which numbers decreased over time.[19]

Student enrollment at Biola shows the opposite development as that in the faculty. With the exception of several years immediately prior to and following World War II, when almost equal numbers of men and women were enrolled, the trend began in the late 1950s toward a significantly greater number of women being enrolled than men. The numbers of men students gradually declined over time, such that after 1978 when men comprised 45 percent of the student body, the percentage of male students never again reached above 42 percent.[20]

Bob Jones University. The faculty composition at BJU, unlike Biola, Moody and Wheaton, always included a significant percentage of women. In fact, between 1936 and 1955 there were a greater number of women—ranging from 54 percent to 64 percent—than men faculty members. Between 1955 and 1965 the percentages were roughly equal, and it was not until 1970 that the ratio changed to more men than women, which remained the same through 1991, approximately 55 percent men and 45 percent women.[21] However, this was not true for the faculty in the School of Religion. With the exception of one woman in 1937 and another in 1940, and those who teach "church administration,"[22] there were no women teaching the core Bible and theology classes.[23]

The student enrollment at BJU, like most other colleges and universities over this same time span, grew at a remarkable rate. In 1930[24] the total enrollment was 108 students, of which 52 percent were female and 48 percent male, By 1935 the total enrollment had grown to 160 students and the percentages had reversed, 53 percent male and 47 percent female, The enrollment figures remained well under 1000 until after World War II when in 1950 total enrollment grew to 2130 students, of which 42 percent were women and 58 percent men. By 1980, total enrollment at BJU had increased to 4404 students of which 51 percent were women, and by 1990, with the enrollment remaining over 4000 students, these percentages had reversed with men comprising 51 percent of the student population.[25]

Relations Between the Sexes

Each school in this study implemented many different types of rules that were meant to govern student behavior. Among these were rules the intent of which was to regulate relations between the sexes such as dating, courtship and marriage. These rules were aimed toward accomplishing several tasks, such as controlling the amount of contact that men and women had with each other, reducing the sexual appeal of the female body, regulating dating and/or marriage partners, controlling inappropriate physical contact, including any sexual activity outside of marriage, and regulating sexuality.

Wheaton. Regulating relations between the sexes does not seem to have been nearly as great a preoccupation at Wheaton as it was at each of the other schools included in this study. While each of the other schools directed much effort in attempting to in effect, "micro-manage" the dating, courtship and marriage relations of their students, Wheaton, as evidenced by the rules that were intended to regulate these relations, opted for a somewhat different path. At Wheaton there were initially far fewer rules, and these rules decreased to a core that remained essentially unchanged until the 1970s, when new rules were added that became a permanent part of Wheaton's rule structure.

In 1927, there were several rules that were intended to govern male-female relationships at Wheaton. The intent of these rules seems to have been to keep students from entering into serious relationships with each other, to provide supervision of certain dating activities, and to discourage physical contact between men and women:

> Students are advised to not become engaged until their education is finished.
>
> Students who marry during the academic year will be asked to leave the school.
>
> Young ladies will not be permitted to leave Wheaton in company with young men without an approved chaperon.
>
> Among young people and adults of opposite sexes, embracing should be reserved for members of one's own family.[26]

By 1929, the rule discouraging "embracing" between members of the opposite sexes had been dropped, and by 1933, students were allowed to marry during the school year, so long as they "secure[ed] faculty and parental approval."[27] This rule remained in effect through 1964, at which time the students were required to submit a "letter of intent to marry...to the Student Personnel Office 30 days in advance of the wedding." This rule remained through 1991.

Through 1975, the main concerns of Wheaton in regard to relations between the sexes, were that students not enter into serious relationships such as engagement and marriage while they were still students, and ultimately, that the school be apprised of the students plans to marry. In 1975 however, new rules were added that explicitly listed activities that had previously been implicit expectations of Wheaton students:

> Practices which are known to be morally wrong by Biblical teaching are not acceptable for members of the Wheaton College community. Included are such specific acts such as...sexual sins such as premarital sex, adultery and homosexual behavior.[28]

These prohibitions remained a part of the rules through 1991.

Moody Bible Institute. At Moody, these rules developed in two different stages, first, in the period from the 1920s to the 1950s, the rules dealt primarily with restricting the types of access that men and women students had to each other, while at the same time growing more specific in their restrictions, and second, from the 1960s to 1991, these rules began to allow greater amounts of individual freedom, while simultaneously providing more codified parameters of behavior. These patterns are similar to those found at Biola, although for Moody, the regulation of dating, courtship and marriage remained a core aspect of these rules, and remained in modified form through 1991.

From the 1920s to the 1950s, relations between the sexes were regulated in various ways. In the 1920s and 1930s, the separation of the sexes seems to have been the primary aim of these rules. Men and women met separately for required group devotions, had separate entrances to the campus post office, and in classes men and women students were seatred on opposite sides of the classroom.[29] When students did manage to make dates to see each other socially, they were only allowed to do so only with the permission of the Superintendent of the school,[30] and should a romance develop, students were told that marriage between enrolled students was officially "disapproved." If students were to marry without the "consent of the faculty," they would be required to withdraw from school.[31]

In the 1940s and 1950s, more extensive rules were listed in the student handbook that set out the established "social hours" during which students could spend time together, and specified the conditions under which unmarried men and women could use automobiles for outings. Social hours were limited to attending Sunday services together and to several hours on Saturday and Sunday afternoons, and Monday afternoon and evening.[32] At this same time, the prevalence of automobiles among Moody students represented a potential problem in male/female relationships because of the privacy and mobility they provided. In response, Moody prohibited couples from using automobiles for social outings unless they had special permission and were accompanied in the car by an approved chaperon.[33] Also listed as prohibited behavior during this time were "public displays of affection" including "hand holding," as these were considered, "not in good taste and will not be tolerated."[34]

Beginning in the 1960s, Moody began to allow greater individual discretion in developing relationships, yet simultaneously set down more specific rules that set the parameters within which individual decisions could be made. For example, students had previously been required to get permission for off-campus socializing, but the 1962/63 handbook stated only that, "Students are expected to know the hours for dating and to plan their dates within these periods. Social regulations govern dating with friends either on or off campus."[35] Similarly, while the "public display of affection" was still prohibited, hand-holding was listed in the 1974 Handbook as the one public display of affection that was specifically allowed: "Students are to conduct themselves as Christian ladies and gentlemen at all times. Public display of affection other than handholding will result in counsel or discipline."[36] By 1991, the Student Handbook was even more specific and instructed the students in the appropriate displays of affection, both public and private: "public displays of affection is to be limited to hand holding or taking an escort's arm (This guideline also applies to Married Students). Private displays of affection should follow the biblical principles of chastity and purity which do not allow for activities known as 'petting'."[37] Students were further advised that, "At MBI we believe that God created men and women as sexual beings...wonderfully made for each other....we believe God intended that this gift only be used within the context of heterosexual marriage (I Cor. 6:12-20)...[and] that sexual activity and expression apart from the marriage relationship is a sin against one's body and violates biblical standards (I Thes. 4:3-8)."[38] Note that Moody did not make nearly as extensive a statement about sexual activity as did Wheaton and Biola, and left implicit issues of homosexuality.

Biola. At Biola, rules regulating the relations between the sexes developed in two distinct stages. From the 1920s through the mid-1960s, these rules dealt primarily with courtship, engagement and marriage, and in their development became more restrictive after their initial adoption before being dropped altogether from the student handbooks in 1976. After these rules were dropped, other more specific rules were instituted, not having to do with the selection of dating partners, but with what might be going on during those dates. That is after 1976, specific rules were established regarding premarital sexual activity, and homosexual activity, that had not previously been listed and had been at most, implicit expectations of the students.

Between the 1920s and the 1960s, socializing between men and women was regulated by various means. In the 1920s, Biola students were allowed to socialize on campus in adjoining men's and women's social parlors, or off campus if the woman wishing to go on the date had been given permission by the Dean of Students.[39] Students whose relationships had become more serious, were instructed that they were not to marry while enrolled without the permission of the faculty.[40] By the 1950s these restrictions were eased somewhat in that only first year women students were required to seek permission from the Dean before going out on a date, while older women students needed only to fill out a "date slip" that indicated her plans. No students during this time period were allowed to date anyone who was not a part of the school "family," nor anyone who was a "non-Christian." Students were informed as well that the "faculty reserv[ed] the right to regulate [the] dating privileges" of the students.[41] By 1965, students were no longer required to obtain permission to go out on a date, and by 1968, all dating regulations had been removed from the student handbook.

Although rules governing dating relations between men and women students were no longer in effect after 1968, rules governing engagements and marriage remained, and in fact became more detailed in comparison to the original prohibition of marriage, finally being withdrawn completely from the Student Handbook. The original form of the rule, that students were not permitted to marry while enrolled as Biola students, served until the mid-1950s, but in 1957 more elaborate regulations were established which allowed students to become engaged and married while students, although under very strict conditions:

> The engagement application form must be obtained from the Chairman of the Student Personnel and Guidance Committee and returned to him upon completion....All women under 21 must furnish the Committee with proof of parental consent....A minimum courtship of six months shall be required of all applicants before submitting application to the Committee.[42]

These requirements were gradually revised such that by 1968 they were presented as a recommendation of a minimum time period for courtship before marriage,[43] and by the mid-1980s all such dating and engagement/marriage regulations had been dropped from the student handbooks.[44]

As formal rules governing dating, courtship, and marriage were taking on less importance within the rules, other rules were instituted that at first implicitly, and then specifically prohibited sexual activity that was premarital, extramarital or homosexual in nature. These rules began in 1971 with general statements about the need for Christian students to refrain from certain types of behavior that were "immoral, illegal, physically harmful to one's self or others, dishonest, profane, divisive, contentious or harmful to one's reputation and witness," which the school viewed as being "detrimental to the individual and also to the larger community."[45] These statements left specific prohibitions of certain types of sexual activity implicit until 1980, when the Student Handbook listed several "practices which are known to be morally wrong by biblical teaching are not acceptable for members of the Biola College community" including "sexual sins such as premarital sex, adultery, and homosexual behavior."[46] These rules remained a part of the rules through 1991.[47]

Bob Jones University. Among the schools in this study, Bob Jones University has developed the most comprehensive system of rules aimed at regulating relations between the sexes, and in general, these rules tended to change only in the direction of more rules being added over time, and are a core characteristic of BJU. These have taken on almost mythic proportions within Fundamentalist and Evangelical Christian circles, particularly in terms of the amount and types of rules which the students must follow. While there are many stories that upon investigation turn out to be apocryphal, they are at least partially based in fact. Perhaps the most famous of these stories says that there are separate sidewalks for men and women at BJU—each appropriately painted pink or blue—and a "six-inch" rule that requires men and women to remain at least six inches apart at all times. These stories are in fact not true, however it is true that men and women, whether they are related or not, may not have any physical contact at any time. In addition, chaperons are required on all dates and at all school functions where both men and women will be in attendance. In fact, for many years men and women could not even walk on campus together unless they had what the BJU Student Handbook termed, "legitimate business" in the same direction. This rule is no longer in effect, however men and women still may not be in the classroom buildings together unless they are actually in class, the professor then acting as chaperon.

For BJU, these male-female rules were instituted early in the history of the school, with the amount of dates a woman could go out on being tied to her year in school—the older she was, the more dates she could have each week. These dates however, were never to be two students alone together, they were always to have a chaperon along. This rule never changed after it was established in the early years of the school.

The concept of "proper Christian chaperonage"[48] was established in the opening year of the school and progressed to the institutionalization of the chaperon for virtually all BJU events in which male and female students would be together. For example, in order for men and women students to attend sporting events on campus—not necessarily to go there together as couples—there must be school sponsored chaperons in attendance. Similarly, men and women had separate times to use the swimming pool and the gymnasium, and further, they were not allowed to be in the gymnasium or swimming pool area at the same time—even with a chaperon.[49]

This also resulted in the "social parlor" that students may use for on campus dates. The social parlor is comprised of two large, upstairs rooms filled with couches and chairs, all under the supervision of a chaperon. The chaperon makes rounds every 20 minutes to make sure that there is no physical contact between the students. There are not individual chaperons for each dating couple in the Social Parlor.[50]

Dress Code

A part of the rules that was closely related to the rules governing relations between the sexes was the dress code. As each school developed its dress code, the primary purpose seems to have been two-fold; first, to ensure that the students dressed appropriately whether they were on or off campus, in Sunday services, or at work, and second, to simultaneously differentiate between men and women in their respective dress styles, and to decrease the potential sexual appeal of women as exhibited through their dress styles. As the number of these rules increased over time, the overriding themes remained essentially the same, that women were to dress modestly, and were not to wear anything that was too physically revealing and thus potentially seductive, and were to exhibit "Christian womanliness" in their dress. Men were expected to wear clothing appropriate to the setting and to be well groomed and by so doing, present themselves as proper examples of "Christian manliness."

Wheaton. Proper personal appearance was an important part of Wheaton's expectations as well, although these did not become formally codified as a "dress code" until the early 1960s. Prior to that time, guidelines regarding proper dress were largely enforced through informal means. Two handbooks published from the mid-1940s to the early 1960s, served to inform students of certain Wheaton traditions and extolled proper etiquette in such areas as dating, dressing, bathing, and women's makeup. For women, "correctness [was] the keynote" in dressing, which included "skirts and sweaters, suits and tailored dresses" and "trim slacks" but the latter only when appropriate such as attending a sports event, but never for "promenading."[51] Neither of these publications presented what was required, or more accurately, prohibited, apparel for particular occasions.

Appropriate Dress for Women. In 1962, the first formalized "Campus Dress Regulations" were published in the Student Handbook, and included different rules for women and for men. Women were expected to wear skirts and dresses in public places such as in the classroom, around campus, and in church services, and as such, the rules put forth the times and places that apparel other than skirts and dresses were allowed to be worn; "Bermuda shorts, jeans, and slacks may be worn only in the following situations: the tennis court, group picnics and other outdoor active sports, casual parties in the gym, and in your own room but not in the dormitory lounge or on the streets."[52]

By 1968, when demands for personal freedom and personal expression were being made in the larger culture, Wheaton revised its dress regulations in an attempt to allow its female students both greater individual freedom and to provide more specific guidelines as to what was acceptable and what was not acceptable dress. Thus, "sport clothes," were allowed to be worn in the same places as previously, and some trouser-type apparel was considered appropriate for the classroom, while other regulations were imposed that were intended to keep women's dress styles from reflecting newer forms of fashion expression such as particularly short mini-skirts and the "braless" look;

> Pant dresses or culottes are to be considered acceptable for classroom attire; denim levis and cut-offs are to be considered acceptable sportswear.
> Though there is at present no rule regarding skirt length, campus opinion suggests that a length of 2 to 4 inches above the knee is maximum.
> College women should use discretion in the choice of wearing apparel, including skirt lengths, undergarments, and the fit of all clothes.[53]

For Wheaton women then, "appropriate dress" was defined as wearing appropriately feminine clothing such as skirts, dresses and blouses, while taking care not to be too immodest by wearing skirts that were too short or too tight, or by going without appropriate undergarments.

Appropriate Dress for Men. The dress regulations for men were less restrictive, and did not change in the same manner as those for women. In the 1962 Handbook, men were informed of acceptable attire:

> Knee-length bermuda shorts are acceptable attire. However, athletic shorts, other shorts and ragged makeshift bermudas are not considered suitable attire for Wheaton men.Levis, jeans and beachcomber pants are not acceptable attire for class and Chapel.
> Altered or makeshift athletic shirts including collarless "T" shirts should not be worn in campus buildings.
> Shoes and socks are expected to be worn.[54]

Thus, for male students at Wheaton, "appropriate dress" was defined as wearing clothing that was sufficiently neat in appearance, that could not be considered unkempt, "makeshift," or sloppy, which was not appropriate for Wheaton men.

Non-gendered dress regulations. In 1970, all references to sex-specific dress standards were dropped, and in their place was a single statement that applied to all Wheaton students:

> Wheaton College encourages its student population to accept the responsibility of making mature choices in every area of life. Therefore, students have the freedom to choose their own form of dress on campus appropriate to the occasion. They are to be guided in their choice by the biblical view of man and social propriety which incorporates modesty and good taste. A student-faculty committee is responsible for applying this level of expectation and for counseling any student who seems to behave irresponsibly in matters of dress.[55]

This statement remained the guiding principle governing campus dress from 1970 through 1978. In 1978 however, Wheaton implemented rules meant to define and prohibit the wearing of clothing that it deemed inappropriate and not in good taste for Wheaton students. Clothing that was considered inappropriate had mostly to do with exposing too much of one's body, and although there was no mention of sex-specific dress regulations, the clothing listed as inappropriate was that which would more likely be worn by women; ". . . in most public places on and off campus, abbreviated tops, short shorts, bare backs, bare feet, and other forms of beachwear are inappropriate."[56]

These regulations continued and in fact, Wheaton added a few more regulations to those listed above. In 1983, the wearing of shorts in classes, offices and chapel was prohibited altogether although ultimately, the school allowed that "some dress shorts might be considered appropriate,"[57] and in 1983 a requirement was added that shirts were to be worn at all times in public places. The final change was the addition in 1988, of the statement that there was to be "no sunbathing on front campus or in public view," which remained through 1991.[58]

Moody Bible Institute. Moody's dress code rules expanded greatly over the years, starting with simple statements in the 1930s and developing into rather complex sets of rules that determined what was permissible apparel depending on the time of day, the location of the student, and whether the student was a male or a female. The development of the dress code over time demonstrates that Moody was aware of fashion developments in the larger culture and, in a manner similar to Bob Jones, decided to implement and maintain a dress code that would set Moody men and women apart from many of these trends, rather than try to negotiate acceptable dress standards that took into account various fashion trends.

Appropriate dress for men. The rules governing dress for Moody men were meant to keep them from dressing too casually while in class, while eating in the dining hall, or attending Sunday church services, and to maintain an acceptable level of personal hygiene. For many years these rules required men to wear ties to class and at meals, and even in 1991, men were still required to wear ties (or turtlenecks) to church services on Sundays. The first listing of these rules in 1950 listed such specific regulations as a required shirt and tie with either a coat or sweater to be worn in the classroom, library, and to dinner, prohibiting such casual wear as t-shirts, and shorts, and making sure that the men remembered that "Fingernails should be clean and hair combed.[59] By 1965, ties were no longer required before the evening meal, but new rules were put in place to specify acceptable and unacceptable "sport clothes," and the manner in which they were to be worn: "Shirts should be worn tucked in....Sweatshirts, leather jackets, wind breakers, "T" shirts and blue jeans are not allowed at any time....Shorts of any kind are not to be worn in public except during participation in athletic contests." These same rules applied for what was acceptable wear "in classrooms, library, and office,"[60] and remained in effect for classroom wear through 1991.

Appropriate dress for women. The aim of the dress code for women was two-fold, first, to ensure that women dressed in a "modest" fashion, and second, to ensure that the normative style of dress for women properly demonstrated "Christian womanliness." The first listing of the extensively codified dress code rules in 1950 was prefaced by an extensive quote from "Dodderidge's *Family Expositor,*" that served to define just what Moody had in mind when it told its women students that they were "expected to dress in styles becoming Christian women, avoiding extremes in fashion:"[61]

> The women. . . are to be. . . particularly careful to adorn themselves only with decent apparel, with modesty and sobriety. . . . Be careful to behave in every respect as becomes those whose happiness it is to be acquainted with the

great principles of Christianity; and particularly consider how they should influence your conduct in the adorning of your persons. . . . let your ornament be of a much more glorious nature. . . a well regulated temper of mind [and a] beautiful and harmonious disposition of a meek and quiet spirit.[62]

Thus, for Moody, personal appearance and the appropriate presentation of self for women was not limited to clothing choices, but to one's demeanor as well.

The 1950 rules show that trousers of any sort were not an option for women, and were otherwise oriented toward requiring women to sufficiently cover their bodies, and to keep them from wearing anything that might be too revealing: "Necklines are to be discreet. Sleeves must be modest in length and closed under-arm so as not to reveal the body. Skirts must be long enough to come well below the knee. The body must be firmly supported by undergarments, and if sweaters are used, they *must* be chosen with discretion and worn with a blouse."[63]

These themes continued through the 1970s, as Moody women were told that, "The guiding principles for Christian women's dress are modesty, neatness, and womanliness,"[64] after which more specific dress requirements were listed, such as the proper length for skirts and dresses was "to the knee," that "Stockings or knee socks are to be worn at all times," and that "Stretch slacks are never appropriate."[65] By 1974, skirts and dresses were allowed to be "no shorter than two inches above the top of the knees," but "extremely tight-fitting garments or low necklines are not permitted."[66]

Between 1979 and 1991, the dress code rules became more specific about what types of clothing women were not allowed to wear because of their immodest nature. In 1979, these were listed as "garments which are tight fitting, sheer or have low necklines; shoulderless dresses and tops; and bare midriffs."[67] By 1991 the min-imum length of skirts and dresses had been lengthened from its previous limit of "two inches above the top of the kneecap," to being required to "reach the top of the kneecap."[68]

Biola. At Biola, these rules were established incrementally, initially more restrictive dress code requirements were added, but these were eventually either withdrawn or modified resulting in a less restrictive, more generally worded dress code. All of the changes can be traced to Biola attempting to come to terms with the dress styles of the day, and at least in part, with the general cultural openness that is found in southern California, while presenting its students as good examples of Christian men and Christian women through their clothing choices.

The first dress code rules were listed in the 1941/42 Student Handbook, which stated only that "informal dress" was to be worn "all school functions."[69] Former president Samuel H. Sutherland noted that one reason for there being no codified dress code prior to the 1950s was that people "didn't tend to dress in extremes in the 1930s and 1940s, [so a dress code] wasn't needed until the 1950s," when broad-er ranges of styles for men and women were being worn.[70] This rule remained the only explicit rule governing student appearance until 1953, when it was expanded to list specific types of clothing that was acceptable for men and for women.

Appropriate Dress for Men. Rules governing men's attire centered around prohibiting clothing being worn on campus that was considered too informal such as "Levi's,"[71] "bermuda shorts,"[72] "shirts without a collar,"[73] or "beach type sandals."[74] As the dress code was adjusted to changing fashion trends in general and college fashion in particular, certain types of more casual clothing were gradually allowed, although the specific types of clothing worn, the time of day, and the particular places it could be worn were highly regulated. Thus by the late 1960s different types of dress were listed, "Standard Dress" and "Casual Dress." Standard dress allowed men to wear "long pants, sport shirts, sandals and tennis shoes," and was appropriate for classroom wear, in the library and in faculty and administrative offices.[75] Casual dress allowed "bermudas [and] sweatshirts" to be worn, but were only allowed "in the dorm areas and for participation in physical activities."[76]

The primary intent of the dress code for men was to keep men from presenting themselves in too informal a fashion and thus not presenting a proper image of Christian manliness, and to keep them from looking too much like their counterparts at the large state and private (secular) universities. The style of dress found on those campuses was inappropriate for Christian young men who not only in the way they were to live their lives, but in their presentation of self, were to look like Christians, which Biola believed was represented in the content of its dress code.

Appropriate Dress for Women. The intent of the dress code for women was essentially as it was for men, to provide a normative dress standard that was in keeping with the image of Christian womanliness that Biola wanted to project. The actual rules governing women's dress however, had less to do with being too informal, as with the men, than it did with issues relating to sexuality and to appropriately feminine clothing. The rules governing women's dress were primarily oriented toward minimizing the potential sexual appeal of women students, and maintaining the boundaries between genders through requiring women to wear such clothing as dresses, skirts, hosiery, and the like, and prohibiting the wearing of masculine clothing such as trousers, unless they were involved in some type of sports or recreational activity.[77]

Women were also required to control the amount of their bodies that was allowed to be seen while in public. Women were instructed that "In their...dorms...women students [may wear] pedal pushers or shorts, but only within the dormitory,"[78] and further that they were not allowed to wear dresses that were "strapless, [had] spaghetti straps, or low necklines,"[79] and "skirts and dresses" were to be "below the knee in length."[80]

As women's dress styles in the larger culture began to change in the 1960s toward more physically revealing fashions, the dress requirements at Biola also changed to take these new developments into account. In response to the emergence of miniskirts, hem lengths on dresses and skirts were officially limited to an exact length, and women were encouraged to use good judgement in their choice of clothing: "Next year's skirt length is not [to be] shorter than three inches above the knee. Irrespective of the maximum dress length, each girl is expected to use good judgement in wearing what is appropriate to her individual appearance."[81] By 1971, women were allowed to wear bermuda shorts, pants and other casual wear in the same places and at the same times as were men, but certain potentially revealing types of clothing were specifically prohibited: "Women students engaging in athletic activities may wear gym suits, capris, pant dresses, pant skirts, and culottes (not shorter than the ordinary dress standard) and shorts (of a length no shorter than mid-thigh, i.e. no shorter than half-way between the top of the knee and the top of the leg). 'Hotpants' and bikinis are definitely prohibited. Swimwear should be of a modest style."[82]

Non-Gendered Dress Code. By the mid-1970s, gender specific dress code rules were replaced by rules that specified that "clothes that are conservative, neat and clean and which complement Christian manhood and womanhood are required."[83] Although women were still "encouraged to consider modest dresses as appropriate for all occasions," the primary emphasis in the newly framed rules was in line with the intent of the rules that had previously governed men's appearance, that of keeping the students from dressing too casually while adding the element of modesty that had guided women's appearance; "Not acceptable for men or women are work-type jeans, work-type levis, work-type overalls, shorts, cut-offs, bare feet or beach-type foot wear, white T-shirts, tank shirts and immodest or 'grubby' clothing," such as "work-type" jeans or overalls, "shorts, cutoffs, bare feet, beach-type footwear, white T-shirts, [and] tank tops."[84]

Even though these rules were presented as non-gender specific, the guiding principle of modesty still resulted in various types of women's clothing being defined as unacceptable, "...at Biola modesty in dress is expected and this modesty is best expressed for women by avoiding halter-type clothing, midriff outfits, and spaghetti-strap dresses." The emphasis on modesty however was no longer limited to womens' dress styles; "Swimwear for both men and women should also be modest. If women's swimwear is two-piece, it should cover the navel."[85] This requirement was not made of men's swimwear.

Between 1976 and 1991 Biola continued to use "modesty" as its primary rationale, while reducing the number of specific dress requirements. Students were informed that, "Attractiveness with conservatism is the keynote of the college dress standard and should reflect the biblical principles of personal care and modesty."[86] Potentially immodest and therefore unacceptable clothing was still listed for women in the early 1980s, including the continuing requirements for women that they, "shall not dress braless nor wear low neck-line clothing, spaghetti strap dresses, halter tops or midriff outfits anywhere on campus except their own residence halls."[87] By the 1990s, the dress requirements had been reduced even further to read simply that "Modesty and good taste should guide choices in dress and appearance at Biola, whether it be in the classroom, chapel, cafeteria or the residence halls. Running-type shorts, tank tops, midriffs, exercise apparel, swimsuits, and other similar styles are not appropriate for chapels or the classroom."[88]

Bob Jones University. For BJU, the development of the dress code rules followed the same pattern of development of its rules governing relations between the sexes—keeping out the ever changing influences of the larger culture by continually adding rules to take into account changes in dress styles in the larger culture. From the earliest available rules, proper appearance was seen as being very important at BJU. Men were to come to the dining room "properly dressed." And for Sunday church service and vespers, the mid-day meal on Sunday and for all evening meals, they were expected to wear coats and ties, with the collar buttoned. By the 1960s, BJU men were required to wear a shirt and tie in public at all times, whether on campus or not. Women were "expected to dress neatly and modestly at all times" and were to have their appearance approved by the "Matron" before attending any social function or participating in any program either on or off campus.[89] They were to wear skirts or dresses which covered the knees at all times, were not to wear slacks outside of the dormitories,[90] and were to wear hosiery at all times.[91]

The dress code also extended beyond the students and their required dress while on campus. Students who lived with their parents or otherwise lived off campus were not to wear anything that was not allowed to be worn on campus. For example, shorts were never to be worn except inside one's own home—slacks (for men) or dresses (for women) were preferred, except in those cases where the type of activity was such that it was more modest to wear work pants (for men) or slacks (for women). Further, the Student Handbook stated that "following the spiritual injunction of letting the man be the head of the family," wives of BJU students were also bound by these same dress requirements, and if at any point she would break the rules by wearing the wrong type of clothing, she would jeopardize her husband's enrollment in the university.[92]

DISCUSSION

The persistence of mechanisms variously used to control gender relations, sexuality, and to control the female body has been observed in each area of analysis—in the gender composition, behavioral rules and dress codes of each school. These were evidenced in the rules governing courtship behavior, proper modes of dress, and the prohibition of various sexual activities. These were also found in the gender composition of the schools, in the decline of women faculty and their absence in positions of leadership. Each school has maintained certain elements of control throughout it's pattern of development, that is, contrary to what was expected, the control of gender remained a dominant category for each school, regardless of whatever other changes may have taken place, either within the school or in the larger society. Yet, these schools varied both across schools in terms of how each has attempted to control gender, and also in their own development which has often oscillated between greater and lesser control over male and female activities.

In his study of American Protestant Fundamentalism and Shi'ite Muslim

Fundamentalism in Iran, Martin Riesebrodt has argued that in these religions, women either "...accept their biological destiny and become agents of God, or they deny this destiny, practice a 'perverse' lifestyle, and become agents of Satan. As agents of God, they fulfill their God-given roles as mothers and housekeepers who lift their husbands and preserve the pious home. As agents of Satan, they seduce men and corrupt youth."[93] The images of women as either the agents of God or of Satan are found throughout the rules that serve to control gender at each school. That women seem always to have the power to seduce men, is implied throughout the rules that govern the relations between the sexes and in the dress code. For example, women and men were alternately kept apart, restricted in their social activities, and required to have chaperons on social outings, and women were required to present themselves in modest clothing that modeled proper Christian womanliness. And, even when gender specific clothing was no longer required, it was primarily women's clothing styles that remained listed as immodest and thus prohibited, such clothing as midriff tops, halter tops, hot pants, and bikinis.

Further, the presence of women and their role in these schools has particular salience in this regard in that not only are young Evangelical women and men being taught acceptable roles and behavior patterns, but these are being modeled by the faculty and the leadership of the schools, and through what each school allows women and men to do. It is not only the rules, but the actual roles that women are allowed to have that are an indicator of the ideology that governs gender in these schools. The declining proportion of women faculty members, despite a significant proportion of the student body being female, and women being systematically kept out of Bible and theology teaching positions, indicates that the fundamentalist gender ideology of women being primarily wives and homemakers persists and is evident not only in the ideology of the schools, but in the practice of these schools, regardless the extent to which it exists in any public ideological statements.

By allowing greater numbers of female faculty members, these schools would sanction role models for their female students that would go against the ideology of the motherhood ideal. That is, their role models would be professional woman, out "mixing it up" with the men in the academic world when they should be at home, or at least in a job that is not a career, supporting husbands and taking care of children. Increased numbers of women faculty members would provide the potential for them to be the opposite of the ideal, being used by Satan as a "temptress," both sexually in regard to male faculty members and perhaps students, and also symbolically, in the sense of tempting young female students to pursue a career, rather than the path ordained by God for the pious young woman, that of being a wife and mother.

It could however be argued that the reason there are so few women faculty members is that as these schools developed their faculties to include more individuals who held doctoral degrees, more men were hired because there were more men than women available and qualified to take these positions. While this may have been true through the 1950s and 1960s, this does not seem particularly plausible from the 1970s on, unless the ideology of "women's place" is taken into account. That is, in an era of expanding opportunities for women, we would expect that more women would have been hired, unless the dominant Evangelical ideology disallowed or discouraged women from pursuing an academic career in the first place.

The reach of this ideology is particularly evident in the systematic exclusion of women from the core Bible and theology faculty, that persisted across time, while being allowed for a time at least, to be a part of the Christian education faculty. For women to teach in the core Bible and theology faculty would require that they teach adult male students, and thus to have a role that was too much like their being a pastor in a church providing spiritual leadership for the congregation. Neither of these was to be allowed.

Christian Education on the other hand was originally the province of women within Evangelicalism, because it was primarily concerned with teaching children in Sunday School and Bible clubs, and who better to teach the children than Christian women who embodied the motherhood ideal? As the field of Christian Education became more professionalized however, as evidenced by the growth in terminal degrees[94] earned by Christian Education faculty, and it expanded to include all ages and not just children, the numbers of women decreased and the numbers of men increased in the faculties of each of these schools. Thus, the more Christian Education became a different facet of Bible and theology, however "applied" it may have been, as opposed to children's work and thus the province of women, the more dominated by men it became.

There is however, a particular incongruity here in that Bob Jones University, as the only remaining self-professing Fundamentalist school in this study, consistently had the highest proportion of women on its faculty.[95] How is it that the school that has the most restrictive prescribed roles for women, and the most restrictions on gender relations, also has such a significantly greater percentage of its faculty made up of women than do the other schools in this study? I would argue that this due to the fact that since the gender relations are more explicitly laid out, there is little if any room for negotiating different roles for women, or of their sharing any authority with men. There is then no threat posed by the presence of women in the faculty, instead they act within the context of the prescribed roles accepted by all in the school. In some ways this allows greater opportunities for women, although only within the context of explicit and implicit role expectations. As one BJU student remarked to me about the student behavioral rules, but that also applies here, "If you have to ask if you can do something, you can't."[96]

For the other schools in this study, each of which have far fewer female faculty members and fewer explicit rules governing gender relations, the accepted range of female roles is less agreed upon. This is especially true in the case of Wheaton and Biola the majority of whose women faculty members have earned their PhD, and thus by virtue of their commitment to their career, likely conceive of their roles differently than do those women at BJU or even MBI. As such they represent more of a threat to the established authority structure, which must resort to other means of maintaining their gender ideology. Their primary means seems to be to control the number of women allowed to teach in the school, and also in what areas they will be allowed to teach, and to use the rules to maintain the separate spheres of men and women and to reduce the potential for temptation that comes through women. This simultaneously reestablishes the patriarchal authority and keeps to a minimum aggressive women with advanced degrees who might challenge the dominant gender ideology.

The importance of these gender issues is that ultimately, these schools are themselves patriarchal organizations which model the ideal gender relations, control of sexuality, and control of the female body, for the larger Evangelical movement. These schools are sites in which Evangelical young people are trained, and as such, they have modeled themselves after the social institution that they believe best suits such training, the "Christian home." It is in the Evangelical Christian home that the father is both the spiritual and practical leader, and where women reach their God-given potential through supporting their husbands and raising their children, so that new generations of moral young people are raised. This is precisely the model that each of these schools have chosen for themselves in pursuing their mission of training each new generation of young people. As Susan Rose has argued regarding Evangelical Christian day schools, which I believe also applies here, these Christian colleges provide a relatively homogeneous Christian environment which reinforces the gender values that the students have heard all of their lives through their parents, teachers, and religious leaders, while limiting exposure both to different gender ideology and practice.[97]

Each of these schools have so far, despite much change, maintained major portions of their gender ideology. Whether this will continue to be the case remains to be seen, although it is evident that schools such as Wheaton and Biola will have to struggle with issues that Bob Jones and Moody will not, namely, how to balance their belief in the need for strong families and the attendant roles for roles for men and women, and the pressure for greater opportunities for women that increasingly comes from internal sources.[98]

NOTES

1 This research was funded in part by a Faculty Research Grant from Biola University.

2 I include Fundamentalists/Fundamentalism in my use of the terms Evangelicals/ Evangelicalism.

3 See Nancy A. Hardesty, *Women Called to Witness: Evangelical Feminism in the 19th Century*. 1984. Nashville: Abingdon; Jannette Hassey, *No Time for Silence: Evangelical Women in Public Ministry Around the Turn of the Century*. 1986. Grand Rapid, MI: Academie Books/Zondervan; Margaret Lamberts Bendroth, .*Fundamentalism and Gender, 1987 to the Present*. 1993. New Haven: Yale University Press.

4 Bendroth, *Fundamentalism and Gender*; Randall Balmer, "American Fundamentalism: The Ideal of Femininity" chapter 2 in *Fundamentalism and Gender*, John Stratton Hawley (ed.), 1994. New York: Oxford University Press.; Martin Riesebrodt, "Fundamentalism and the Political Mobilization of Women," chapter 10 in *The Political Dimensions of Religion*, Said Amir Arjomand (ed). 1993. Albany: SUNY Press.

5 James Davison Hunter, *Evangelicalism: The Coming Generation*. 1987. Chicago: The University of Chicago Press.

6 see Mark Chaves, "Intraorganizational Power and Internal Secularization in Protestant Denominations." *American Journal of Sociology* 99:1 (July) 1-48).

7 Note that there were many more rules included in the Student Handbooks aimed at governing student behavior, than were relevant to this paper. This paper only analyzes a subset of the entire range of student behavioral rules—those that directly bear on gender issues.

8 See Table 1, Wheaton College Faculty, 1920-1990.

9 There were two women listed as Instructors and Assistant Professors of Bible during the 1930s and 1940s, however, according to Bendroth, these women were actually the first Christian Education professors at Wheaton. Bendroth, *Fundamentalism and Gender*, p. 87.

10 See Table 2, Wheaton College Faculty: Departments and Gender, 1920-1990.

11 See Table 3, Wheaton College Student Enrollments, 1920-1990.

12 See Table 4, Moody Bible Institute Faculty, 1945-1990.

13 See Table 5, Moody Bible Institute Faculty: Department and Gender, 1980-1990.

14 Complete data for student enrollment prior to the 1950s is not available. The annual Registrar reports date to 1963 and the Moody student yearbooks listed only seniors prior to the 1950s. The figures for student social composition are based on both the available school records and tallies from the Moody Bible Institute student yearbook, *The Arch*.

15 See Table 6, Moody Bible Institute Student Enrollment, 1938-1990.

16 See Table 6.

17 See Table 7, Biola University Faculty, 1950-1990.

18 I have defined religion faculty to include those faculty members teaching Bible, Theology, Christian Education, and Missions.

19 See Table 8, Biola University Faculty: Department and Gender, 1950-1990.

20 See Table 9, Biola University Student Enrollment, 1927-1990.

21 See Table 10, Bob Jones University Faculty, 1936-1990.

22 Church Administration courses are church secretarial training classes.

23 See Table 11, Bob Jones University Faculty: Department and Gender, 1936-1990.

24 The administration at BJU did not allow me to have access to any student enrollment records. Consequently, these are reconstructed from the school yearbooks by counting men and women students and faculty.

25 See Table 12, Bob Jones University Student Enrollment, 1927-1990.

26 *Wheaton College Student Handbook*, 1927, p. 10-11.

27 *ibid.*, 1933-34, p. 28.

28 *ibid.*, 1975/76, p.29).

29 Moody Bible Institute, Information Booklet for Students, 1929-1930, p. 20. *ibid.*, 1934-1936, p. 21.

30 *ibid.*, 1924-1926, p. 13.

31 *ibid.*, 1929-1930, p. 18.

32 *ibid.*, 1940-1942, p. 14.

33 *ibid.*, 1940-1942, p. 14.

34 *MBI, Handbook for Women*, September 1950, p. 12-13; *Through the Arch, Handbook for Men*,
     September 1950, p. 8.
35 *MBI Student Handbook*, 1962/63, p.38
36 *ibid.*, 1974/75, p.25).
37 *ibid.*, 1991/92, p.9.
38 *ibid.*, p.9.
39 *Biola Student Handbook*, 1928-29, p. 15.
40 *ibid.*, p. 19.
41 *ibid.*, 1957/58, p.28.
42 *ibid.*, 1957/58, p.28.
43 *ibid.*, 1968/69, p. 25.
44 *ibid.*, 1985.
45 *ibid.*, 1971/72, p.35.
46 *ibid.*, 1980/81, p.7.
47 *ibid.*, 1990/92.
48 Bob Jones College Catalog 1927.
49 One informant told me that because of the practical aspects of getting chaperons (the
     chaperons are "recruited" from within the BJU community) for the different events on
     campus, the result can be that one or the other sex is not allowed to attend a particular
     event. Thus, men may not be able to attend sporting events that women's teams are
     playing, or vice versa.
50 BJU Social Parlor Chaperon, interview with the author, 10/92.
51 Wheaton College, Tradiquette, 1950.
52 Wheaton College Student Handbook, 1962/63
53 *ibid.*, 1968-69, p. 36.
54 *ibid.*, 1962-63, p. 25.
55 *ibid.*, 1970/71:33.
56 *ibid.*, 1978/79.
57 *ibid.*, 1986-87, p. 10.
58 *ibid.*, 1988/89; 1990/91).
59 MBI, *Through the Arch*, Mens Handbook, September 1950, p. 13.
60 MBI, Men's Handbook, 1965-1966, p. 14.
61 *ibid.*, 1950, p. 17.
62 *ibid.*
63 Moody Bible Institute Handbook, p. 18.
64 *ibid.*, 1974-1975, p. 22.
65 *ibid.* 1969-1970, p. 29-30.
66 *ibid.*, 1974-1975, p. 22.
67 *ibid.*, 1979-1980, p. 23.
68 *ibid.*, 1991-1992, p. 10.
69 Biola Student Handbook, 1941/42.
70 Samuel H. Sutherland, interview with the author, 5/7/91, Carol Stream, IL.
71 Biola Student Handbook 1955/56.
72 *ibid.*, 1958/59.
73 *ibid.*, 1959/60.
74 *ibid.*, 1973/74.
75 *ibid.*, 1967/68, np.

76　*ibid.*, 1967/68, np.

77　*ibid.*, 1953/54, p.17.

78　*ibid.*, 1959/60

79　*ibid.*, 1960/61, p.41.

80　*ibid.*, 1961/62:40.

81　*ibid.*, 1969/70, p.24.

82　*ibid.*, 1971/72, p.39.

83　*ibid.*, 1976/77, p.8. As reported by a Biola Student Affairs Administrator, the non-gender specific rules were due to the passage of Title IX of the Educational Amendments of 1972, which outlawed sex discrimination in educational programs, and the interpretation of that law by the regional accrediting agency, the Western Association of Schools and Colleges. With the passage of this law, Biola was told that it could not have rules, including dress code rules, for one sex that it did not have for the other sex. Interview with the author, 12/90.

84　Biola Student Handbook 1976/77, p.8.

85　*ibid.*, 1976/77, p.7.

86　*ibid.*, 1980/81, p.10.

87　*ibid.*, 1980/81, p.11.

88　*ibid.*, 1990/92:10.

89　Rules of The Bob Jones College, 1933, np.

90　BJU Student Handbook, 1951/52-1991.

91　*ibid.*

92　*ibid.*, 1963-64.

93　Martin Riesebrodt, "Fundamentalism and the Political Mobilization of Women."

94　Such degrees as EdD, PhD in education; For a discussion of the professionalization and upgrading of the faculties of these schools, see Richard W. Flory, "Development and Transformation within Protestant Fundamentalism: Fundamentalist Bible Institutes and Colleges in the U.S., 1925-1991." 1995. Unpublished dissertation, University of Chicago, Department of Sociology.

95　In 1991 this was 45%.

96　Informal discussion with female undergraduate student, Bob Jones University, 10/92.

97　Susan D. Rose, "Gender, Education and the New Christian Right," pp. 59-66, *Society*, 26:2, January/February 1989.

98　See Diana Hochstedt Butler, "Between two worlds," *The Christian Century*, March 3, 1993, pp. 231-232 and Nancy Hardesty, letter to the editor, *The Christian Century*, April 14, 1993, Pp. 414, for a first-hand discussion and a follow-up comment on these issues.

Table 1
Wheaton College: Faculty Gender, 1928–1990

Year	Men		Women		Total
1928	22	(67%)	11	(33%)	33
1931	23	(61%)	15	(39%)	38
1935	24	(57%)	18	(43%)	42
1940	47	(60%)	31	(40%)	78
1945	58	(59%)	40	(41%)	98
1950	73	(63%)	43	(37%)	116
1955	91	(73%)	34	(27%)	125
1960	100	(74%)	35	(26%)	135
1965	114	(83%)	24	(17%)	138
1970	131	(83%)	26	(17%)	157
1975	133	(85%)	23	(15%)	156
1980	128	(80%)	32	(20%)	160
1985	139	(82%)	31	(18%)	170
1990	139	(80%)	34	(20%)	173

Table 2
Wheaton College Faculty: Department and Gender, 1928–1990

Year	Religion Faculty		Christian Education		Other Disciplines		Total
	Men	Women	Men	Women	Men	Women	
1928	2			1	20	10	33
1931	1			2	22	13	38
1935	2			2	22	16	42
1940	5			3	42	28	78
1945	6		1	6	50	34	98
1950	12		2	6	59	37	116
1955	14			4	77	30	125
1960	20			4	80	31	135
1965	16			2	98	22	138
1970	19		1	2	111	24	157
1975	14			2	119	21	156
1980	16		3		109	32	160
1985	15		6		118	31	170
1990	12		7		120	34	173

Table 3
Wheaton College: Student Enrollments, 1920–1990

Year	Men		Women		Total
1920	94	(47%)	105	(53%)	199
1925	152	(44%)	191	(56%)	343
1930	299	(47%)	343	(53%)	633
1935	439	(55%)	355	(45%)	794
1940	561	(51%)	535	(49%)	1096
1945	413	(30%)	920	(70%)	1333
1950	928	(54%)	799	(56%)	1727
1955	963	(52%)	894	(48%)	1857
1960	1060	(55%)	883	(45%)	1943
1965	1016	(52%)	921	(48%)	1937
1970	1014	(50%)	997	(50%)	2011
1975	1318	(52%)	1217	(48%)	2535
1980	1363	(50%)	1375	(50%)	2738
1985	1256	(49%)	1315	(51%)	2571
1990	1208	(47%)	1340	(53%)	2548

Table 4
Moody Bible Institute: Faculty Gender, 1945–1990

Year	Men		Women		Total
1945	18	(75%)	6	(25%)	24
1950	18	(64%)	10	(36%)	28
1955	24	(75%)	8	(25%)	32
1960	25	(81%)	6	(19%)	31
1965	34	(83%)	7	(17%)	41
1970	43	(90%)	5	(10%)	48
1975	69	(91%)	7	(9%)	76
1980	64	(85%)	11	(15%)	75
1985	74	(89%)	9	(11%)	83
1990	79	(85%)	14	(15%)	93

Table 5
Moody Bible Institute: Department and Gender, 1980-1990

Year	Religion Faculty		Christian Education		Other Disciplines		Total
	Men	Women	Men	Women	Men	Women	
1980	29			2	32	9	75
1985	31				43	9	83
1990	33				46	14	93

Table 6
Moody Bible Institute: Student Enrollments, 1938-1990

Year	Men		Women		Total
1938	59	(54%)	50	(46%)	109
1941	121	(49%)	137	(51%)	258
1944	97	(35%)	183	(65%)	280
1947	64	(27%)	175	(73%)	239
1953	187	(46%)	223	(54%)	410
1956	265	(53%)	235	(47%)	500
1959	429	(50%)	432	(50%)	861
1961	477	(51%)	451	(49%)	928
1965	500	(52%)	464	(48%)	964
1970	503	(54%)	433	(46%)	936
1975	695	(54%)	601	(46%)	1296
1980	780	(58%)	555	(42%)	1335
1985	779	(61%)	496	(39%)	1275
1990	829	(60%)	550	(40%)	1379

Table 7
Biola University: Faculty Gender, 1950-1990

Year	Men		Women		Total
1950	22	(61%)	14	(39%)	36
1955	43	(75%)	14	(25%)	57
1960	50	(78%)	14	(22%)	64
1965	59	(78%)	17	(22%)	76
1970	88	(81%)	21	(19%)	109
1975	108	(80%)	27	(20%)	135
1980	148	(82%)	33	(18%)	181
1985	129	(80%)	33	(20%)	162
1990	120	(78%)	34	(22%)	154

Table 8
Biola University Faculty: Department and Gender, 1950-1990

Year	Religion Faculty		Christian Education		Other Disciplines		Total
	Men	Women	Men	Women	Men	Women	
1950	10		2	4	12	9	36
1955	17			3	26	11	57
1960	16		1	1	33	13	64
1965	16		6	1	37	16	76
1970	20		3	1	65	19	109
1975	29		4	2	75	25	135
1980	51		5	4	92	29	181
1985	29		6	1	94	32	162
1990	27		7	1	86	33	154

Table 9
Biola University: Student Enrollments, 1927-1990

Year	Men		Women		Total
1927	139	(42%)	190	(58%)	329
1930	91	(42%)	124	(58%)	215
1938	146	(46%)	173	(54%)	319
1940	204	(50%)	202	(50%)	406
1945	153	(21%)	586	(79%)	739
1950	397	(51%)	375	(49%)	772
1955	373	(56%)	298	(44%)	671
1960	349	(49%)	361	(51%)	710
1965	391	(42%)	535	(58%)	926
1970	272	(41%)	385	(59%)	657
1975	864	(44%)	1063	(56%)	1927
1980	943	(42%)	1327	(58%)	2270
1985	744	(39%)	1178	(61%)	1922
1990	517	(38%)	839	(62%)	1356

Table 10
Bob Jones University: Faculty Gender, 1936-1990

Year	Men		Women		Total
1936	9	(41%)	13	(59%)	
1940	12	(39%)	19	(61%)	
1945	19	(40%)	20	(60%)	
1950	41	(45%)	49	(55%)	
1955	47	(45%)	57	(55%)	
1960	65	(50%)	66	(50%)	
1965	77	(49%)	80	(51%)	
1970	104	(53%)	90	(47%)	
1975	111	(52%)	103	(48%)	
1980	132	(49%)	135	(51%)	
1985	159	(54%)	134	(46%)	
1990	169	(56%)	135	(44%)	

Table 11
Bob Jones University: Department and Gender, 1936-1990

Year	Religion Faculty		Christian Education		Other Disciplines		Total
	Men	Women	Men	Women	Men	Women	
1936	2				7	13	22
1940	2				10	19	31
1945	4		1	1	14	28	48
1950	8		1	5	32	48	90
1955	11		3		34	57	105
1960	11		2	2	52	64	131
1965	13		4	1	60	79	157
1970	15		7	2	84	88	196
1975	22				89	100	214
1980	24				108	132	267
1985	26				133	131	293
1990	23				146	131	304

Table 12
Bob Jones University: Student Enrollments, 1927-1990

Year	Men		Women		Total
1927	49	(58%)	36	(42%)	85
1930	52	(48%)	56	(52%)	108
1935	86	(54%)	74	(46%)	160
1940	192	(53%)	168	(47%)	360
1945	209	(32%)	437	(68%)	646
1950	1239	(58%)	891	(42%)	2130
1955	1156	(57%)	869	(43%)	2026
1960	1112	(55%)	911	(45%)	2034
1965	1195	(51%)	1166	(49%)	2361
1970	1431	(50%)	1438	(50%)	2870
1980	2182	(50%)	2221	(50%)	4404
1985	2015	(50%)	1974	(50%)	3991
1990	1921	(46%)	2032	(54%)	4137

THE SEARCH FOR SELF AND SOCIAL JUSTICE IN THE SPIRITUAL JOURNEY OF MARY WOLLSTONECRAFT: LESSONS FOR TODAY

Don Hufford
Kansas Newman College

Mary Wollstonecraft (1759 - 1797) has been considered by literary critics and social historians to be an eighteenth century spiritual progenitor and political grandmother of the twentieth century "Feminist Movement." Her 1792 publication, *The Vindication of the Rights of Woman*, continues to be a powerful, evocative emotional/intellectual stimulus for those who understand that the battle for human rights is an unfinished task—a battle not won until freedom, equality, and justice are achieved by all people. She was also a teacher and educational theorist, a journalist, a literary translator, an autobiographical novelist, a political analyst, and a social critic. Her life and written work provide intellectually challenging interpretive possibilities for the educator, the political scientist, the sociologist, the historian, the psychologist—even the theologian. For the purposes of this paper, however, Mary Wollstonecraft was first a "person"—an individual in search of a personal identity. It is a thesis presented here that the "person" and the "search" may be studied for twentieth century androgogical implications.[1]

Wollstonecraft was a radical thinker whose efforts to define her "selfhood" led her to defy the social mores, cultural precepts, institutionalized religious conventions, and educational philosophy of her historical era. Her literary and life-style challenges to an unjust social/political/religious power structure were outer, objective expressions of an inner, subjective struggle for self-definition. It was the emotional intensity of the struggle that caused her to understand "what a long time it requires us to know ourselves."[2] This paper explores basic philosophical assumptions underlying one woman's personal efforts to achieve the power "to be" (self-realization) and "to do" (active involvement in constructive social transformation)[3]

Wollstonecraft's search for self-validation is here interpreted as a spiritual journey—a bildung in literary terms.[4] It is suggested that her journey may be used as a self-teaching tool for those who continue on a similar journey. An analysis of Wollstonecraft's life and writings opens up the intellectual opportunity for one to engage in an hermeneutical process.[5] One may interpret that many of her life choices were influenced by an existentially defined continuing quest to find answers to the age-old theologically based—and philosophically speculative—question, "Who am I?" To ask the question is, of course, to confront the existential necessity of continually questioning the answers.

Wollstonecraft's eighteenth century struggle for meaningful selfhood may be understood in relationship to divergent principles and assumptions which give rise to many of the discordant notes characterizing twentieth century social/political discourse. To engage in analysis and interpretation of Wollstonecraft's spiritual journey is to engage (confront) universal themes found in "Everyperson's" quest. It is to wrestle with "who am I?" as a three part question —one involving theological, philosophical, *and* sociological answers.[6]

Wollstonecraft's radical reformist challenges to eighteenth century educational, political, religious, and economic practices provide historical precedent for today's social activists.[7] She challenged the status quo. She encouraged an awareness of how unjust social and economic power structures and inequitable educational systems deny to many the opportunity for full realization of the possibilities of the self.[8] She reminded those who would listen: "I think the female world oppressed, yet the gangrene which the vices produced by oppression have produced is not confined . . . . but pervades society at large."[9] Her life and writings provide interpretive possibilities for an understanding of how issues of social justice and individual self-realization are intertwined. Wollstonecraft raised questions regarding many of the same religious, political, and economic issues which are part of the 1990s contentious social justice debates. She knew—as is evident today—that answers are too often based on unchallenged assumptions, misplaced priorities, and on the vested interests of those who wield economic power and political privilege.

The questions regarding self and society are seeking answers today, even as they were during Wollstonecraft's historical era when human and social perfection were thought to be only a matter of time and the wise use of reason. For the purpose of this study Wollstonecraft's lived answers to fundamental questions were viewed within the context of her spiritual journey. It was this journey—her search for selfhood—viewed as educational process, which called for interpretive reflection.[10]

Wollstonecraft sought for herself —and other women—the rights and responsibilities of free, rational human beings. She sought both a freedom *from* and a freedom *to*. Her selfhood would be achieved only as she gained liberation *from* the restrictive bonds of sexually defined oppression, and achieved freedom *to* "be" the self she was capable of becoming. And she understood that sexual oppression was inextricably bound to other social injustices. The process of liberation—integral to her spiritual journey—required her to become a rebellious iconoclast. She broke social, political, economic, and religious "icons" representing the injustices holding together the power structures of her place and time.

She dared to be person in her own right. She insisted on the right to *think* as well as to feel. She inserted herself into an "old boy" network, and found a measure of success and acceptance in a male dominated profession.[11] She travelled internationally as an equal of men.[12] In her personal relationships with men she allowed her romantic inclinations—both sexual and philosophical—to override social and religious conventions. It was as she reminded her sister, Everina, in a 1788 letter: "You know, I am not born to tread the beaten path."[13] Later she was to describe her unconventional, iconoclastic life journey as a "thorny path."[14]

Even a "thorny path" may facilitate a spiritual journey, and such it was for Mary Wollstonecraft. As she travelled this path on her spiritual journey she continually encountered polarities of life-choice possibilities. Time and space constraints applied to this paper necessarily limited the issues which could be placed under the hermeneutical microscope. Therefore, three polar themes—which at various times either lighted or darkened her path—have been selected as worthy of interpretive evaluation: (1) Reason/Emotion, (2) Nature/Nurture, and (3) Religion/Spirituality.

1. Reason/Emotion

Mary Wollstonecraft's life and writings gave testimony to her struggles to deal with the basic reason/emotion dichotomy which is part of an individual's search for answers to the "who am I?" question. Her answers did not come easily, and the struggle caused her to prophesy: "Till I can form some idea of the whole of my existence, I must be content to weep and dance like a child—long for a toy, and be tired of it as soon as I get it."[15] The "whole of her existence" included the effort to hold in creative tension the often diverging demands of reason and emotion. She described herself when she portrayed her fictional Mary as one whose "reason was as profound as her imagination was lively,"[16] and she lived a personal drama in which the "profound" and the "lively" were often in conflict.

She was in—and of—the "age of reason," and described herself by reference to "this primary human characteristic."[17] She challenged the eighteenth century sexual stereotype that women were basically frivolous, emotional, irrational creatures. She knew that women would have to be accepted as fully rational human beings before they could hope to achieve political, legal, and social freedom. She subscribed to John Locke's political philosophy that a person derives natural and political rights through the possession and use of reason.[18] In the age of "enlightenment" women were considered to be deficient in this human quality, and were—therefore—easily victimized, oppressed, and denied natural and political rights.

Wollstonecraft wanted women to have equal access to formal education, to be allowed to fully exercise the powers of reason—to *think*.[19] Only then would women be liberated. Consistent with Enlightenment era philosophy, Wollstonecraft believed that the educated use of reason was "the first step to form a being advancing gradually toward perfection."[20] She understood herself to be a reasoning being. Her rationalist strivings were, however, continually challenged by her emotions. She wrote of her "sacred emotions that are the sure harbingers of the delights (she) was formed to enjoy, and shall enjoy, for nothing can extinguish the heavenly spark."[21] Try as she would, she could not give herself totally to a rationalist worldview. She wrote: "I must fly from thought, and find refuse in a strong imagination,"[22] and "without the aid of the imagination all the pleasures of the senses must sink into grossness."[23]

In eighteenth century terminology Wollstonecraft was a creature of "sensibilities." For her:

> Sensibility is the most exquisite feeling of which the human soul is susceptible . . . . It is this quickness, this delicacy of feeling, which enables us to relish the sublime touches of the poet, and the painter; it is this which expands the soul, gives an enthusiastic greatness, mixed with tenderness .... Softened by tenderness the soul is disposed to be virtuous.[24]

Part of Wollstonecraft's psychological unease, her psychosomatic illnesses, and her attempts at suicide resulted from a failure to hold reason and emotion in balance—a failure to find a way for reason to live at peace with emotion. Her dedication to reason as "the primary human characteristic" caused her to be ill at ease with her emotional sensibilities. She believed "the heart of sensibility understands a superior language,"[25] but understood "my imagination hurries me forward . . . . but reason drags me back."[26] In a letter to one of her mentors, Joseph Johnson the publisher, she described a concern regarding the emotion/reason dichotomy: "I am a mere animal, and instinctive emotion too often silences the suggestions of resolution."[27]

Wollstonecraft's search for self-definition was hampered by her sense of this reason/emotion turmoil in her life. She understood the integrative possibilities that exist for reason and emotion—the cognitive and the affective—to work collaboratively to strengthen the personality. She was aware of "the grace which results from the imagination mixing with the senses."[28] She was, however, not always able to maintain a creative tension between the two aspects of the self.

She believed that emotion unchecked by reason leads to misdirected passion, and that reason divorced from feeling is creatively sterile. But her challenge to the prevailing dominate/subordinate concept of male/female relationships led her to place emphasis on her power to reason at the expense of her ability to feel. She understood that there is truth beyond reason—that there is another dimension of the self. She wrote of those "half alive beings who seem to have been made by Prometheus when the fire he stole from Heaven was so exhausted that he could only spare a spark to give life, not animation, to the inert clay."[29] For Wollstonecraft emotion was the animation which -when added to reason—allowed for the development of "the feeling mind."[30] This she understood. But her psychological need to prove her rationality in a male dominated "age of reason" caused her—in many situations—to be existentially "inauthentic" with regard to her emotional reality.

2. Nature/Nurture

Mary Wollstonecraft's defiance of the eighteenth century dictum that "men think and women feel" led this woman of intense feeling to attempt to subdue natural "sensibilities," and to place them under the control of reason. She sought to give, in her words, "the indulgence of feeling the sanction of reason."[31] Wollstonecraft argued against the concept that there are significant innate differences in male/female characteristics, and insisted that "the sexual distinction which men have so warmly insisted upon, is arbitrary."[32] She would not accept the thinking that the male is innately strong, resolute, adventurous, assertive, and rational while the female is by nature weak, indecisive, yielding, giving, and emotional. She also challenged the collateral belief that men and women are by nature destined for different "spheres of activity," and are, therefore, innately imbued with differing character qualities designed for success in separate spheres of life. She believed "women may have different duties to fulfill, but they are *human* duties, and the principles that should regulate the discharge of them . . . must be the same."[33] She was particularly adamant in her insistence that both men and women have innate reasoning capacities.

Wollstonecraft challenged the theory that male and female characteristics are naturally different, yet designed to be complimentary. She argued against Rousseau's statement that "in the union of the sexes, each alike contributes to the common end, but in different ways."[34] This makes it all too easy to assume that in the metaphysical scheme of things there is a "man's place" and a "woman's place." Such a philosophical assumption—ignoring cultural conditioning and situational expectations—provides justification for assigning an inferior social status to women, and gives the *imprimatur* of natural law to male subjugation of females. Wollstonecraft understood the reality that "such is the force of prejudice, that what was called spirit and wit in him, was cruelly thought forwardness in me."[35]

Wollstonecraft recognized that the idea of separate female/male innate characteristics allowed the power structure (male) to assign to the female second class citizenship, subordinate marital status, and lowered educational expectations. She recognized that the idea of separate male/female natures leads to an expectation that women should be sensitive, intuitive, and obedient rather than rational, reasonable, and self-disciplined. In defiance of this social/sexual norm she claimed for women the potential—and right—to have and use the power of full rationality; and, therefore, to be afforded full social, political, economic, and educational equality.[36]

It is at this point that education, a nurture component, was viewed by Wollstonecraft as vital in answering the "who am I" question. She proclaimed that equality of educational opportunity was the key to freedom for women. She viewed perceived differences between male and female as the result of different experiences resulting from educational inequities. Wollstonecraft argued that personality *and* ability differences between male and female result more from nurture than from nature. In her thinking such differences were not related primarily to innate sexually defined characteristics, but resulted from the differing quality of educational experiences.

Wollstonecraft applied Locke's *tabula rasa* theory to women as well as to men, believing that with equal educational experience women would be the equal of men in the ability to use the human potential to reason. She argued that women are endowed by nature with the same reasoning potential as men, but are denied full realization of their innate possibilities by a lack of education (nurture), by misplaced expectations, and by the consequences of a "self-fulfilling prophecy."

3. Religion/Spirituality

As a child of the Enlightenment Mary Wollstonecraft believed that "a love of order and beauty leads directly to admiration of its author."[37] As a closet literary Romantic—whose work influenced Coleridge, Wordsworth, Southey, Byron, and Shelley—[38] she spiced her reason with imagination, and believed it would necessitate "a philosophical inquiry . . . to trace the spontaneous feelings and ideas which have produced the images that now frequently appear unnatural. . . ."[39] Religion—as an organized system of belief—had an impact on Wollstonecraft's life journey, but caused her a degree of discomfort. She experienced conflicting moral demands between the ritualized imperatives of institutionalized religion and her inner spiritual longings. She was reared an Anglican, but gradually divorced herself from a religion of "irksome ceremonies and unreasonable restraints."[40] She sought a more personal connection to the creative, sustaining power of spirituality.

Wollstonecraft was called deist, agnostic, humanist, heathen, atheist.[41] But throughout her writings were scattered descriptive references to a God familiar to those with a more theistic theology. At various times—and in various moods—she wrote of a Providence, Supreme Being, Master of the Universe, Author of All Good, Deity, Father of Nature, Almighty Friend, Lord Omnipotent, Father of Spirits, Author of All Perfection, etc. She imbued personal meaning to these descriptions by making connections to both her faith in reason *and* her sense of a spiritual reality transcending the power of reasoning. Her spirituality was manifested in the existential "I" contemplating the awesomeness, mystery, and wonder of the universe. In her moments of contemplation it was her poetic spirituality—not her rational religion—that found expression in the self.

She had a spiritual faith in the human possibility to create a world of justice and peace based on compassion, love, and joy. She believed that "where Love and Joy appeared the flowers sprung up . . . . the sun shone with a brighter radiance, and all nature seemed embellished by their presence."[42] She felt the oneness of nature and humanity, "the simple yet sublime harmony of that system which unites men to each other."[43] There was an understanding that religious truth must be true to humankind's reasoning powers, but also that spiritual truth brings knowledge of the irrationality which makes the human psyche whole. Wollstonecraft wrestled with this apparent inconsistency in the self. The rational, progressive, liberal, and scientific ideas of the Enlightenment were part of "who" she was, and influenced her religious thought. Yet her philosophically romantic inclinations allowed for a spiritual interpretation of life which went beyond rational understanding. She was aware that she was "struck with a mystic kind of reverence"[44] in which her "imagination still could dip her brush in the rainbow of fancy, and sketch futurity in glowing colors."[45]

So it was that even with her dedication to reason she remained an intensely spiritual woman, relating to others and the world of natural wonders in a personal and intimate way. She sought meaning, direction, hope, and purpose in life outside the established institutional religious structures. Such structures had been necessary to her religious life prior to her association with a group of English dissenters led by Dr. Richard Price. But, influenced by religious free-thinkers she gradually began to engage in a more questioning, challenging attitude toward religious orthodoxy.

She began to distance herself from ceremony, creed, ritual, and ecclesiastical authority—from the "religion (whose) clear stream (had) been muddied by the dabblers, who presumptuously endeavored to confine in one narrow channel, the living waters that ever flow towards God—the sublime ocean of existence."[46] As organized religion became less a part of her life she continued to seek comfort in a spiritual connection to a power beyond the self that could cause her to feel as if "everything seemed to harmonize into tranquility . . . . my soul diffused itself into the scene, and seeming to become all senses . . . . . . melted into the freshening breeze."[47]

Mary Wollstonecraft was a rationalist dedicated to reason, but the powerful psychological drives put in motion by her "exquisite sensibility"[48] could only be tempered by "inquiries which expand the soul."[49] Her intellect had sought a religion of rational coherence. This was not sufficient for a woman who experienced "emotions that trembled on the brink of ecstasy,[50] and who, "for years endeavored to calm an impetuous tide—laboring to make (her) feelings take an orderly course. It was striving against the stream."[51]

She was especially "spiritual" when caught up in the wonder, awe, and beauty of the natural world. It was at such moments—when "grand and sublime images strike the imagination"[52]—that she could imagine "eternity is in these moments . . . airy stuff that dreams are made of,"[53] and be "absorbed by the sublime sensibility which (flows into) consciousness of existence . . ."[54] As a novelist she described the spirituality of her alterego:

> She would gaze on the moon . . . .observe the various shapes the clouds assumed, and listen to the sea . . . . The wandering spirits, which she imagined inhabited every part of nature, were her constant friends and confidants. She began to consider the first great cause.[55]

CONCLUSION

Mary Wollstonecraft was still on her spiritual pilgrimage of self-discovery when, at age thirty-eight, she died from complications arising from the birth of her second child. Answers to the "who am I" question remained unresolved—suspended somewhere in a philosophical/theological space between a rationalist's worldview and a romantic's skepticism regarding the ultimate power of reason. She did not reconcile within her own psyche the perfectionist expectations of the Enlightenment with the counterpoint romantic reactions to this age of reason. She did, however, leave hermeneutic possibilities for those who might seek insights from her spiritual journey—for those who continue a quest on the "thorny path" of self-discovery.

The interpreter becomes involved—perhaps unconsciously—in an heuristic learning activity—a process of questioning, validating, and/or redefining his/her personal values, understandings, ways of thinking, and ways of perceiving the world. An academic exercise is translated into a learning experience with personal meaning. This is, by broad definition, a spiritual experience. There is heightened awareness—even if not total acceptance—of the existential human predicament in which choices *must* be made and consequences lived with. Questions are raised. Previously held answers are questioned.

There is an intensified understanding of the need to seek connections—not dichotomies—between thinking and feeling—between "being" and "doing." Wollstonecraft wanted females—and by extension, all people—to be educated to be reasoning/thinking *as well as* emotional/feeling beings. She understood that "reason strikes most forcibly when illuminated by the brilliancy of fancy."[56]

Perhaps to gaze with an interpretive eye into the becoming "self" of another is to continue to "know thyself." Wollstonecraft understood that as we "obtain a knowledge of others at the same time we become acquainted with ourselves."[57] It is this connecting of "self" to "other" that translates to a social consciousness. Here the interpreter recognizes the critical theorist in Wollstonecraft.[58] It was not *just* the sexually based inequalities of the eighteenth century which she challenged with her pen and by her lifestyle. She wrote about—and lived a response to—other social, political, economic, and religious injustices affecting both women and men. She knew—and helps her interpreter to understand—that such injustices represent forces which are the results of the very structure of society.[59] It was the structure—the status quo—which she challenged.

There was within Wollstonecraft's life journey a concern for both personal growth and the transformation of the social system—a connection between the search for self and the search for a better society. This was not a self/other dichotomy, but a linking of the self to the larger whole. Herein was the essence of Wollstonecraft's spiritual journey. "To be spiritual is to perceive our oneness with everybody and everything, and to act on this perception."[60]

NOTES

1. Androgogy - as distinguished from pedagogy - is defined as the "art and science of help-ing adults learn." (Malcolm Knowles, *The Modern Practice of Adult Education* [New York: Association Press, 1970], 38). The term was first used by Eduard Lindeman, and defined as the "effort toward self-mastery." (Eduard C. Lindeman, *The Meaning of Adult Education* [Montreal: Harvest House, 1961]. For the purpose of this paper a Mary Wollstonecraft research effort provides insights for the researcher's personal "effort toward self-mastery."

2. *The Works of Mary Wollstonecraft*, ed. Janet Todd and Marilyn Butler, vol. 6, *Letters Written in Sweden, Norway, and Denmark* (New York: New York University Press, 1989), 289.

3. Wollstonecraft's search for self-definition was made in the context of an historical era. She understood that her self-transformation from oppressed female to emancipated per-son was inextricably bound to transformation of the basic structures of society.

4. In literary terms the *bildungsroman* is a novel depicting the self-development of a protag-onist. The term derives from the German, *bildung*, the informal process of education in which a person is continually educated by the self-learning opportunities inherent in life situations and circumstances.

5. *Hermeneutics* is a process familiar in philosophical, theological, legal, literary, and educa-tional contexts. It relates to the "how," "why," and "who" of a textual interpretation. For the purposes of this paper it is recognized that an interpretation of the written work and life experiences of Mary Wollstonecraft will not be totally objective. The interpreter is influenced by personal experiences, conditioned biases and prejudices, and a par-ticular philosophical worldview. Elements of the interpreter's existential "I" enter into any analytical evaluation. The result is not a scientific outcome, but is a creative understanding of "who" Wollstonecraft was and who she was "becoming." For a look at hermeneutical possibilities and constraints see Shaun Gallager, *Hermeneutics and Education* (Albany: State University of New York Press, 1992).

6. To interpret the "self" of Mary Wollstonecraft is to deal with a literary reality. To ask the question "who am I?" is to open the door to many answers - often divergent and para-doxical. Her life underscored that "to know who I am is to (be) many facetted, complex, aware of numerous and often conflicting claims, incapable of meeting all, and therefore required to decide and to sacrifice, standing in different relations to different peopl . . . . to all the manifold contrasts of life." (George Morgan, "The Human Revolution: A Search for Wholeness," *Prophetic Voices*, Ned Gorman, ed. [New York: Random House, 1969,54]).

7. Wollstonecraft's writings and activities were eighteenth century reformist preliminaries to the twentieth century activists who base their challenges to the status quo on a Critical Theory philosophical foundation. Critical Theory is a philosophical thought process which goes back to the Frankfort School in Germany in the 1920s and 1930s; and is asso-ciated with such thinkers as Max Horkheimer, Herbert Marcuse, Theodor Adorno, and Jurgen Habermas. The aim of Critical Theorists is the emancipation of individuals and social groups from the exploitation of unjust political and economic power systems. Critical Theorists are interested in the transformation of society by way of more just, equitable, and humane relationships.

8. Wollstonecraft encouraged her fellow citizens - female and male - to challenge these unjust systems. She was concerned that "men . . . . submit everywhere to oppression . . . . Instead of asserting their birthright they lick the dust and say, let us eat and drink, for tomorrow we die. Women are degraded by the same propensity to enjoy the present moment." (Mary Wollstonecraft, *A Vindication of the Rights of Woman*, ed. Carol H. Poston [New York: W.W. Norton Company, 1975, 52.])

9. Wollstonecraft, *Vindication*.

10. Wollstonecraft understood the importance of reflecting on and interpreting different points of view. She understood the philosophical process in which "good and solid arguments take rise from different points of view," and she could "rejoice to find that those she could not concur with had some reason on their side." (Wollstonecraft, *Works*, vol. 1, *Mary a Fiction*, 29). She believed that those who "have not the power of concentering seeming contradictions (represent) the empty voice of ignorance." (Wollstonecraft, *Works*, vol. 6, *Analytical Review*, 229). She also understood "that people who have but one criterion for excellence, whose minds have a confined range will ever be intolerant." (Wollstonecraft, *Works*, vol. 7, *Analytical Review*, 228)

   In spite, however, of her willingness to consider divergent points of view - and to reflect on them - she remained firmly convinced that "paradoxes need fixed principles." (Wollstonecraft, *Works*, vol.. 7, *Analytical Review*, 49).

11. Wollstonecraft was allowed social and intellectual intercourse with such stimulating and "radical" thinkers as Thomas Paine, William Godwin, and William Blake. See Ralph M. Wardle, Mary *Wollstonecraft: A Critical Biography* (Lincoln: University of Nebraska Press, 1951), 93-94-95.

12. Wollstonecraft's *An Historical and Moral View of the Origin and Progress of the French Revolution and the Effect It has Produced in Europe* and her *Letters Written in Sweden, Norway, and Denmark* give evidence of her continental travel.

13. Found in G.R. Sterling Taylor, *Mary Wollstonecraft: A Study in Economics and Romance,* (New York: Haskell House, Ltd., 1969), 77.

14. Wollstonecraft, *Works*, vol. 1, *Mary, a Fiction*, 22.

15. Wollstonecraft, *Works*, vol. 6, *Letters to Johnson*, 359.

16. Wollstonecraft, *Works*, vol. 1, *Mary, a Fiction*, 60.

17. Found in Carolyn Korsmeyer, ed., *Women and Philosophy: Toward a Theory of Liberation,* (New York: Capricorn Books, 1976), "Reason and Morals in the Early Feminist Movement: Mary Wollstonecraft," by Carolyn Korsmeyer, 53.

18. Wollstonecraft also indicated an understanding of Locke's philosophy regarding the necessity to reflect upon sensation (sense data) in order to develop ideas. She wrote: "It is reflection which forms habits and fixes principles indelibly on the heart; without it the mind is like a wreck drifted about by every squall." (Mary Wollstonecraft, *Thoughts on the Education of Daughters*. Microfiche Publication. [London: British Library, 1978], 111)

19. Wollstonecraft's treatise on raising daughters was specific: "I wish them to be taught to *think*." (Ibid., 22).

   Wollstonecraft understood "thinking" to be a basic purpose of an educational system. She proposed a system of coeducational national education that would equalize such educational opportunities between male and female. William Godwin, her husband, however, opposed a national system of education. He feared such a system would be used to stifle reason, and produce compliant, docile citizens unprepared to challenge social injustices. Godwin believed the content and process of a national education system would be shaped by the narrow, self-serving interests of those holding political and economic power.

20. Yet she had an awareness that "imperfection is mixed with every work of man; it slides imperceptibly into every plan." (Wollstonecraft, *Works,* vol. 7, *Analytical Review,* 57).
21. Wollstonecraft, *Works,* vol. 6, *Letters to Imlay,* 419
22. Wollstonecraft, *Works,* vol. 6, *Letters Written in Sweden,* 294.
23. *Ibid.,* 250.
24. Wollstonecraft, *Works,* vol. 1, *Mary, a Fiction,* 59.

    She also defined her sensibilities as "those involuntary sensations which are like the beauteous tints of an evening sky, (and) are so evanescent that they melt into new forms before they can be analyzed." (Wollstonecraft, *Works,* vol. 7, *On Poetry,* 8). In an imaginative work she offered another definition:

    > To give the shortest definition of sensibility I should say that it is the result of acute senses, finely fashioned nerves, which vibrate at the slightest touch, and convey such clear intelligence to the brain, that it does not require to be arranged by the judgment . . . . Exquisite pain and pleasure is their portion; nature wears for them a different aspect than is displayed to common mortals. (Wollstonecraft, *Works,* vol. 1, *The Cave of Fancy: A Tale,* 201).

25. Wollstonecraft, *Works,* vol. 7, *Analytical Review,* 213.
26. Wollstonecraft, *Works,* vol. 6, *Letters in Sweden,* 308.
27. Wollstonecraft, *Works,* vol. 6, *Letters to Johnson,* 358.

    She also made descriptive reference to herself when writing of those "eccentric characters, comet like (who) are always in extremes." (Wollstonecraft, *Works,* vol. 1, *Mary, a Fiction,* 61).

28. Wollstonecraft, *Works,* vol. 1, *The Cave of Fancy: A Tale,* 195.
29. Wollstonecraft, *Works,* vol. 6, *Letters in Sweden,* 314.
30. Wollstonecraft, *Works,* vol. 7, *Analytical Review,* 329.
31. Wollstonecraft, *Works,* vol. 6, *Letters in Sweden,* 294.
32. Wollstonecraft, *A Vindication,* 193.

    It is interesting to note that in the United States John Adams thoroughly read A Vindication, making notes in the margins of his copy. His notes indicated the kind of "sexual distinction" Wollstonecraft referred to when he noted: "This is a lady of masculine masterly understanding." (Found in Eleanor Flexner, *Mary Wollstonecraft* [New York: Coward, McCann, and Georghegan, 1972, 197.])

33. *Ibid.,* 51.
34. This statement is from Rousseau's Emile. Wollstonecraft made frequent negative references to Rousseau in her Vindication. One passage summarizes her concern: "He denies woman reason, shuts her out from knowledge, and turns her aside from truth." (Ibid., 104)   But in spite of her harsh criticism of Rousseau's "sexism" she also writes: "Rousseau alone, the true Prometheus of sentiment, possessed the fire of genius necessary to portray the passion, the truth which goes directly to the heart." (Wollstonecraft, *Works,* vol. 1, *The Wrongs of Woman: or, Maria,* 96.) She further writes:

    > The Confessions of J.J. Rousseau will ever be read with interest by those persons of sensitivity who have pondered over the movements of their own hearts . . . He speaks to the heart . . . It is impossible to pursue his simple descriptions without loving the man, in spite of the weakness of character that he himself depicts. (Wollstonecraft, *Works,* vol. 7, *Analytical Review,* 409.)

35 Wollstonecraft, *Works,* vol. 1, *Wrongs of Woman, or Maria,* 124.
36. And yet, in letters to both her "pretend" husband, Gilbert Imlay, and her legal husband,

William Godwin, she defines her own female nature in contradistinction to their male natures. For an elaboration on this issue see *Works*, vol. 1, "General Introduction," 22.

37. Wollstonecraft, *Works*, vol. 7, *Analytical Review*, 317.
38. For an elaboration of this theme see *Works*, vol. 1, "General Introduction," 21-22-23.
39. Wollstonecraft, *Works*, vol. 7, *On Poetry*, 8.
40. Wollstonecraft, *Vindication of Woman*, 161.
41. Horace Walpole called Wollstonecraft a "hyena in petticoats." Other less-than-flattering descriptions used in response to her lifestyle challenges to the status quo were: "philosophizing serpent" and "shameless wanton."
42. Wollstonecraft, *Works*, vol. 4, *The Female Reader*, 167.
43. Wollstonecraft, *Works*, vol. 7, *Analytical Review*, 66.
44. Wollstonecraft, *Works*, vol. 6, *Letters in Sweden*, 286.
45. *Ibid.*, 310.
46. Wollstonecraft, *Vindication*, 160.
   Note the connection here to the Buddhist concept of *Nirvana*. An analogy for *Nirvana* (enlightenment) is the transmigrated soul finally being absorbed into Reality like a drop of water is absorbed into the ocean.
47. Wollstonecraft, *Works*, vol. 6, *Letters in Sweden*, 280.
48. Wollstonecraft, *Works*, vol. 7, *Analytical Review*, 231.
49. Wollstonecraft, *Works*, vol. 6, *Letters in Sweden*, 256.
50. *Ibid.*, 248.
51. *Ibid.*, 280.
52. Wollstonecraft, *Works*, vol. 7, *On Poetry*,
53. Wollstonecraft, *Works*, vol. 6, *Letters in Sweden*, 252.
54. Wollstonecraft, *Works*, vol. 1, *Wrongs of Woman*, 96.
55. Wollstonecraft, *Works*, vol. 1, *Mary, a Fiction*, 11.
56. Wollstonecraft, *Daughters*, 51.
57. Wollstonecraft, *Vindication*, 112.
58. See Note Number 7 for a definition of Critical Theorist.
59. Example: "The preposterous distinction of rank, which renders civilization a curse, by dividing the world between voluptuous tyrants, and cunning, envious dependents, corrupt almost equally, every class of people." (Wollstonecraft, *Vindication*, 144.)
60. James Moffett, *The Universal Schoolhouse: Spiritual Awakening Through Education* (San Francisco: Jossey-Bass Publishing, 1994), xix.

MANAGING AND PRODUCING ETHNIC AND RELIGIOUS IDENTITIES: GREEK IMMIGRANT MEN AND WOMEN CHURCH VOLUNTEERS

Anna Karpathakis

Department of Sociology
Nebraska Wesleyan University

The immigrant and American born ethnic women's contributions to the construction and reproduction of their group's ethnic identity has been widely documented (Gabbaccia 1994; Iacovetta 1992; Di Leonardo 1984; see also Rosaldo and Lamphere 1974 for an early theoretical exposition of women's positions and relations in public spheres). Less, however, has been written on the Greek immigrant women's contributions to their community's organizations and thus their group's constructions and maintenance of its identity (see Alba 1990; Waters 1990, for the importance of public institutions in the reconstruction of group ethnic identities).

Perceived cultural traditions and identities are constitutive of social relations and are possible and created only within historically and spatially defined interactions and institutional structures (see for example Verkuyten, de Jon and Masson 1995; Hernandez and Rosalva 1994; Bottomley 1991; Brunt 1989). Religious institutions are fora in and through which group religious and ethnic identities are constructed (see Mohl and Betten 1981; Gjerde 1986; Yoon 1995; Palinkas 1984; Breton 1965 for immigrant churches and their roles in the construction of their groups' ethnic and religious identities).

The numerous volunteer groups the laity establish and run in the Greek Orthodox Church provide institutional settings for Greek immigrants and the American born to construct their religious and secular Greek ethnic identity (see Bruneau 1993; Kourvetaris 1990; Costantinou 1989; Tsorvas 1989; Veglery 1988 for the role the Greek Orthodox Church plays in the maintenance of Greek ethnic identity). The Greek Orthodox Archdiocese of North and South America (G.O.A.N.S.A.) has a history of unprecedented laity involvement; it was the Greek immigrants of the late 19th and early 20th centuries themselves who established the local parishes, writing to the Church of Greece for the assignment of clergy. G.O.A.N.S.A. has, like other immigrant churches, (see for example Dolan 1985; Bankston and Zhou 1995; Shaw 1991) been charged (by its original immigrant creators) with three primary responsibilities: i. help immigrants enter and adjust to American society; ii. maintain and transmit the home society's culture, heritage and history to the American born; iii. maintain and transmit the home society's religion to the immigrants and the American born (see Chapin 1991; Kiriazis 1989; Moskos 1989; Scourby 1982, 1989; Jusdanis 1991; Georgakas and Moskos 1991). The Church has, in other words, been charged with the responsibility of maintaining and recreating the group's religious and ethnic identities. The resultant daily tasks and chores to be accomplished in this long term project are many and the Church has come to rely on numerous formal and informal volunteer groups to fulfill its responsibilities and goals.

The paper looks at how Greek immigrant men and women laity, working in the Church's volunteer groups differentially contribute to the construction of their group's ethnic identity. Gender specific behavior, as defined by the Church's teachings, is reproduced in the immigrants' volunteer work; the traditional gendered division of labor (men as managers and leaders and women as workers) is recreated in the Church's formal and informal structures and is thereby given legitimacy in the immigrants' volunteer work (see West and Zimmerman 1987 for a theoretical statement regarding the reproduction of gender relations in institutional settings). The institutionalized gender specific behavior has important ramifications regarding the nature of men's and women's contributions to the construction of their group's ethnic and religious identity.

While both men and women immigrants and American born are active in the Church related groups and organizations, there are important differences in the genders' volunteer activities and the nature of their participation in these groups. The genders differ on the types of groups and committees they volunteer for, the positions of power they hold in these groups, and the nature of the work they both volunteer for and are assigned. The men volunteer for the community's governing and managerial bodies deciding on the parish's policies and long or short term projects and goals. These are highly visible and prestigious parish wide groups, and tend to require intermittent and only seasonal work and meetings. The women, on the other hand, serve on less powerful, less prestigious and less visible committees and groups which lack parish wide decision making powers; the women tend to enter and create support groups carrying through work and projects decided upon by the higher order committees and groups. Furthermore, the women, independent of their group membership, are called upon on a regular basis to organize, co-sponsor, raise funds or other resources, or to simply coordinate projects decided upon by higher order committees and bodies (which are dominated by men). The women in other words, serve as a reserve army of volunteers; by being called upon to work and complete a variety of projects defined and initiated by committees and groups dominated by men, the women are the mass producers of their group's ethnic and religious identities.

As a result of this gender defined participation and as will become clear throughout the paper, the men dominated clergy and laity committees (the managers of the community's public life) define the content and parameters of the long and short term projects in and through which the group's ethnic and religious identities are constructed. The women, on the other hand, forming the reserve army of volunteer labor, produce the projects and thereby the group's ethnic and religious identities.

Methods, Sample and Site Description

Research for this paper was begun in December of 1989 as part of dissertation research on Greek immigrants of Astoria, New York. I have since returned to the field for numerous projects, extending the research beyond the Astoria community to other parts of New York City. While only twenty interviews of the original sample were used for this paper, an additional twenty five interviews carried out since then with immigrants and the second generation American born active in Church related groups, have also been used for this paper. Only interviews with immigrants active in the Church and its related groups have been included in this paper. The later (1994-1996) interviews were carried out with women active in numerous parishes throughout the City, including Brooklyn, and other towns of Queens and Nassau County. I have also carried out participant observation and even contributed to a number of Church sponsored events and meetings in Astoria.

While a variety of parish and other community sites were visited throughout the research, data from these sites have been used only for their general insights. The detailed analysis is based on the two Astoria sites (the parish and the Cultural Center offices) primarily because they are the largest, most active and most frequented by parishioners, and thus offered the greatest information. To overcome this regional bias and thus gain a more accurate picture of the community as a whole, however, interviews with women active in various parishes throughout the City have been used.

Astoria, located in the north western part of the borough of Queens, is home to the largest Greek immigrant community in the United States. While the first Greek Orthodox parish in the Astoria/Corona area was established by the immigrants in 1928, there are currently a total of four churches serving the Greek immigrants, two of which are under the auspices of the Greek Orthodox Archdiocese (the focus of this paper). The community grew from a mere eight families in the early 1920s, to twenty thousand by the mid-sixties, to approximately eighty to one hundred thousand by the late seventies and early eighties; there are currently between thirty-five and forty-five thousand Greek immigrants and their American born descendants living in Astoria. It is currently the largest and most active of the parishes in the country in terms of laity participation and fund raising capacities. The parish, incorporating two churches, averages two thousand five hundred dues annual dues paying member families.

The major formal Church related organizations on the parish level include two churches, the full-time grades K-12 parochial school (approximately eight hundred students), a part-time afternoon Greek language instruction program for public school students (approximately two hundred students), the Hellenic Cultural Center, the Parents-Teachers Association (PTA), (the single most active volunteer group in terms of hours and projects worked on), the Greek Orthodox Youth Association (G.O.Y.A.), the Philoptochos (Friends of the Poor) and the parish board (responsible for the overseeing of parish affairs). Each of these organizations and bodies in turn houses or serves as the locus of a number of loosely related groups and committees. The Hellenic Cultural Center for example, has been responsible for creating a number of additional volunteer groups and associations which are now loosely related to the Church's other groups and considered as additional lay fora. There is thus an intricate interweaving between the Church's formal structures and the volunteer groups as each of these formal organizations and groups cooperate with informal or ad hoc groups on various projects and thereby create additional temporary or longer term groups and committees.

Immigrant men active in Church related groups tend to be owners of small businesses and members of the educated middle classes. The more prestigious, visible and powerful the group or committee, the more likely that its members will be among the more successful of the lower middle and middle class men immigrants. While the women serving on special project committees tend to be college educated and some even professionals, those serving as the core group of volunteers tend to be mothers, married to small business owners or professional husbands, and not gainfully employed. While the numbers for the current sample are small, it is nevertheless appropriate and necessary that they be presented since they exemplify the patterns that Simon (1977, 1979) discovered twenty years earlier. Sixty-seven percent of the men volunteers (N = 15) appearing in the sample are small business owners, twenty two percent are middle class professionals, and the remaining eleven percent are members of the working class. Among the women (N = 30), seventy percent are married to small business owners, ten percent are married to working class men, and the remaining twenty percent are professionals; of the women volunteers, only the professionals are gainfully employed.

Gender Specific Volunteer Groups

Looking unto a group of eight women gathered at the Cultural Center on a Friday night, a clergy member whispered: "we wouldn't have anything if it wasn't for all these people volunteering their time. We rely on volunteers for the running of this Church." Indeed, projects ranging from lecture series, to weekly newsletters, from a survey of the community to art exhibits, from school programs to after church service refreshments, i.e., the very projects which the official hierarchy acknowledges as pivotal in the continuation and relevance of the Church in the community, hinge on the existence of volunteer labor.

Both men and women, immigrants and the American born, volunteer time, energy and funds to produce a variety of community projects. There are differences, however, in the type of volunteer positions and projects in which the two genders are found as well as the types of tasks they carry out in these projects. Men tend to be found in the more prestigious, more powerful and more visible positions and groups; higher level professional men volunteer their services by sitting on this or other prestigious parish level committees (such as the finance, investment and legal committees) responsible for overseeing and managing particular parish wide projects. These are the bodies which, in cooperation with the clergy, define the parish's goals, policies and even long and short term projects. The parish board, for example, historically a male body, is responsible for overseeing and managing parish wide projects; it has over the last few years undertaken the financing and overseeing of both the school and church buildings physical renovations, and in cooperation with the school officials continues to oversee a summer camp program in Greece for high school students.

The women, on the other hand, are found in the less prestigious and less powerful positions and groups. The two largest and most active women's laity groups are the Parents Teachers Association (PTA) and the Ladies' Philoptochos (Friends of the Poor). Although these groups accord the women in them status and prestige in relation to women not active in these or other committees or groups, they are nevertheless less prestigious and less powerful than the committees and groups the men enter. Both of these major women's groups are support groups, not governing bodies; the PTA works to support the school while the Philoptochos works to raise money for the Church and the parish as well as to aid the poor and other immigrants in need. The women's Church related groups, in other words, lack the power to make parish wide decisions.

When one of the school buildings was in need of renovation, the school principal contacted the PTA officers and together they met with the parish board and presented their case. The parish board voted on whether to further investigate the need for renovations; once this initial decision was taken, a committee was formed to create a committee of professionals to research the costs, contact general contractors and accept estimates of cost. Once this was done, the parish board took another vote to pursue the project, and a number of task oriented committees were formed from among the parish board and other men professionals who were recruited to sit on these highly visible and highly prestigious committees. One of the committees formed was the fund raising committee and this was the only committee on which the PTA was asked to be represented on.

While both of the traditionally women's groups could ostensibly vote for and initiate community wide projects, they in fact work closely with and act as the executors or coordinators of projects decided on by the clergy, parish board or professional groups, and always under the guidance of the bishop or another clergy member.

During the annual fund raising festival the parish holds, for example, the parish board plans on and decides the structure of the event; the board decides on the number of game, food and other gift stands, the number of rides, the prices charged for food and beverages, the nature of the dinner dance on the last night of the festival; the board will eventually also decide on how funds are to be distributed throughout the parish and the numerous ongoing projects. While both the PTA and Philoptochos representatives are present at the numerous meetings for this event, these groups' contributions come at a later point. The women's groups are called on to carry out the specific tasks necessary for the festival; volunteers must, for example, price (and negotiate with merchants) and purchase food and beverages, solicit donations and contributions in money and kind for the lottery drawing, recruit more volunteers to work in the gift and food kiosks, to prepare and set up the grounds, the vendors must be called and organized, the event must be advertised in the community's mass media. The women, in other words, are called upon to take on and carry out the detailed and often tedious tasks so necessary in the completion of this and other projects.

Even in the mixed gender professional volunteer groups, the men assume the managerial roles while the women assume the roles of support. When the Cultural Center decided to organize a non-profit bookstore on its premises so as to make Greek language religious and history books available to the immigrants, the bishop called on the PTA for names of potential volunteer librarians. Within two months, the Bishop gathered a group of four librarians to index and catalogue books. Despite the fact that a woman in the group was a senior librarian for a college, the only man in the group was introduced to the women librarians as "the one who knows what has to be done;" while the only man in the group was given detailed explanations as to the intended group's purposes prior to the first meeting, the women were given general explanations. As a result, while the clergy decided on the types of books to be sold in the bookstore, the man librarian immediately assumed the leadership position in the group by assigning himself the task of researching and selecting particular books to be included in the bookstore, organizing schedules, tasks and time tables; the women, on the other hand, were assigned the actual cataloguing and organizing of the books and pamphlets. When a woman visitor asked "will you have books on the early Church? On women in the Church?", the man librarian quickly responded, "there aren't any in Greek."

During events organized by both men's and women's groups, the men tend to take on the more prestigious and visible roles of chairpersons and moderators, while the women remain invisible. As a result of working backstage in preparing projects and events defined by the male dominated committees, the women receive little public recognition for their services. One of the administrative assistants, also active in the PTA, recounted an incident with dismay.

"He came to us and said that it would be nice if Mr . . . were one of the speakers for the lecture series. We organized, we set up the whole event. Set up the room and refreshments for after the talk. Mr... (one of the parish board members) who knew the speaker and did no work at all to make this event possible was given the honor of presenting the event and the speaker. Not a mention was made of our work. It's not fair and it happens all the time. Ah you get used to it after awhile You don't like it but there is nothing you can do. What are you going to do? Create trouble? Be seen as a troublemaker? It's not worth it. We do this for the children. Someone has to do the work. I just wish we had more I don't know say so in things."

Working backstage in the support groups often means that the women lack the power to initiate particular projects or even define the content of the projects. The lecture series is a vital part of the Cultural Center's outreach efforts; its aim is to transmit the history and cultural heritage of Greece, the Church and the immigrants to the community. When one woman volunteer asked that a well known feminist theologian be invited to present on her research on the women's roles in the early Church, one of the clergy members immediately retorted: "She's controversial. I'm not sure it's a good idea . . . well, some of the men won't like it and we'll be sowing conflict and disunity when our aim here is to create unity among the Greeks and Greek Americans. "

To summarize, while the men volunteers work on the more visible and prestigious groups with decision making powers (on long and short term goals and projects), the women enter groups which serve as support mechanisms for the parish's formal governing bodies. As a result, the men in effect become the "managers" of projects and events which recreate the group's ethnic and religious identity, while the women become the producers of these projects.

Core Volunteers

There is a core group of thirty women who can be relied upon to help organize a variety of events and projects; while these women are officially part of the PTA or the Philoptochos, they are found working on a variety of projects at any one time. This core group of women attend the various functions acting as hostesses and support staff; they act as translators, prepare and serve beverages and cakes after meetings or lectures, organize fundraisers, help organize and financially support after school programs and extra curriculum activities for the students, cook and prepare meals for clergy and other meetings and gatherings in the parish, raise funds for school supplies and equipment, on major holidays visit and bake Greek sweets for the residents of the Church sponsored nursing home, finance printing charges for newsletters and other mailings, on major holidays bring Greek holiday sweets and gifts to the residents of the children's home sponsored by the Church, raise funds for adult Greek language courses, call on and send sympathy and get well cards to parishioners, organize and fund holiday parties and festivities for children, teach the Greek language courses, help the maintenance crew clean the room after exhibits or meetings.

In addition, as one mother of two school aged children said laughing, the women also provide "bodies. We need people to come to these affairs. Part of my job is to call women I know who may be interested in the topic and come with me to the talk. Now depending on the topic or the event this is easier or harder. Sometimes I get ten women to come sometimes one or two. Last week I got no one. The talks on AIDS and the history of Greek immigration to the United States we got a room full of people. Ah, some days are better than others."

Another woman, eavesdropping on the conversation added,

"I have learned more things in the last three years I've been doing this than in all my years in school. Sittin' here listening to these professors, artists, writers, listening to things about ancient Greece, the Byzantium, immigrants, psychology, health . . . I go home and teach my kids and even my husband about Greek history and poetry and anything and everything... I'm tellin' ya. I deserve a college degree by now."

Since the volunteer Church groups are gendered by participation as well as by the positions and tasks assigned, there are also differences in the number of hours and seasonality of the work the genders contribute. The women tend to work throughout the year and contribute more hours per week, while the men's volunteer work requires monthly and even only seasonal meetings and other work contributions. The parish wide committees on which the men are found, for example, meet monthly, semi-annually or once every quarter. The men meet to decide on projects and then delegate tasks to be completed by the women volunteers; while the men's work is completed through these meetings, the projects decided upon are then carried out by the women's groups. The groups that the women enter thus are active throughout the year despite the fact that these groups are officially active only while school is in session; women are called upon to work on "extra" projects going on throughout the year when school is closed. Christmas and Easter parties and other events require that the women, as one woman said,

"we celebrate New Year's at the parish. We have a Greek Santa Claus we try to have a Greek party. It's a family affair. Kids, my parents, who ever was going to come over my house I tell them to come to St. . . . instead. It's fun. I shouldn't be complaining . . . I haven't spent a quiet New Year's Eve at home with my kids for oh, over six or seven years. It's fun though."

Again, the March 25th Greek Independence Day (from the Ottoman occupation) is celebrated in the schools with the students reciting poetry and staging one-act plays, all in the Greek language. The PTA women are important contributors to this since there is limited paid staff to produce these celebrations; the women help in the rehearsals, they set up the stage and the auditorium and make the appropriate costumes. None of the volunteers found at the school after hours during the preparations for these celebrations are men.

During the laity-clergy conference of 1996 held in early July, one of the PTA officers was responsible for organizing a group of volunteers to prepare the meeting packets for one thousand two hundred conference delegates. Another was responsible for the printing of the program, while another was responsible for organizing volunteers to be present at the three day workshops. Maria, a thirty-five year old mother of two said, "we're on call these days twenty four hours a day. (Laughing). My husband jokes that I must find priests more interesting than him because I spend more time with them than with him." While the parish board will not convene for the summer months, the core group of women volunteers will be available for translation work, to host visitors to the parish, to, as Maria said, "you never know things always happen."

Recruiting Men and Women Volunteers Outside the Formal Groups

Professional men are recruited to volunteer for parish wide and project specific groups and committees; while some of these committees tend to be temporary, lasting anywhere from six months to two years, they are also decision making bodies. Professional men are the least likely to volunteers their services by sitting on committees or projects with intensive and regular work schedules. One of the committees formed during the school building's renovation, included three newly recruited professional men whose legal and financial expertise were lacking among the parish board members. This particular committee met every three months for an average of three to four hours; in the committee's two year existence, only two emergency meetings (one lasting eight hours) were called.

The professional women volunteers, on the other hand, are asked to contribute to projects which are more labor intensive and time consuming. When in the Spring of 1994 the Cultural Center produced a radio program, to (as a clergy member said) "inform the community of Greek and religious affairs", a man director/producer was hired to spearhead the station and program; part of his responsibility was to solicit professional volunteers to produce their own thirty or sixty minute weekly program. Six months into the radio station's existence, the overwhelming majority of volunteer radio producers were women professionals. As the director said, "a couple of them (men) are from the men's organizations . . . but mostly they are women . . . the professionals are women . . . it's nice to have a doctor being interviewed on one program, a social worker on another, a poet . . . the women show up week after week. They do good work . . . The men show one week they don't show another. (Laughing.) Like my wife says I guess men are lazy."

Given the shortage of funds allocated to projects, both Project Directors and the officers of volunteer groups must turn to the secular organizations to recruit volunteers and other resources. There are important differences as to the type of resources requested and received from the secular men's and women's organizations. Church activists are more likely to recruit volunteers from the women's organizations and funds from the men's organizations. Furthermore, the few men who are recruited tend to work on a particular project and will cease their volunteer work once the project is completed; the women recruited from the secular women's organizations, on the other hand, are more likely to remain active in the Church related groups taking on responsibilities for other projects.

The women's secular organizations also serve as a reserve army of volunteer labor of the last resort. When during an annual parish fundraiser the organizers realized that more volunteers were needed, women active in Church related groups were asked by the committee chairman to call women from secular organizations and recruit volunteers. It was this way, for example, that the President of one woman's secular organization, recruited five women from her organization to do volunteer work at the parish's fundraiser; two of these women have since become active members of the PTA.

In sum, while the women's volunteer labor can be relied upon as a steady pool of labor, the men's voluntary activities are more project or committee oriented with a less demanding work schedule. Men do not become part of the reserve army of volunteers.

Women Church Employees and Volunteer Groups

A little note on the men and women Church and parish employees is in order. While the numbers here are small (N = 16), (the totality of this subgroup is not part of the interview sample), the patterns are unwavering (and also hold for other parishes in the City.) While all six of the administrative assistants are women, all of the project directors are men; the only general parish and Church manager is a man, while the maintenance crew for the buildings consists of three men. Only one woman holds a lower level managerial position of Assistant Director.

Furthermore, while the women tend to be hired under broadly defined job titles and overlapping responsibilities (in particular sub-divisions of the hierarchy), the men tend to be hired as directors of particular projects with more specific job titles and job descriptions. One woman was hired as the "administrative assistant of the parish," while another was hired as the "administrative assistant for membership and clergy." At the same time, one man, was hired to raise funds for the Cultural Center and the radio station, another to produce and direct the radio program. The only managerial level position with a broad description is held by a man who has the support of two administrative assistants.

Hired women personnel become part of the pool or reserve army of volunteers called upon to perform and complete projects unrelated to their job titles. Given the women's broadly defined job categories and the shortage of paid personnel, the women support staff, although hired for specific sub-divisions within the parish and the Center, work on a variety of projects external to their job assignments and departments. Volunteers turn to the women employees for help in the various stages of the ongoing projects. When a project sponsored by the Cultural Center required a lengthy Greek document to be typed, a clergy member called one of the parish administrative secretaries and, as he said, "asked her for a favor." The women support staff are, as one secretary said, "shuffled back and forth. There's an extra project that comes up, we're calling . . . That does not replace or excuse us from our work. I'm not complaining and I want to help but this is too much."

A certain amount of volunteer work is unofficially expected of the women staff, which as the women have pointed out, is not expected of the men. As one of the women staff said,

> "I have spend many Friday and Wednesday nights here. I go home for a couple of hours after work and then return because there is some affair and someone who works here must be here . . . the super does it once in a while but he's so nasty to people it's hard to have him as a host . . . last week when I couldn't be here Kathy (another woman) came in for me . . . The men? Huh. Once they leave they leave. At most they'll go to a Christmas party. They'll go to meetings in the evenings but only if it is important for their work. Somehow you can't ask the men to do these things. They're extra. We (the women) have to do them."

While the men may be invited to meetings relevant to their own department, they are not asked to host events or provide their services for projects unrelated to their departments. When one of the directors was asked if he attended any of the ongoing lectures he laughed:

> *George:* "of course not. They're held on Thursday and Friday nights and I'm busy then. I have a social life too. I want to be home with my family or with my friends."
> *Interviewer:* "Have you attended any of them?"
> *George:* "One. I (needed to be there for [my own] work . . . I (had to do something very specific). That was the only one."

Given this gender difference and the overall shortage of paid personnel, the few women employees find that their time and labor are freely used and freely assumed, and it often becomes part of the volunteer labor sustaining the Church.

Women's Labor as a Reserved Army of Volunteer Labor

The projects that the Church related groups sponsor are numerous and range from fund raising activities, to student poetry and play productions, from art exhibits to music concerts, from a weekly newsletter to religious and secular holiday gatherings and parties, from numerous lecture series to raising funds for charity, from creating and running a non-profit bookstore to scouting the community to learn of immigrants needing financial relief, from a sociological survey of the community to running a radio station . . . The list can go on ad infinitum. These projects are an essential element and process of the Church fulfilling its responsibilities and mission in the immigrant community. It is through these projects that the group constructs and defines its heritage as well as religious and ethnic identities.

While the employed parish and Church staff is minimal, these and all other projects sponsored by the Church are dependent on the women reserve army of volunteer labor. Two examples will serve to illustrate our discussion of how men manage and direct these projects (through which the group's ethnic and religious identities are constructed) while women serve as the reserved army of volunteer labor called upon to carry out and complete projects defined by men.

The Hellenic Cultural Center sponsors weekly lectures on a variety of topics. These tend to be initiated by the auxiliary bishop who creates ad hoc groups by inviting professionals to form such lecture series or manage projects in their areas of work or specialization. After the bishop's initial meeting with these professionals, the project is carried on by the volunteers themselves; they scout their professional circles, do the necessary research, in cooperation with the Assistant Director of the Center make a schedule of events, make the contacts and extend the invitations. Once this is done, the PTA women are called by the Assistant Director; while the Assistant Director advertises the events through the community's formal mass media, the PTA advertises through the schools, the secular organizations they may be active in and other informal channels so as to recruit attendees; lastly, the PTA hosts the lectures by providing refreshments, cakes, and audience.

A group of eight social scientists were in November of 1993 invited to a meeting by the auxiliary bishop of Queens and Long Island (Nassau County) who put forth a strong case of volunteerism: he asked those gathered to

> "think about how you can contribute to the community. There are a lot of problems from what I see . . . You are working as professionals, contributing to the world we live in. You are helping to make this a better world. You are committed to servicing humanity and that is why you have chosen your work. You get paid for this. This is how you earn your living. What I now come to ask you is what can you as social scientists contribute to make this a better world for Greek immigrants and their children. Remember there is no money involved, a lot of work but desperately needed work. This is what God tells us. To help those who need help. Goods and talents not shared for the service of one's community are wasted."

After a long discussion, it was decided that it was first necessary to understand the problems that the immigrants and the community face, and a group of two volunteered to work on a survey of the community. By working after hours and subsidizing the expenses, the group completed the English version of the survey eighteen months later. A PTA ex-president, educated in the university in Greece was called by the bishop and asked to translate the survey into Greek. The Greek version of the survey was typed by one of the administrative assistants in the Cultural Center who was asked by the bishop for "a favor"; by working in the evenings, with no monetary remuneration, the woman completed the survey (in its numerous revisions) within two months. Immigrants with copy machines in their businesses printed the survey over the next two months. The bishop then called the parochial school principals and the PTA presidents who were asked for their cooperation in the distribution of the survey; while the principals sent letters to parents, the PTA officers discussed and informed their members of the survey. In collaboration with teachers or school principals (all of them women), the surveys were distributed and collected by the group members. One of the City University colleges offered to house the survey and make it part of its on going work and research on Greek immigrants in New York City—this entailed no monetary remuneration but only the institutional affiliation necessary to lend legitimacy to the project.

Conclusion

The Greek Orthodox Church has been charged by its lay membership to maintain, transmit and reconstruct their group's ethnic identity; to achieve this, numerous volunteer groups form, initiate and complete a variety of projects. Men and women immigrants volunteer their time, energies, money and other resources to the completion of these projects. However, the ways in which men's and women's volunteer labor is used varies. The men volunteer for and enter specialized committees with decision making powers, i.e., the parish's governing groups; in cooperation with the clergy (all male), these groups manage and define the parish's policies, goals and projects. These committees, meeting seasonally and only a few times a year, then delegate tasks to the lower order support groups and committees consisting of women. These women's groups take on the responsibilities of carrying through projects to their completion. As a result of the gender structured participation in the laity groups, the men are the managers of the parish's projects and affairs, and the women are the producers; the women constitute a reserve army of volunteer labor from which free labor is recruited and used in the completion of these ethnic and religious identity projects. To the extent that the group's identity is constructed in and through these ongoing projects and it is the men dominated committees who define the long and short term projects, it is the men who manage and define the group's identity and the women who then produce it.

References

Alba, Richard. 1990. *Ethnic Identity: The Transformation of White America*. New Haven: Yale University Press.

Bankston, Carl, L. III., Zhou Min. 1995. "Religious Participation, Ethnic Identification, and Adaptation of Vietnamese Adolescents in an Immigrant Community." *Sociological Quarterly* Vol. 36, No. 3. Summer, 523-534.

Bottomley, Gillian. 1991. "Culture, Ethnicity, and the Politics/Poetics of Representation." *Diaspora*. Vol. 1. No. 3: 303-320

Breton, Raymond. 1965. "Institutionalized Completeness of Ethnic Communities and the Personal Relations of Immigrants." *American Journal of Sociology* 70: 193-205.

Bruneau, Michel. 1993. "The Orthodox Church and the Greek Diaspora." *Social Compass* Vol 40. No. 2. June. 199-216.

Brunt, Rosalind. 1989. "The Politics of Identity", in, Stuart Hall and M. Jacques, eds. *New Times*. London: Lawrence and Wishart.

Chapin, Helen Geracimos. 1991. "The Greeks of Hawaii", in Dan Georgakas and Charles C. Moskos, eds. *New Directions of Greek American Studies*. New York: Pella Publishing.

Di Leonardo, Micaela. 1984. *Varieties of Ethnic Experience: Kinship, Class and Gender among California Italian Americans*. Ithaca: Cornell University Press.

Dolan, Jay. 1985. *American Catholic Experience: A History from Colonial Times to the Present*. Garden City, New York: Double Day.

Gabaccia, Donna. 1994. *From the Other Side: Women, Gender, and Immigrant Life in the U.S., 1820-1990*. Bloomington: Indiana University Press.

Georgakas, Dan and Moskos, Charles C. 1991. eds. *New Directions of Greek American Studies*. New York: Pella Publishing.

Gjerde, Jon. 1986. "Conflict and Community: A Case Study of the Immigrant Church in the United States." *Journal of Social History* Vol. 19. No. 4. Summer. 681-697.

Hasiotis, Ioannis K. 1989. "Continuity and Change in the Modern Greek Diaspora." *Journal of Modern Hellenism* No. 6. Winter. 9-24.

Hernandez, Castillo, and Rosalva, Aida. 1994. "Collective Identities in the Periphery of the Nation: Ethnicity and Religious Change among the Mames of Chiapas." *Nueva Anthropologia* Vol. 13, No. 45. April. 83-105

Iacovetta, Franca. 1992. *Such Hardworking people: Italian immigrants in postwar Toronto*. Toronto: McGill Queens University Press.

Jusdanis, Gregory. 1991. "Greek Americans and the Diaspora." *Diaspora* Vol. 1. No. 2. 209-223.

Karpathakis, Anna. 1994. "'Whose Church Is It Anyway?' Greek Immigrants of Astoria, New York, and their Church." *Journal of the Hellenic Diaspora* Vol. 20. No. 1. 97-122.

Kiriazis, James W. 1989. *Children of the Colossus: The Rhodian Greek Immigrants in the United States*. New York. AMS Press Inc.

Kourvetaris, George, A. 1990. "Conflicts and Identity Crises among Greek Americans and Greeks of the Diaspora." *International Journal of Contemporary Sociology* Vol. 27. Nos. 3-4. July-October. 137-153.

Mohl, Raymond, A., Betten, Neil. 1981;"The Immigrant Church in Gary, Indiana: Religious Adjustment and Cultural Defense." *Ethnicity* Vol. 8, No. 1. March. 1-17.

Moskos, Charles 1979. *Greek American: Struggle and Success*. New Brunswick: Transaction Books.

Palinkas, Lawrence. 1984. "Social Fission and Cultural Change in an Ethnic Chinese Church." *Ethnic Groups* Vol. 5. No. 4. Feb. 255-277.

Rosaldo, Michelle Zimbalist and Louise Lamphere, eds. 1974. *Woman, Culture and Society*. Stanford: Stanford University Press.

Scourby, Alice. 1982. "Three Generations of Greek Americans: A Study in Ethnicity." in, Harry J. Psomiades, Alice Scourby, eds. *The Greek American Community in Transition*. New York: Pella Publishing Co., Inc.

_____. 1987. "The Interweave of Gender and Ethnicity: The Case of Greek Americans." in, Peter Kivisto, ed. *The Ethnic Enigma: The Salience of Ethnicity of European-Origin Groups*. Philadelphia: The Balch Institute Press .

Shaw, Stephen Joseph. 1991. "The Catholic parish as a way-station of ethnicity and Americanization: Chicago's Germans and Italians, 1903-1939." *Chicago Studies in the History of American Religion*. Brooklyn, NY: Carlson Publications.

Tsorvas, Ourania. 1989. "Highlights of a Study of the Mobility and Social Characteristics of the Greek Population of Bridgeport, Connecticut, 1900-1970." *Journal of the Hellenic Diaspora*. Vol. 16. Nos. 1-4. 95-103.

Veglery, Anna. 1988 "Differential Social Integration among First Generation Greeks in new York City." *International Migration Review*. Vol. 22. No. 4. Winter. 627-657.

Verkuyten, M., de Jong, W., and C.N. Masson 1995. "The construction of ethnic categories: discourses of ethnicity in the Netherlands." Vol 18. No. 2. April. 251-276.

Waters, Mary C. 1990. *Ethnic Options: Choosing Identities in America*. Berkeley: University of California Press.

West, Candace and Zimmerman, Don. H. 1987. "Doing Gender." *Gender & Society*. June 1: 125-151.

Yoon, In Jin. 1995. "The Growth of Korean Immigrant Entrepreneurship in Chicago." *Ethnic and Racial Studies*. Vol. 18. No. 2. April. 315-335.

JUST SAY WAIT:
A FIRST LOOK AT THE TRUE LOVE WAITS CAMPAIGN

J. Shawn Landres

Department of Religious Studies
University of California, Santa Barbara

"Believing that true love waits, I make a commitment to God, myself, my family, my friends, my future mate, and my future children to be sexually abstinent from this day until the day I enter a biblical marriage relationship."

The True Love Waits campaign is an inter-denominational program that promotes premarital chastity. It is led by the Southern Baptist Sunday School Board with the cooperation of 27 other Christian denominations,[1] and as of late 1995, 250,000 young people in the United States have signed the True Love Waits pledge.[2] Various denominations have created rituals of commitment to accompany the pledge, and some youth have begun to wear a white purity ribbon, analogous not only to the red AIDS ribbon of the 1980s and 1990s, but also to the temperance movement of the late 1800s, during which young people made pledges to God and their community, and publicized their commitment by wearing white.[3]

The purpose of this chapter is to provide an initial report on the True Love Waits campaign, to describe the phenomenon in general terms, and to locate it in the contemporary situation. To do so involves three inter-related tasks:

• first, to interpret the campaign as a means of selling a complete identity, both individual and collective;

• second, to consider the campaign as representative of popular American Protestantism; and

• third, to reflect on the campaign as a marketing strategy, one with targets, niches, and messages.

A single metaphor drives this descriptive enterprise: selling identity. This is an expansion of the title metaphor of R. Laurence Moore's book, *Selling God*, which he describes as "a study of religious influence in determining the taste of people who were learning to purchase 'culture' as a means of self-improvement and relaxation."[4] In my view, the True Love Waits campaign attempts neither to sell culture, nor to market self-improvement and relaxation, but rather to offer an entire way of being in the world, and of indicating one's relationship to the world in which one lives. To that end, this study somewhat may resemble a market research analysis, focusing on three central issues: the targets of the campaign, whether they are in the evangelical community or in society at large, the message it promotes, and the context within which it operates. In other words, to whom is it trying to sell its product (whether in the conservative Protestant sub-culture or in the "wider" secular world), what product is True Love Waits selling, and what "market segment" does it occupy?

The True Love Waits campaign's market niche is located within what Wayne Elzey has called "popular American Protestantism."[5] Within this rubric Elzey includes a number of characteristic traits:

- an extra-ecclesiastical community;
- a developed iconographic and artifactual tradition;
- a highly personalized conception of the object of religion;
- a primary concern with the individual, rather than with the group, the society, or the nation;
- the aim of establishing and maintaining a devotional or 'bhaktic' relationship between the believer and the object of worship;
- a dualistic view of the world;
- the tendency to express 'doctrines' by means of concrete images and symbols rather than in abstract language and systematic theologies;
- the sacralization of the ordinary and commonplace;
- conversely, the de-emphasis of traditionally 'sacred' texts, institutions, and actions; and
- the ritualization of moral behavior.[6]

The portrait of True Love Waits presented here will take up each of these traits in turn, relating it to the three central issues of target, context, and message.

First, it is important to consider the targets of the True Love Waits campaign. This will provide a reference point in relation with which to place the message and context of the campaign. The target membership is not American teenagers in general, but rather "churched" teenagers already within the conservative Protestant fold. As Wayne Elzey points out, "the real target has always been precisely the people who attended regularly, the urban, middle-class Protestants. . . . They were to be thought about, and not to be converted."[7] The wording of the "Sample News Release" provided in the "True Love Waits Emphasis Planning Kit," which is sent to group leaders who wish to start a local campaign, is intended to "coincide with planned church True Love Waits . . . celebration event[s]." The news release is to be distributed to all "community media" outlets, secular and religious:

> "The purpose of the emphasis is to inspire, inform, and call youth to adhere
> to the biblical mandate from God and commit to refraining from sex before
> marriage, (*pastor's name*) said. (*Pastor's name*) said over (*number*) teenagers

have signed commitment cards promising to abstain from sex from now until marriage."

The message transmitted here is not intended to bring outsiders in, but rather to gather in unregenerate church members and to demonstrate to the "wider world" the strength and integrity of the movement. The extent to which the "community media" might completely ignore these events would also highlight the power of the movement to persevere in the face of social stigma.[8]

Different kinds of statistical evidence are cited by the True Love Waits campaign in its "For Your Information" fact sheet, in order to provide a contextual justification for the campaign; that is to say, the planning kit documents a continuing decline of morality among America's youth, such that a new movement is needed, one that will elevate falling moral standards. The nature of the statistical evidence, however, demonstrates that the campaign's target is churched youth, not the "wider world." While the sheet contains the by-now standard mantra about promiscuity, sexually transmitted behavior, and generally moral vapidity of America's youth, it also uncovers the following:

> A survey conducted during the 1992 Winter Youth Celebrations at Ridgecrest Conference Center, NC, revealed that the majority of youth surveyed were Christians—95%. The survey also revealed that one out of every five youth have had sex already. Of those who have had sex already, 41% admitted to being sexually active at the time of the survey.

Such survey results are confirmed by the investigations done in the early 1980s by sociologist James Davison Hunter and in the mid-1990s by youth minister Josh McDowell: sexual activity among "churched" youth increased from the 1960s to the 1980s, and then soared to a peak in 1987. Since 1987, although the proportion of sexually active "churched" youth has declined, so has the proportion believing that pre-marital sexual contact, including intercourse, is "always morally wrong." In other words, fewer people are having premarital sex, but not because they think it is *wrong*; this suggests to authors like McDowell that young people have lost their moral compass. The True Love Waits campaign thus concentrates on chastity in the individual while cultivating an increased sense of moral commitment and solidarity within the church community.

Let us now take up Wayne Elzey's categories of popular Protestantism. The campaign is "extra-ecclesiastical" in that it is sponsored by a coalition of evangelical, fundamentalist, pentecostal, and holiness groups, and does not claim to replace any of them as a "church"; rather, it seeks to supplement existing teen ministry programs. To the limited extent that the campaign is moving beyond the evangelical sub-culture into the so-called "wider world," the campaign keeps to a minimum the kinds of "brand-name" references that would tag it as of interest only to a particular group, but it nonetheless retains a strongly conservative Protestant tone.

True Love Waits has developed a powerful iconographic and artifactual tradition, which has led to the commodification not of sex, but of abstinence. The campaign assumes that for teenagers of the 1990s, image is everything, and the "True Love Waits Emphasis Planning Kit" includes a number of related materials that may be purchased: in addition to "TLW" logos that may be photocopied or made into stickers and buttons. The planning kit provides ordering information for T-shirts, caps, "commitment" rings, compact discs and cassettes, banners and posters, mugs and plates, and, not to be outdone by the secular fashion industry, "True Love Waits Active Wear," including T-shirts and sweatshirts. One of the most compelling aspects of the True Love Waits logo is that in the contemporary marketplace of clothing, where a wide variety of initials and messages is imprinted on shirts and sweaters, the True Love Waits logo is not immediately recognizable to outsiders. To those "in the know," however, the True Love Waits identity is instantly communicated. Not only does this phenomenon echo the "ΙΧΘΥΣ" insignia of the early Church, but it visually establishes a sense of solidarity—and hence community identity—among its wearers. The campaign thus uses "concrete images and symbols," such as the covenant card and the "TLW" logo, to convey its message. The duplicating instructions included in the planning kit suggest that "the quality of the card reflect the depth of the commitment being made," and include ordering information for acrylic holders to preserve the cards after they have been signed. Furthermore, the order form for the commitment ring (which costs $29.00) indicates that "a gold ring is a symbol of the 'True Love Waits' commitment. The ring is a daily reminder of the vow and serves also as a witnessing tool. It is suggested that the ring be worn until marriage and given to the marriage partner on the wedding night as their gift of purity." The True Love Waits planning kit's list of "Church Worship Ideas" further notes that the ring "can also provide opportunities to teenagers to share their commitment to abstinence with their peers when asked about the ring"—in other words, it becomes a concrete, material witnessing tool.

The message of the True Love Waits campaign promotes "a highly personalized conception of the object of religion" and seeks to establish and maintain a "devotional ...relationship between the believer and the object of worship." Teenagers involved in the True Love Waits campaign believe that God (in the conservative Protestant tradition this is a highly personal, involved, authoritative father figure) wants them to remain "sexually pure" not only for the sake of their future mate but also for His sake. Furthermore, the campaign is concerned primarily with the individual promise-maker, rather than with any larger social group. All it asks of the believer is that he or she take a vow of chastity until marriage. The campaign pursues no larger social or political goals; it has even stayed out of the sex education controversy in public schools. When True Love Waits held a rally—a "stake-out" of over 211,000 "covenant cards" (as the signed pledge cards are called)—on the Mall in Washington, DC, on July 29, 1994, it appeared only to seek to demonstrate the sheer number of young people who had taken the pledge, and at most to document a "cultural trend," not to make any larger social statement.[10]

The campaign articulates "a dualistic view of the world." Pre-marital sexual intercourse constitutes an expression of "false love";[11] "true" love requires sexual "purity," defined as chastity before marriage and selfless sexual union within marriage. In his book *Innocent Ecstasy*, Peter Gardella relates how Joshua McDowell, the popular Christian educator cited earlier, develops the notion of "maximum sex," the idea that sexuality expressed within marriage offers the greatest opportunity for spiritual and physical pleasure.[12] The phrase "innocent ecstasy" itself illustrates the dualistic notions that drive popular movements like True Love Waits. By channeling "impure" desires and expressions into "pure" venues such as prayer and, more importantly, "Biblical marriage relationships," True Love Waits offers a bridge for living a pure, Godly life in an impure, human, body. One way of doing so is to combine the Christian message with the "innocently ecstatic" medium of popular contemporary music. The planning kit includes sheet music for two songs to be used at home and in church, "This Promise I Made" and the "True Love Waits Anthem." Furthermore, the True Love Waits compact disc/cassette includes such popular artists as Grammy award-winners DC Talk and Petra, as well as Newsboys and Lisa Bevill, all of whom are superstars in the conservative Protestant sub-culture. Many of the songs, if pure in their message, are frankly sexual in their backbeat and texture, illustrating Wayne Elzey's observation that "the erotic techniques of salvation ought to be as obvious as the content of the sermon which equates eroticism and sin. Neither can be understood apart from the other. Conversion involves eliciting 'sinful' attitudes which save people from their 'sins.'"[13] The True Love Waits audio products thus seek to re-channel normal, human, erotic desires into a purely Christian outlet, such physical pleasure becomes a means toward a spiritual end.

One of the implicit messages of the True Love Waits campaign is that sex is more pleasurable if each partners abstains until marriage. As Elzey observes, "opposing and contrary beliefs and symbols are held together . . . . by the fact that each finds the existence of the other to be necessary to its own existence."[14] Thus, within the context of the True Love Waits campaign, the spiritual and physical pleasure found in sexual relations is actually created through the process of chastity and abstinence. Conversely, pre-marital promiscuity robs young people of true sexual pleasure, through sexually transmitted diseases, pregnancy, and the social stigma associated with sexual impurity.

Just because the campaign encourages its members to remain sexually pure, however, does not mean that it excludes sexually active teenagers. In fact, the campaign specifically targets these teenagers by placing the emphasis on the campaign not on virginity, but rather on chastity. The campaign creates a category of "secondary virginity" that allows—indeed, welcomes—young people who have been sexually active to alter their behavior. Focusing on "acquired" purity over "original" purity not only places the campaign firmly within a Protestant tradition that emphasizes conversion experience over inherited religious affiliation, but also reiterates the campaign's overall message that sexual purity is achieved only through a personal relationship with God and with one's future spouse, and it does not just "happen." Christian sex-education books aimed at teenagers often make this point quite strongly; Greg Johnson and Susie Shellenberger put it this way:

> Maybe you . . . have already blown it. God is willing to forgive and forget. So what is your responsibility? To seek His forgiveness. *And* to start over . . . .

> Isaiah 43:19 says, 'I'm going to do a brand new thing!' (TLB). And that's exactly what He wants to do in *your* life. It's called a 'second virginity.' If you've had sex, you're no longer a virgin. But God wants to forgive and *forget*, remember? In other words, He wants to wipe your slate completely clean—as if you'd never blown it!

> What a wonderful and powerful God, huh? So, through His forgiveness and cleansing, you can claim a 'second virginity.' In *His* eyes—because He's blotted out your past—you're starting all over, a *virgin!*"[15]

This passage demonstrates at least popular Protestant traits, such as an intensely personal relationship between God and the believer, one which is dependent on the believer's continued devotion to God (the "responsibility . . . to seek His forgiveness"), and a dualistic worldview: "Either you're in with God, or you're not. It's your choice." Furthermore, the passage, as well as the True Love Waits campaign as a whole, not only "de-emphasizes traditionally 'sacred' actions,'" insofar as it presents sexuality as having been commodified and devalued by the secular consumer culture. It also "sacralizes the ordinary," that is, renders sacred the act of admitting to and repenting for premarital sexual activity. The sacred and the ordinary are again inverted when the positive decision to remain chaste—in the form of the True Love Waits pledge—is elevated to a position of importance. A decision *not* to have sex, even if one has already been sexually active, becomes a sacred act. Conversely, admitting and repenting sexual impurity simply removes it from the divine tally sheet.

One consequence of elevating sexual purity to such a high level, however, is that it raises the question of when purity ends and impurity begins. This is an especially difficult question with regard to masturbation, which Christians traditionally have strongly opposed but which one might reasonably expect to be preferable to sexual intercourse. The Roman Catholic Church, for example, declares masturbation to be "an intrinsically and gravely disordered action. The deliberate use of the sexual faculty, for whatever reason, outside of marriage is essentially contrary to its purpose."[16] By contrast, conservative Protestant educators Bill Ameiss and Jane Graver counsel, "Infrequent self-stimulation provides a release of sexual tension and should not be a cause for concern or shame." They caution, however, against using masturbation to compensate for loneliness and against fantasizing about using another person as a "toy made for your sexual pleasure."[17] Perhaps purposefully more vague than either of these two other positions, Johnson and Shellenberger point out that "to be sexually fulfilled by someone other than your husband/wife is *wrong* in God's eyes";[18] they do not indicate, however, whether masturbation falls into this category.

Wayne Elzey's last category concerns the "ritualization of moral behavior." Indeed, the True Love Waits campaign appears to have a ritual for nearly every action. The planning kit includes "Family Worship Ideas" and "Church Worship Ideas," both of which contain suggestions for incorporating into the formal liturgy a ritual for taking the sexual purity vows, and for re-affirming those vows on a regular basis. In the case of church worship, this is done in call-and-response form to ensure the support and participation of the entire congregation. One element of the ritual is a "ring ceremony," during which the teenager receives the commitment ring "as a constant reminder of the commitment made." Johnson and Shellenberger, in a book entitled *258 Great Dates While You Wait*, describe one family's ring ceremony, which takes place on the occasion of the young woman's thirteenth birthday, itself a ritual occasion of passage into the teenage years. "Someday when I'm out with a guy and he reaches for my hand," the authors quote Shauna Menefee as telling them, "I'm going to feel my ring against his flesh. That's a pretty powerful reminder of my commitment. And even now, when I catch myself daydreaming in class, I start fiddling with my ring—you know, twisting it round and round. And I smile deep inside, knowing that someday I'll present this very ring to my husband on our wedding night as a symbol of the most important gift I can give him—my virginity.'"[19] This statement not only captures the power of materiality in the True Love Waits campaign, but also illustrates the extent to which ordinary activities—holding hands and daydreaming in class—are sacralized to become opportunities for a ritual of memory and commitment.

The way the True Love Waits campaign has employed these characteristics of popular Protestantism indicates the extent to which the campaign is not just selling chastity, but rather marketing an entire identity. Indeed, playwrights Kathie Hill and Travis Cottrell have expanded the concept of waiting for marriage and sexual activity to include an entire identity constructed on "waiting on the Lord." The True Love Waits planning kit promotes their play, entitled *Waiters: A Youth Musical About Waiting on the Lord*; with a pun on the meaning of the word "waiters," the play is set in a trendy restaurant called Masterson's (an allusion to the churched life with the Master's Son, Jesus Christ). The play promotes "wait training," an "acquired Christian discipline" to be "applied] to our lives." The waiter should be "punctual" but "patient"; he or she should seek to know God's "purpose" and "plan," and acknowledge God's "presence." The only thing for which one should *not* wait is "making Jesus Savior and Lord." This is a priority," and waiters should learn to be "sensitive to the *prodding* of the Holy Spirit"; finally, true waiters "know the *product* of waiting is service to others."[20]

Difficult though this regimen may be to keep, the spiritual rewards (salvation) and material rewards (sexual pleasure in marriage—and in the context of the play, college scholarships as well) are generous. Sociologists Rodney Stark and Roger Finke would characterize the True Love Waits campaign, then, as a "high cost-high reward" movement. Such movements, they argue in *The Churching of America*, have been the most successful in attracting and retaining members:

Sectarian members are either in or out; they must follow the demands of the group or withdraw. The 'seductive middle-ground' is lost.

For those who do join, high costs increase their level of involvement because it makes activities outside of the group more costly. The flow of rewards for displaying high levels of commitment have been substantially increased.

...The higher the costs of membership, the greater the material and social, as well as religious, benefits of membership.[21]

This is clearly evident in the sense of identity and community cultivated by the True Love Waits campaign. In a secular world where sexuality has been commodified, and virginity devalued, if not ridiculed, taking a vow of chastity is a high-cost either-or proposition. "Seductive" though it may be, there is no middle ground. As a result of making this commitment, however, teen believers may feel uncomfortable in the "wider world" for at least two reasons: not only might they be teased mercilessly for "wimping out" on sex, but they might find the sexual temptations (which are apparent everywhere, from prime-time sitcoms to public billboards) too overwhelming to resist. Thus they would seek a home within the church community, and more specifically, the youth community as defined to include others who have taken the chastity vow; the church community, in turn, provides social, material, and religious rewards for the teens' loyalty.

Notes

1 These include: "American Christian Cause; Assemblies of God; Baptist World Alliance; Campus Crusade for Christ; Christian Camping International; Church of God Cleveland; Church of the Nazarene; Evangelical Covenant Church; Evangelical Fellowship of Canada; Family of the Americas; Fellowship of Christian Athletes; General Association of General Baptists; Grace Brethren Fellowship of Churches; Mennonite Church; National Federation for Catholic Youth Ministry, Inc.; National Network of Youth Ministries; Open Bible Standard Churches; Pentecostal Church of God; Reachout Ministries; Sonlife Ministries; Student Discipleship Ministries; The Salvation Army; The Wesleyan Church; Youth America; Youth for Christ; Youth Specialties; and Youth With a Mission. In addition, well-known Christian authors James Dobson and Josh McDowell and contemporary Christian recording artists Steven Curtis Chapman, Michael W. Smith, DC Talk, Petra, and Lisa Bevill have expressed support for the campaign." True Love Waits-A Fact Sheet, Southern Baptist Sunday School Board (October 1994), 1.

2 *Living the Word: Teens, Sex, and God*, part 2, KCAL-TV Channel Nine, Los Angeles, California, May 1995. Hereinafter referred to as KCAL-TV. A Valentine's Week rally in Atlanta, in February 1996, sought to raise the figure from 250,000 to one million.

3 I am indebted to Julie Ingersoll and Diana Butler for pointing out the parallels between the True Love Waits sexual purity pledge and the WCTU temperance pledge.

4 R. Laurence Moore, *Selling God: American Religion in the Marketplace of Culture* (New York: Oxford University Press, 1994), 5.

5 Wayne Elzey, "Liminality and Symbiosis in Popular American Protestantism," *Journal of the American Academy of Religion* 43 (December 1975), 741-756.

6 Elzey, 742.

7 Elzey, 753.

8 See Elzey, 752: "Continued failure is the only sure mark of success."

9 James Davison Hunter, *Evangelicalism: The Coming Generation* (Chicago: University of Chicago Press, 1983), 59-63. Josh McDowell and Bob Hostetler, *Right from Wrong* (Dallas: Word Publishing, 1994), 267-280.

10 Nancye Willis, "Sexual Purity Pledges Catch World Interest," Baptist Press (news release), July 30, 1994.

11 True Love Waits Church Worship Ideas, 1.

12 Peter Gardella, *Innocent Ecstasy: How Christianity Gave American an Ethic of Sexual Pleasure* (New York: Oxford University Press, 1985), 4-5.

13 Elzey, 750.

14 Elzey, 746.

15 Greg Johnson and Susie Shellenberger, *What Hollywood Won't Tell You About Sex, Love, and Dating* (Ventura, CA: Regal Books, 1994), 206-207.

16 *Catechism of the Catholic Church*, III:2:1:6 (2352). Catechism of the Catholic Church (New York: Image/Doubleday, 1995), 623-624.

17 Bill Ameiss and Jane Graver, *Love, Sex & God* (St. Louis, MO: Concordia, 1995), 28-29.

18 Johnson and Shellenberger, 192.

19 Johnson and Shellenberger, *258 Great Dates While You Wait* (Nashville: Broadman & Holman, 1995), 33-39, esp. 35.

20 Kathie Hill and Travis Cottrell, *Waiters: A Youth Musical About Waiting on the Lord*, libretto and cassette (Nashville: Genevox/GMG, 1994), 91-92.

21 Roger Finke and Rodney Stark, *The Churching of America 1776-1990: Winners and Losers in Our Religious Economy* (New Brunswick, NJ: Rutgers University Press, 1992), 254-255.

WHY MEN AND WOMEN LEAVE THE MINISTRY: HYPOTHESES FROM RESEARCH ON CLERGY AND FROM ROLE EXITERS OF OTHER STATUSES

Adair Lummis

Center for Social and Religious Research
Hartford Seminary

Research on clergy dropouts from parish ministry or any kind of paid church ministry suggests that leaving the clergy career follows similar trajectories followed by those exiting from other master statuses or going through religious disaffiliation generally. Yet, stories from Protestant clergy dropouts and reason analysis of why they consider leaving or have left church employment also add dimensions to understanding dropouts generally.

Rapid Versus More Gradual Departure from the Clergy Role

A crisis in clergy's personal life or congregation can precipitate an abrupt departure from church paid work. But as with those who disaffiliate from sects (Wright 1988), clergy choice of withdrawal from a ministerial career is likely to be a more gradual realization that parish ministry (Jud, Mills, Burch 1970) or even some other kind of ministerial career—is not for them. Some who leave parish ministry become happily employed in work as chaplains, denominational staff, interims, parochial school or seminary staff. Others want nothing more to do with the church in a clergy status and seek secular employment soon after exiting their church employment.

Not all clergy who leave the ministry initially want to depart. Clergy in these enlightened times can be thrown out of the ordained ministry for sexual abuse of minors, lay members of their congregations, or other legally punishable crimes that can get denominations sued. But focus in this paper will be given to clergy who—even if pressured to leave by lay leaders, church executives and their own burnout —leave church paid positions and do not seek other paid ministry positions by their own volition.

Research on apostasy and role exit from other master statuses indicate that there seems to be several typical steps in the disengagement process (Bromley, 1988; Ebaugh, 1988, Wright 1988):

1) a crisis and/or unavoidable realization that things are worse than expected and/or unjust;

2) reevaluation of situation, and possible disillusionment, occasioned by a sense of personal failure, emotional and physical exhaustion, loss of faith in leaders' or system's integrity, leading to seriously considering withdrawal.

3) decision to withdraw, and firming of their rationale for leaving, exploration of alternatives, shifting reference groups, withdrawal from associates in group being left and formation of new social circles.

Reasons for Protestant Clergy's Dropping Out of Ministerial Work

Reasons for Protestant clergy's leaving a ministerial career have been found or postulated by other researchers (Carroll et. al., 1993; Charlton, 1994; Fletcher 1989; Judd, Mills and Burch 1970; Lee and Balswick, 1989; Marciano, 1990; Mickey and Ashmore 1991; Mills 1988, and Norell, 1989) to include the following:

1) **Difficulty in setting boundaries between work and private life in congregational ministry particularly.** Too often clergy are expected to put in sixty hour weeks, be always available for crises, and generally make their congregation the most vital, growing, wealthiest one in the area—at the same time they and their immediate family are expected to set high standard for how they conduct their so-called "private lives".

2) **Dissonance between what clergy expected on ordination to find in theirministry work and settings** and the realities they experience. This dissonance is a problem for newly ordained clergy especially. Recent seminary graduates may be unrealistic about how much time and energy certain routine activities take up, too idealistic about how involved members would be in the congregation, or how well lay, clergy and denominational executives would treat one another.

3) **Perception of inequity in rewards and insufficient compensation for the amount of time, energy and personal assents clergy bring to the ministry** becomes more of a factor in decisions to leave church employment for clergy somewhat later in their careers. As clergy come to realize that job conditions for them will not improve much or at all in the church, they look for employment alternatives in the secular arena.

4) **Low or weak professional self-concept as competent in core ministerial activities** is certainly a factor leading some clergy to try an find another line of work. Low professional self-assessment occurs when clergy feel too inexperienced, inadequately prepared, or lacking the requisite spiritual and personal qualities to enable them, in their own opinion, to competently carry out their ministerial work. Persons with low 'professional self-concepts' in terms of one occupation do not necessarily have low self-esteem in considering themselves as individuals, family

members or possible practitioners of other occupations (though there may well be a negative carry-over).

5) **Lack of professional support from other clergy**, denominational executives or pastoral counselors to counteract either a negative self-evaluation or sense of being trapped in a particular ministerial position or kind of ministry—is a factor contributing to dropout. For potential dropouts, either isolation from clergy peers and church executives, or little positive affirmation from those such clergy are in contact with, will accelerated any inclinations they may have to leave the ministry.

6) **Burnout**—or some degree of (a typically gestalt combination of) spiritual, emotional, physical breakdown or crisis (Retiger 1981, Warner and Carter, 1984) can develop and be triggered by any one or combination of the preceding five factors precipitating dropout. In a severe case of burn-out, clergy literally feel they must get out of ministry or die physically and spiritually.

7) **Little hope that one's future *as clergy* will become brighter** is a final reason for deciding to get out of church employment. Loss of hope can occur because dropouts feel they will never be competent as clergy, or congregations will never be appealing places to work, or at least they personally will never be able to get a decent (or any) clergy position in a healthy congregation, or even that they no longer want to be part of a denomination where the leaders are inept or corrupt.

8) **More rewarding experiences in secular employment than in ministry** (financially, intellectually, socially, emotionally), or perceived probability that this would be the case—provide positive incentives for leaving church employment.

9) **Reversabilty** (Ebaugh 1988:186-188) or how **easy it is to either *leave* or rescind the decision to leave** *the ordained ministry* is apt to affect clergy's decision to dropout. In a way it **easier** for unhappy clergy to dropout if their denomination has clear rules that are enforced on who may be **considered clergy** if they have **no church employment**. At the same time, the very clarity of withdrawal may extend the time they take to make a final decision to dropout. For example, clergy in the Episcopal Church are ordained a "priest forever" unless they are deposed or give up their orders; whereas in the Lutheran Church if they do not have a church position for over three years, they may no longer be considered clergy (although they may be formally reinstated). In most denominations, however, even if ordained men and women who are not church employed are still clergy, they are unlikely to have 'legal' church standing for voting in their judicatory or receiving continuing denominational education funds, medical and other insurance.

Intervening and Mediating Variables on Retention and Dropout

Clergy of different genders, ages, races who have different family statuses and other personal characteristics, will vary in how they view the same set of circumstances as well as how they respond to similar situational assessments. Those who enter the ministry with less experience in the church, with different priorities, and outlooks are going to assess the importance of their remaining in ministry differently in times of strain.

Values certainly affect perceptions and actions, but how the same values will affect actions may change over time. In illustration, in the seventies, young single women seminarians and graduates who held a strong **feminist** advocacy position that more women should be ordained in their denominations, **expected** problems on coming as the first women pastors to congregations. They grit their teeth, and stayed with the congregation in face of at least covert opposition from a strong minority. But by 1980, women seminary faculty were expressing apprehension that women seminarians were neither as "feminist" nor as realistic about what they would be facing after seminary as were the women students as five to ten years earlier (Carroll, Hargrove, Lummis 1983)—and hence might not have the same staying power to remain in the church as did the women who earned their M.Div.'s in the early seventies.

It would at least seem that church feminism in the nineties has differentiated into several strands. In addition to feminist advocacy of ordaining more women to overcome 'the sexist nature of the church', for example, spiritual feminist centering on God as in part, female, seems to be more associated with disinterest in, if not scorn for, the value of setting anyone aside through ordination. (Winter et. al., 1994; Zikmund, 1994). Being "feminist" may therefore not be as motivating a force in 1995 in clergywomen's resolve to grit their teeth and stay in difficult congregations for the good of all women in the church as may have been more the case for clergywomen twenty years ago. Further, contemporary clergywomen who believe their church careers are going to be substantially blocked because of sexist attitudes of lay leaders and judicatory executives, may decide that the ministry is just not worth it—especially when secular occupations are more and more accepting of women in top leadership positions.

In considering the costs and benefits of staying in the ministry rather than seeking employment outside the church, actual income is part of the equation. Can clergy afford to stay in low paying church positions—especially if it is possible that they could obtain secular work which would give their families a better standard of living? Regardless of whether clergy can live comfortably on their present income, money also is an indicator of worth. In looking around at what members of their congregation make compared to what they are paying their pastor, or even what pastors of other congregations are paid, they may decide that they are being exploited. This may trigger their wondering if they should leave the ministry for the secular world which may treat them more fairly than has the church.

DATA, DEFINITIONS AND METHODOLOGY

These are some of the hypotheses and issues that are investigated in a study of over 4,500 clergy in fifteen denominations. This study, conducted by Barbara Brown Zikmund, Adair T. Lummis, and Patricia M.Y. Chang, and supported by the Lilly Endowment is predominantly of clergy **considered active** by their denominations. We wanted to get a sample of "drop-outs" from church employment. This proved somewhat difficult because denominational offices, and seminaries simply do not keep lists of those who are not longer working as clergy. The best method we used in locating dropouts was to ask clergy respondents on the survey: "Do you know of any clergy who have left the ordained ministry—as "ex-pastors" or "dropouts" from a church career or from the church altogether?" If they did, a second part of the question was to supply the names and addresses of these "dropouts". Far more had an idea of who dropped out among their seminary classmates and colleagues, than where these people are now. All of those whose names and addresses we received through this snowball sampling were sent questionnaires.

A problem of this method for *defining dropouts* is it relies on **others'** definitions. Many "ex-pastors", as Jud, Mills, and Burch (1970) found, who left the parish ministry still predominantly considered themselves "ministers" in their non-parish church position or even secular positions. Further, it is important whether ordained men and women who are no longer church paid think of themselves as 'clergy' in how active they will be in church work. For example, music students who earn their living by driving taxicabs but believe themselves to be "really" musicians rather than taxicab drivers, are more likely to continue practicing and creating music (Kadushin 1969). Similarly, ordained women and men who are secularly employed full-time but think of themselves still as clergy probably do a lot more volunteer or part-time paid ministry than those for whom the clergy status is no longer salient. It is certainly possible that the "tent-maker" minister who earns his or her living outside the church but gives fifteen hours weekly without financial compensation to pastoring a small congregation, may be showing greater commitment to the clergy role than the senior minister of a wealthy parish.

Survey definition of "Dropout". Few if any seminarians go through the often expensive education and ordination process to take secular employment on graduation, although they may be more interested in a chaplaincy or specialized ministry than parish ministry. Even if they must work in a secular job to survive financially, clergy can also have a part-time job in a congregation. Clergy who have no paid church work, however, are more likely to be those who have left ministry completely—whether they have taken a secular position or are unemployed. Therefore, for analysis of survey data presented in this paper, **clergy who were under 68 and had** *no* **"regular paid church related work"** when they completed the survey are considered probable *dropouts*. About 75 of the returned questionnaires of clergy who fit this category across denominations were pulled to be examined more closely to see if they were **really** dropouts. Twenty of those who seemed to have left ministry or be on the verge of so doing, have been interviewed to date.

Not all clergy who have seriously considered leaving church related employment for some other kind of work, do so. But as a study of Catholic priests showed, those who often thought about leaving the ministry in the last year, eventually did so (Schoenner and Young 1992). Analysis for this study of Protestant clergy suggests as well, that "dropouts" had thought about leaving ministry for a while before they gave up on pursuing a church career. Overall, close to a third of the clergywomen

(31%) and nearly that proportion of clergymen (28%) indicated that during the last year it was at least sometimes the case that they "thought seriously about leaving church-related ministry for some other kind of work." Several clergy who followed through on such feelings and left church employment, would say that these percentages **underestimate** the extent of clergy discontent, as illustrated by comments from one man:

> If pastors are being honest, most would admit that from time to time during a average month, 'dropping out' of the parish ministry has crossed their minds. The frustration of dealing with persons in the congregation out to get the pastor is not what most expected the parish ministry to be."

Depth interviews with both clergy who have left and those who intend to stay in parish ministry at some point within at least the last few years (if not the 'last year')—do suggest that probably over half have given serious thought as to what they might do to earn their living other than working for the church. Obviously, far fewer follow through with actually getting out of church-paid ministry. Less than a sixth of the clergy (13% of the women, and 8% of the men) in our sample have no regular paid church employment. Several explanations come to mind. One obvious one is that those who have dropped out are less likely to than active clergy to be on denominational mailing lists, known to other active clergy, or be interested in answering long surveys sent out by seminaries. Another likelihood for a number of clergy who would love to leave ministry is that their M.Div. degree does not prepare them for much else. But another possibility is that despite problems ordained women and men face in their clergy positions which lead them to wonder if God really expects them to continue in ministry all the way to the cross, some who stay anyway may have particular supports that those who exit the clergy role do not to the same degree.

INSIGHTS FROM DEPTH INTERVIEWS

Inability to get *any* full-time church work or full-time church that pays a living wage is a depressing factor affecting seemingly more and more recent seminary graduates, especially women, to wonder if perhaps they have made a mistake or misunderstood what God was calling them to do with their lives. Eventually they must get secular work to eat, and may become so discouraged they resign themselves to getting a secular job and never try to get church-paid work again. In illustration the following clergy woman dropout explains:

> * "Since I couldn't get called to a full-time ministry position after four years 'searching' in the U.C.C.—I left church work." (Special Education Teacher)

Several other women, who are surviving on part-time church work and still hopeful for full-time church employment, are coming closer to thoughts of leaving the ministry. As one interviewee muses:

*"It is disconcerting in my part-time church positions to realize that I am making less now with three advanced degrees than I was in my first year of college. It does raise some questions... Yes, I think about dropping out of ministry from day to day, moment to moment. But I am still determined—with the support of my congregation and (clergy) husband— to stay in and fight for a full time parish job....But will the bishop ever think of his part-time clergy as serious applicants for the better positions?"

Difficulty in setting boundaries between church work and personal life, and trying to meet often impossible demands as a parish minister—is a major reason for wanting out of church employment. Clergy talk of the unrealistic expectations of what they can accomplish as parish minister put on them not only by those in the congregations but also by their regional denominational executives. To quote another who is thinking about dropping out—of at least parish work:

* "I sometimes wonder if this is really what I was called to do. A lot of clergy men and women go though a period of questioning what they are doing with their lives after pastoring certain congregations for a while. The 'nit-picking and whining' get to you, as does the demand that the pastor get the congregation to grow in numbers (even though the population in the area is declining), as does the conference executives allowing congregations to do anything they want for fear of losing their support... Why haven't I left? Because I have a call to the ministry; because I made a commitment in being ordained—although right now I am not sure this 'call' is to the parish ministry any more."

Another difficulty with ministry is that the job is so amorphous, as several pointed out, it is hard to know if one has been successful in the pastoral role. So often, clergy complain, if one group in the church thinks they are doing a great job in all areas, there will be other groups or individuals that are variously displeased with their preaching, administration, counselling, sociability or whatever.

Congregational ministry, as described, is **typically** a fifty-hour week, six day a week job. It is also a sort-of 'fish bowl existence' for pastors whose public and private activities are of great interest to many of their parishioners. It is this very aspect of parish ministry—the difficulty in setting boundaries between church work and personal time—which was drives some clergy out of the ministry altogether, as illustrated by the reflections of the following dropout:

* "My leaving ordained ministry was *not* about being female. It was about having a personal life, a job with professional boundaries and time limits. I *need* a job *separate* from my life! ...I am troubled by lack of professional boundaries in the church. To me, that connects with clergy sexual abuse and other unhealthy behaviors. I believe very few clergy can handle the diffusion of boundaries in the church." (Chemical Dependency Counselor)

Clergy have family statuses that may increase their difficulties in setting effective boundaries between church and private life. First, clergywomen with young children may have a particularly hard time fulfilling both church demands and the demands of being a mother in so some denominations perhaps more so than others. The itinerancy system in the Methodist Church, according to one informant, is the major reason a good number of young clergy women she knows went to part-time work or dropped out altogether: either they could not keep moving to a new church every few years if they had young children; or they felt with a baby or young child one parent should work only part time—and most husbands refused to do that. Sometimes in the struggle of being a pastor, being a mother gets lost.

A clergywoman recounted that one evening when she kissed her three year old son goodnight as she was going out yet again that week to an evening meeting at her conflicted church, that she hadn't seem much of her child or husband for months. She was worried about losing her job, she was close to burn-out, but worst of all she realized she had sacrificed too much to her view of herself as "a career woman who happened to be a mother". Very soon thereafter, she resigned her church position, took a three month leave to decide what to do. Her decision was to get a doctorate in business and become a free-lance organizational development consultant—a "mother who happens to have a career". Although she is still technically part of the clergy, she said: "I consider myself a dropout...I have done some consulting for the denomination, but I know I can never go back into a congregation as a pastor—I would feel trapped. I have an emotional connection to this Church, but I do not want to return to paid church work."

Single clergy find parish ministry, particularly in small towns difficult, because they cannot carry on a romantic life easily being the pastor. In more conservative denominations where women are expected to remain virgins until married, a single woman pastor has even greater difficulty meeting men. Leaving the parochial setting for secular professional employment allowed one thirty-something single woman to at least "get a life" and maybe soon, a husband! She is never going back to the parish ministry—or any church-related work for that matter—again.

If single heterosexual clergy have difficulty in having a personal life while a parish ministry, these difficulties are compounded for gay and lesbian clergy. Four who have dropped out said that their sexual orientation was the major factor. First, there is so much competition for the congregations that will hire out-homosexuals that it is very difficult to get those job where their known sexual preference would not void the call. Second, if they are not "out" then they struggle with whether they want to work as clergy and hide their sexual identity. It can be easier to just get a secular position where their being gay or lesbian is fairly irrelevant. One gay clergy man who is now a business executive commented that he knew 15 other men that had left ministry—

"All of them are gay. We've pretty much written ordained ministry off. Its just not worth the stress, and the ignorance is too dense and tedious. I've worked through my bitterness and I've made a better life than the church would ever have given me. Still, I'm haunted by the thought that I'm still ordained."

One lesbian clergywomen, now working as a clerk while she earns her doctorate, knows 4 women and 2 men who left the church because of their sexual orientation. She comments:

"I have become rather anti-clerical of late and am seriously considering surrendering my credentials. Ordination seems to me to be too power-oriented; it tends more to divide than to join clergy and laity...Then there's the issue of sexuality, which the Church wants to condemn when it doesn't ignore it. I'm tired of having to hide myself as a lesbian in the church, especially being ordained."

It seems many young single and married clergy find the rural and small town congregations where they are sent as first calls or appointments particularly difficult—so different from the expectations of ministry they held on ordination, that they seriously consider leaving the clergy. Several dropouts interviewed, both male and female, indicate that pastoring these rural/small town congregations was an experience indeed leading them **out** of ministry. Although these newly ordained clergy were typically "loved" by the members of their churches, and helped to "grow up" as clergy in many ways, they found little opportunity to do much in the way of innovative programming and the kind of ministry they envisioned while in seminary. They typically pastored churches where they preached to less than 60 people who were mainly over sixty on a typical Sunday morning, including farmers and factory workers, and a high proportion of retired people from these occupations. These seminary graduates became bored as well as impoverished financially, intellectually and socially. They felt "burned out", not from too much stress, but too much isolation.

What can happen to commitment to a ministerial career of recently ordained clergy who take rural or small town parish portions, is illustrated in the stories of several interviewed. Two unrelated dropouts interviewed, a woman and a man who started their clergy careers as full-time pastors of rural churches, realized after about a year that they could not pay off their seminary debts and other bills on their church salaries. Further there seemed to be no one in the church or community who had college education anywhere near their ages, let alone any clergy with whom to share experiences. So they "moonlighted" part-time as teachers or administrators in educational institutions, both to earn enough to pay their debts as well as for the intellectual stimulation and social relationships. These two decided that really their part-time secular work was much more fulfilling financially, emotionally, mentally, and socially than their full-time work in the rural church. They resigned their church positions, told their regional executives and denominational deployment officers to forget them, and are now happily working full-time as educators in secular institutions. Similar stories were told by small town church clergy who decided that they would be happier as a self-employed carpenter, or a shop keeper, or a nurse, or a free-lance consultant, or in the same business as their secularly-employed spouse—but nearer a cosmopolitan, urban area.

Church Crises Leading to Voluntary or Involuntary Termination of Pastors have happened to clergy in urban, suburban and rural congregations. These are major precipitating events leading ordained women and men to consider seriously getting out of the ministry for good. From their stories, undoubtedly true, of the horrible ways in which they were treated by senior pastors, old guard lay leaders, and other nasty people, it is perfectly understandable why they would go screaming from the church never to return. However, there are clergy in our sample who also went through minor hells in their parish, denominational or chaplaincy portions, and yet stayed in the system eventually getting better positions or making their present lot more livable.

Newly ordained clergy may be particularly vulnerable to having their commitment to a ministerial career derailed by a bad first parish or chaplaincy experience. If they get two devastating church experiences in a row, without a lot of support from denominational officials and counsellors they are likely to think very seriously often about finding a secular job, and do so.. Survey data indicates that young women are particularly apt to wonder if they should be in the ministry. Women ordained in their twenties may have unrealistic expectations of how much they will be loved in the parish at the same time as they receive little serious recognition of their worth as clergy from ordained peers and executives in their judicatory.

Support from Significant Others in Ministry. One difference seems in whether ousted pastors and chaplains remain or quit the ministry, is whether they have peer support and affirmation of their worth from ordained friends or clergy groups and especially whether they see their judicatory executive as sympathetic and helpful. Those who have such support not only can recover from the traumatic church situation better, but look forward to future opportunities in other ministry settings for improving their abilities to handle difficult church situations. Clergy who have had to leave a position and do not have such peer support and affirmation from their regional executives, are apt to have their secret fear that they are not competent as clergy reinforced. Or, they may decide that even if they could be more effective in another church position, will not be given the chance because of this failure, and so they might as well forget a church career.

All too often the dropouts' stories of what occurred in their last positions include references to feeling "betrayed" by their regional executive. They had obviously expected their bishop, district superintendent, conference minister, presbyter, or judicatory deployment officer to be on **their** side in church fights, not on the side of nasty good old boys on the congregational governing boards or supporting their unethical or unfair senior pastors. They typical describe the actions of their denominational executives as motivated mainly by money—i.e. they see their denominational executives as far more concerned with keeping congregational dollars flowing up to support the executives and the denomination than they are about the fate of individual clergy in their care. In interviews they attribute at least part of their "burnout" in the position to lack of support and assistance from their regional executive when they asked for help.

Dropouts from church employment and from all contact with the denomination are those who feel their denomination has lost legitimacy. Clergy who resign a church position to go into secular employment for whatever combination of reasons often do attempt to maintain some ongoing relationship as clergy with their denomination and judicatory by serving on committees or helping out in congregations temporarily if needed. But clergy who have dropped out not only from a career in the church, but in effect from their denomination as well, usually have done so because they perceive that it is not just one or two denominational executives who are unworthy of the position, but a plurality of their denominational leaders who are cowardly or unethical. Five or six spoke or wrote of physical abuse or sexual harassment of women which they themselves brought to the attention of church executives, who subsequently refused to confront or punish the offender. These were described as the critical incidents which made the clergy woman or man realize that they not only wanted out of church employment, they wanted out of the denomination that supported such cowardly executives and immoral clergy. In illustration:

> One woman told of a situation in which a clergyman was known by the police to be a wife batterer in another state, a fact she brought to the attention of the church officials on the credentials committee of which she was a member. They helped the batterer get a church in their area anyway, and wondered in her presence if she really should have been on this committee. After all maybe her being sexually abused as a child and recently giving up her parish for a college position—was clouding her judgment about not wanting this poor, dear man given church employment.

> A clergyman who once served on a seminary committee to decide whether seminarians should be recommended for ordination, told of an incident in which he heard and verified a story that one of the women seminarians had been given poor evaluations by her clergy supervisor because she rejected his sexual advances. The church executives in charge of the seminary said that though charge was probably true, in light of the fact that this clergy supervisor and his congregation were among their biggest contributors, they would do nothing. In fact, he should get off his high moral horse, and

be more realistic and less idealistic, especially since he decided to switch from being a pastor to secular employment himself.

A divorced clergywoman with three children in her care was working hard to impress the married senior minister. He was impressed all right - he said he found her ankles "so sexy during worship, he could not concentrate on leading the prayers." She told him not say such things; he continued, and one day he backed into her hard while she was xeroxing, throwing her down over the xerox machine. This time she was sufficiently scared and angry that she went directly to the judicatory executive. and to the lay elected leaders of the congregation. They did nothing. The senior minister became very hostile, she finally resigned for her own health and that of her family. This was a few years ago...perhaps it could not happen today with all the attention on clergy sexual misconduct....But she doesn't really trust her church executives any more..Fortunately she has a good position in a social service agency now... No she will never, never go back to the parish ministry. Although she tries to be understanding and forgiving, no, she really does not want to serve as a member of the clergy for this denomination in any capacity, any more...at all. The sole reason she had not yet resigned her orders is a financial one: if her secular job lost funding or her children needed more money, she could still work as an interim or supply minister to augment her income. So though she is technically perhaps not a dropout, in reality she *is*.

Less dramatically, but probably more prevalently, are the cases of secularly employed clergy who would like to donate their services as pastoral supply to needy churches, but are not accepted as clergy by judicatory executives. Denominational officials on the national level may acclaim the noble "tent makers" who support themselves in secular jobs so they give of their time to pastor to in impoverished rural and inner city churches. But on the regional level, nonstipendiary clergy are often treated as nonentities. As two interviewed related with hurt surprise, nonstipendiary clergy can be designated by judicatory executives as having "left ministry". If others in official church capacity continue to define the "tent maker" as ministry dropouts, the definition will likely be prophetic.

Dropping in again after five years out is difficult. Clergy who drop out of church employment and standing can drop in again, but it is not all that easy — given the current clergy job market.

Some who graduate from seminary, or leave a parish position or a nonparochial church position because of dissatisfaction with the position, do not initially intend to leave church-paid ministry. But if they are unable to find a church-paid or church related position may, in order to survive, take secular work. After several years of secular work, many of these clergy may well decide not to return to church employment.

There are also clergy who leave a church position and then do not work on a regular basis in *any* job for years... Some of these clergy are those who have only physically survived a disastrous last church position or psychological breakdown due to other causes. There are also clergy who leave full-time church employment because of a new marriage and/or new child and find that when they are ready to reenter the full-time clergy job market, they cannot easily do so. They have often lost their connections with persons who might help them get positions. They may also have lost their credibility as being motivated clergy with judicatory executives and deployment officers.

Indeed, not all clergy who left may be very motivated to return to a church career. Two women who resigned full-time ministry positions for marriage and children, one from a parish and one from a hospital chaplaincy, almost seemed relieved that while their family situation allowed them to reenter the clergy job market now, they have been unsuccessful in getting any parish or chaplaincy work. These two it should be noted have husbands with very good salaries. In our sample there are clergy well below retirement age who are simply not working at all—mainly because their spouse's salary makes it at least possible for them to be housewives or househusbands. These clergy are likely dropouts from all church employment on a permanent rather than just temporary basis.

Even self-proclaimed 'permanent' dropouts. as well as those who said they had not yet but are seriously considering leaving church employment forever, indicated some ambivalence in interviews over forsaking the church career for which they were ordained. Several sort of wistfully indicated that if their denominations "really" wanted them back to do some kind of ministry, they might consider agreeing— if the particular ministry is important, appreciated and presented to them by their judicatory executives 'just right'. But these dropouts are unlikely to be sought after by church leaders to return to clergy employment, as most probably realize. Four interviewed who had been out of church-related work of any kind for over two years are currently wrestling with the question of whether they want to be technically still considered clergy or just make a clean break and give up their orders.

Depth interviews suggest that while many unpleasant aspects of ministry may lead clergy to consider leaving church employment, whether they actually do so may depend on whether other conditions are present. What these are likely to be is suggested by analyses of survey responses.

Insights from Survey Analysis

There are denominational differences among clergy in whether they have recently at least sometimes seriously considered leaving church-related work, as well as in whether they are now without paid church employment. Many factors may have combined variously within denominational clusters to account differently for the percentages of those women and men who have thought of leaving and those who have left ministerial employment (see Table I). In partial illustration, women clergy in the Southern Baptist denominations are among the most likely to have contemplated leaving church related ministry and have actually done so. From other findings, we know that Southern Baptist clergywomen are among the most feminist in the sample while Southern Baptist clergymen are among the least—easily symptomatic of conflicts within congregations and Baptist associations that would make women want out of church work.

Church of God and Assemblies of God clergywomen are even less likely than Southern Baptist clergywomen to be church-employed; but at the same time they are least likely to think seriously about "leaving church-related ministry". Clergywomen in the Church of God and Assemblies of God are more traditional in their theology and view of women's role than clergywomen in other denominations; hence ordained women in these denominations may have less problem with the fact that it is clergymen, rather than clergywomen, who are get full church employment. Hence, clergywomen in these more conservative denominations may be more apt to view themselves as "in church related-ministry" without full or any paid church work than would clergywomen without church employment in the more liberal denominations.

In the total sample of clergywomen and of clergymen *feminist values and perspectives* on women, God and the church **have** *no* significant relationship to either wanting to leave church-related work or actually leaving church employment. In the nineties, feminist perspectives may work as a double-edged sword keeping some within the church fighting for its transformation, and drive others out by highlighting the divergences between what they expected or wanted and what the church seems content to be.

Although relative *youth* may predispose women clergy especially to be disturbed and disappointed by what they find ministry actually like after seminary, there is no evidence that younger women clergy will leave ministry any more readily than older women clergy. In our sample, women who started seminary in their twenties are somewhat more likely to have thought seriously about leaving ministry during the last year. But in accord with findings of Nesbitt (1995), younger age at ordination has no significant effect on dropout of women or men from a church career.

Lack of ability to manage boundaries and potential role conflicts between church and private life (See Table II) increases to some degree both clergy women and men's thoughts of leaving ministry. But other correlations suggest that clergy's inability to manage boundaries will mainly increase their doubts about whether they should be in ministry at all, especially if their **overall health** is undermined. Clergy who are in poor overall mental, emotional, spiritual and physical health—or close to burnout—are definitely going to think more seriously about leaving the ministry, even with other important influences on their exit considerations controlled by regression (see Table IV). At the same time **burnout** does not necessarily lead to actual drop-out, if sufficient support and hope for the future is present.

Feeling insufficiently competent in clergy roles, **or having a low professional self-concept,** is a major factor in both women's and men's wondering if they should leave church employment. The following clergy characteristics both contribute to a strong professional self-concept among clergy and have some independent effect on clergy women and men's feeling committed to ministry: 1) clergy's belief they are fairly compensated for their ministerial work; 2) they are appreciated by their judicatory executive for their leadership abilities; 3) and they are involved with a regularly meeting group of clergy colleagues. These supports help clergy not only avoid constant wishing they could leave the ministry in the first place, but also apparently help retain disenchanted clergy in church employment.

IN SUMMARY: Being a minister in the contemporary church although it has its rewards, often entails as well: long hours, low pay, nasty people, difficulty in being sure when one had done a good job, uncaring judicatory executives and deployment officers, little opportunity for upward career mobility, and other problems leading many to consider whether they would not be better off employed outside the church.

Yet these analyses suggest that even clergy considered disaffiliating themselves from a church career because the reality of ministry is so dissonant from what they anticipated, who find sexism still present and equity far from fully achieved, who are close to burnout from overwork or church conflicts—will still remain in paid ministry if they have hope and support from ordained leaders.

Isolation in ministry is one major factor in clergy's considering leaving church employment. Yet at the same time there is evidence that clergy who decide to dropout and do so, often do not maintain friendships with former clergy colleagues. Whether this is because they have totally lost interest in ministry and friends still in the ordained 'life', or because they feel shame that they do not expect any affirmation from judicatory executives or believe they can get a better church job eventually and hence avoid former ordained friends and associates—is not always clear even in a depth interview.

Depth interviews and short interviews with clergy, as well as survey analyses, however, do suggest that many clergy feel their judicatory executives are distant, self-absorbed people, who do not care about the clergy in their care. A substantial proportion of clergy who are seriously considering dropping out of all church employment would still stay in ministry, even possibly working for the church without compensation, if they got some affirmation from their denominational leaders directly and through provision of denominational resources such as counselors, clergy discussion groups, and continuing education opportunities. But so many clergy say they do not get even minimal support along these lines from their judicatories. Why not? That is the real paradigmatic question!

References

Bromley, David G. 1988. "Religious Disaffiliation: A Neglected Social Process". Pp.9-28 in David G. Bromley, editor, *Falling from the Faith: Causes and Consequences of Religious Apostasy*. Newbury Park: Sage.

Carroll, Jackson W., Barbara Hargrove, Adair Lummis. 1983. *Women of the Cloth: New Opportunity for Churches*. San Francisco: Harper and Row.

Chang, Patricia M.Y. 1994. "In Search of a Pulpit: Sex differences in the transition from seminary training to the first parish job." Paper presented at the Society for the Scientific Study of Religion, Albuquerque (November).

Charlton, Joy. 1995. "Dropping Out/Staying In: Revisiting Clergywomen in Mid-Careers." Paper presented at the Annual Meeting of the Religious Research Association, Albuquerque, New Mexico (November).

Ebaugh, Helen Rose Fuchs. 1988, *Becoming an Ex: The Process of Role Exit*. Chicago: University of Chicago Press.

Fletcher, Gordon. 1989. *The Lost Shepherd: Why Individuals are Leaving Full-Time Ministry in the Pentecostal Assemblies of Canada, Alberta District*. D.Min. Dissertation, St. Stephens College.

Jud, Gerald, Edgar Mills, Jr., and Genevieve W. Burch. 1970. *Ex-Pastors, Why Men Drop out of the Parish Ministry*. Philadelphia: The Westminster Press.

Kadushin, Charles. 1969. "The Professional Self-Concept of Music Students." *American Journal of Sociology* 75:389-404.

Lee, Cameron and Jack Balswick. 1989. *Life in a Glass House: The Minister's Family in Its Unique Social Context*. Grand Rapids, Michigan. Zondervan Publishing House.

Lummis, Adair and Roberta Walmsley. 1993. *Healthy Clergy, Wounded Healers: Their Families and Their Ministries*. (to be published in 1996, Episcopal Church Hymnal Corporation.

Marciano, Teresa. 1990. Corporate Church, Ministry, and Ministerial Family: Embedded Employment and Measure of Success." *Marriage and Family Review* 15"171-193.

Mickey, Paul and Ginny W. Ashmore. 1991. *Clergy Families: Is Normal Life Possible?* Grand Rapids, MI: Zondervan Publishing House.

Mills, Edgar W. 1988. "Review of Recent Social Science Research on Stress." Pp. 38-67 in Loren B. Mead, Barry Evans, Edgar W. Mills, Jr., and Clement W. Welsh, eds. *Personal and Professional Needs of the Clergy of the Episcopal Church*. New York: The Episcopal Church Foundation.

Nesbitt, Paula D. 1995. "First- and Second-Career Clergy: Influences of Age and Gender on the Career-Stage Paradigm." *Journal for the Scientific Study of Religion*. 34:152-171.

Norell, Elizabeth J. 1989. "Clergy Family Satisfaction: A Review." *Family Science Review* 4:69-93.

Retiger, Lloyd. 1981. *Coping with Clergy Burnout*. Valley Forge, Pa: Judson Press.

Schoenherr, Richard and Larry Young. 1993. *Full Pews and Empty Altars*. Madison, WI:University of Wisconsin Press.

Warner, Janelle and John D. Carter. 1984. "Loneliness, Marital Adjustment and Burnout in Pastoral and Lay Persons." *Journal of Psychology and Theology*. 12:125-131.

Winter, Miriam Therese, Adair Lummis, Allison Stokes. 1994. *Defecting in Place: Women Claiming Responsibility for Their Own Spiritual Lives*. New York: Crossroad.

Wright, Stuart A. 1988. "Leaving New Religious Movements: Issues, Theory and Research." Pp. 143-165 in David G. Bromley, editor, *Falling from the Faith: Causes and Consequences of Religious Apostasy*. Newbury Park: Sage.

Zikmund, Barbara Brown. 1995. "Changing Understandings of Ordination in American Protestantism." Paper to be presented at the Annual Meetings of the Society for the Scientific Study of Religion, St. Louis (October).

TABLE I
THOUGHTS OF LEAVING MINISTRY AND <u>ACTUALLY</u> LEAVING PAID MINISTRY
By Gender and Denomination

DENOMINATIONS	Last Year, Sometimes or Usually Thought Seriously About Leaving Church Related Ministry <u>For Other Kind of Work</u>		Under 68 & Do NOT <u>Have Paid Church Work</u>	
	WOMEN	**MEN**	**WOMEN**	**MEN**
"People-Centered"				
Unitarian Universalist (w=236, m=242)	23%	26%	6%	12%
United Ch.of Christ (w=283, m=229)	38%	31%	12%	7%
Disciples of Christ (w=265, m=204)	36%	27%	11%	7%
Brethren (w=86, m=61)	33%	21%	9%	15%
American Baptist Ch. (w=227, m=183)	33%	30%	16%	7%
Southern Baptist (w=116, m=107)	40%	24%	21%	4%
"Church Centered"				
Presyterian Church (w=252, m=179)	31%	31%	12%	9%
U.Methodist Church (w=211, m=197)	44%	23%	14%	6%
Lutheran (ELCA) Church (w=254, m=220)	31%	34%	7%	5%
Episcopal Church (w=236, m=191)	23%	25%	11%	9%
"Spirit-Centered"				
Church of God (w=67, m=58)	18%	28%	25%	12%
Nazarene (w=128, m=109)	23%	31%	19%	3%
Other Holiness (Free Meth.,Wesleyan) (w=64, m=78	15%	25%	8%	8%
Assemblies of God (w=41, m=14)	10%	21%	29%	0%

TABLE II
INDICES

All Scale Items scored as follows: 1 "usually true" to 4 "usually false".

I. BOUNDARY MAINTENANCE INDEX
(Managing Boundaries, Time Demands, Role Conflicts Between Church Private Life)
(low scores= good ability, high scores poor ability)
    a. I was able to maintain a separation between my ministerial duties and my private life.
    b. I felt I did have enough time to do what was expected of me by my family or spouse/partner.
    c. I usually had enough time to be alone for reflection, hobbies reading and recreation.
    d. I felt I did (not) impose unrealistic expectations on myself.

standardized item alpha: **clergywomen .68   clergymen .70**

II. OVERALL PHYSICAL, SPIRITUAL, MENTAL, SOCIAL HEALTH INDEX
(low scores good health, high scores = poor health, **burnout).**
    a. I felt physically healthy and energetic.
    b. I felt spiritually whole and growing in spiritual health.
    c. I (did not) feel lonely and isolated.
    d. I (did not) feel the need for confidential counselling.

standardized item alpha: **clergywomen .66   clergymen .68**

III. PROFESSIONAL SELF-CONCEPT INDEX
(low scores strong professional self-concept, high = weak p.i.)
    a. I felt accepted, liked and appreciated my most in my church or ministry position.
    b. I felt I was really accomplishing things in my ministry.
    c. I (did not) feel bored and constrained by the limits of this church position, resources or people.
    d. I have been successful in overcoming difficulties and obstacles in my ministry.

standardized item alpha: **clergywomen .61   clergymen .64**

CORRELATIONS AMONG INDICES and Other Indicators

	(good to poor) Boundary Maintenance		(good to poor) Overall Health		(strong to weak) Self-Concept	
	Women	Men	Women	Men	Women	Men
Overall Health	.40	.40	—	—	50	56
Self Concept	.20	23	50	56	—	—
Equity: Suff.Paid.	15	20	.21	.28	.26	31
Den.Exec. Recognizes						
Leadership Ability	n.s.	.07	.15	.23	.17	.22
In Clergy Support Grp	n.s.	n.s.	.11	n.s.	.07	.07
Considering Leaving	-.18	-.24 -.42	-.50	-.42	-.44	
Left Church Employ	n.s.	n.s.	n.s.	n.s.	.13	.10

TABLE III
CORRELATIONS

	Seriously Considered Leaving Church For Other Career		Not CHURCH Employed At All	
	WOMEN	**MEN**	**WOMEN**	**MEN**
Dropout: Not Church Employed	.16	.18	—	—
Age Began Seminary (young to old)	.21	n.s.	n.s.	n.s.
Ability to Set Boundaries (negative = inability)	-.14	-.22	n.s.	n.s.
Good Overall Health (negative = burnout)	-.39	-.48	n.s.	n.s.
Strong Profes. Self Concept (negative = weak)	-.40	-.43	-.10	-.09
Felt Suffic. Compensated for Ministerial Work (negative=insufficently)	-.21	-.24	n.s.	-.06
Ease of Getting Another Ch Position Slightly Better (negative = difficult)	-.15	-.12	-.12	-.1
Den. Executive Recognizes Your Leadership Abilities (negative = not well)	-.17	-.20	-.15	-.12
Member: Clergy Support Group (negative = not member)	-.15	-.11	-.16	-.16

All correlations over .08 significant at .001 level

T A B L E   IV
MAJOR INFLUENCES ON DROPOUT

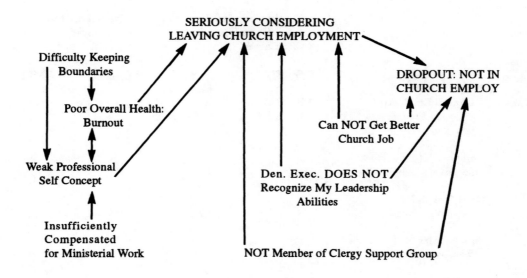

Beta's

	Seriously Considering Leaving the Ordained Ministry		No Longer Any Paid Regular Church Work	
	Women	Men	Women	Men
Seriously Considered Leaving Ordained Min.			.11	.13
Age At Seminary	.15	n.s.	n.s.	n.s.
Health-Burnout Sc.	-.21	-.32	n.s.	n.s.
Suff. Paid Min. Wk.	-.11	-.08	n.s.	n.s.
Easy Get Bet.Ch. Job	-.07	n.s.	-.08	-.07
Abilities Recognized Well by Denom. Exec.	-.06	-.06	-.06	-.06
Strong Profes. Self-Concept	-.21	-.21	n.s.	n.s.
Member of Clergy Support Groups	-.07	-.07	-.14	-.11
MULTIPLE R	.50	.54	.24	.22
Multiple R sq	.25	.29	.06	.05

GENDER ROLE EDUCATION IN SUNDAY SCHOOL

Gail Murphy-Geiss

Iliff School of Theology
University of Denver

Introduction

About two years ago, my then 4 year old daughter came home from Sunday School, eager to share what she had learned that morning, proudly announcing that Adam had named all of the animals. Teaching Feminist Theology at the time, I quickly added that Eve may have helped. My daughter responded firmly that Adam had done it alone because Eve was not smart enough. Her teacher had said so. Needless to say, we continued the discussion. This was my first overt awareness that my female child was learning about her gender's secondary status in Sunday School, the place where we learn what is sacred. I then began to more seriously study the materials she brought home and regularly ask questions about what was taught.

Again, my awareness was peaked during last December's Christmas pageant. A real baby was "playing" the part of Jesus, and he started to cry. Unable to console him, the girl playing Mary handed the baby to the boy playing Joseph, and went out into the congregation to find the real mother who had his bottle. For those few minutes, we were left with a nativity scene that consisted only of Joseph holding the baby Jesus. I felt jarred out of my pageant complacency. Had I ever seen Joseph holding the baby Jesus, all by himself? I was sure I had not, and began to look at the nativity images all around, especially in Sunday School materials. Indeed, whenever Joseph held Jesus, which was not often, Mary was also holding him in a kind of joint effort. I began to wonder what these kind of images do to the developing gender notions of children in Sunday School.

Even more recently, my daughter, now 6, brought home from Sunday School a page to color which she had not finished in church. Two years had gone by since our first discussion, and my attention had waned. In looking at the picture, I saw only boys gathered around a rabbi during what was supposed to be Jesus' time. I asked my daughter if it bothered her that there were no girls pictured. She responded that there were girls in the picture, but when I asked her to identify one, she could not. Still, she maintained that girls were present because "Everyone looked the same back then." Why was she seeing androgynous figures where I saw males? What were these Sunday School materials trying to communicate? Despite that, how were they perceived?

My initial curiosity has grown into this initial study of pictures in Kindergarten and 1st grade Sunday School curricula and their part in gender role education and sacralization. Based on these three experiences and the cursory observations to which they led me, I hypothesized the following:

1. Sunday School materials depict largely traditional gender roles.

2. More conservative publishers depict more people in traditional gender roles than do more liberal publishers.

3. Sunday School materials depict largely traditional family scenes.

4. More conservative publishers depict more overtly traditional family scenes than do more liberal publishers as a way of encouraging girls to see their roles as wives and mothers as sacred.

This paper will show how two of these hypotheses can be accepted as correct (#1 and #2 partially), but also how the materials are more complex than initially expected and consequently, how gender role counting can be confusing. As a result, I will share both the quantitative results obtained through content analysis as well as some qualitative observations. Neither one alone fully represents the reality of these materials.

Review of the Literature

Although gender role analysis has been done with children's secular education (e.g., Weitzman, Eifler, Hokada and Ross, 1972; Stacey, Béreaud and Daniels, 1874; Andrée 1986; Scrase 1993), I could find no previous work that specifically analyzed Sunday School curricula for their depictions of gender roles. Still, much has been done that provides a foundation. One unique work that specifically deals with pictorial representations of gender in religion is Thomas Boslooper's *The Image of Woman* published by the Unification Church (1980). Because gender relations are significant to that group, this book is an attempt to show the historical gender "errors" in Christianity and bring us to the present, when women can be spiritually powerful through Unification Theology. His analysis is helpful in that it brings together religious art and theology which is usually done by artists rather than theologians, and certainly not Sunday School writers, editors, teachers, etc., but the specifics of his critique are not pertinent here.

More helpful and much more common is the mass of work within feminist theology in which scholars cite the bias, and even harm done by solely male-centered religion. Two of the classic works in this field continue to be Mary Daly's *Beyond God the Father (1973)* and Rosemary Radford Ruether's *Sexism and God-Talk* (1983). In these works and many others (e.g. Trible, 1978; Christ and Plaskow, 1979; Fiorenza, 1984; Russell, 1985; McFague, 1987; et. al.) , patriarchal Christianity is deconstructed especially looking at language and theology, but only peripherally through pictures.

Another bank of information is that of secular feminist studies. The history of women's roles, both in religious communities and without is covered in Elise

Boulding's *The Underside of History* (1976) and Averil Cameron and Amélie Kuhrt's *Images of Women in Antiquity* (1983). These works, and others like them, are more likely to deal with pictorial imagery because often, that is the only resource available. For example, Egyptian hieroglyphics often provide the richest source of information on women's everyday lives in ancient Egypt. These sources are helpful in studying Biblical scenes as depicted in the Sunday School materials, but they are not as useful in analyzing modern scenes. They can provide a guide to gender roles for ancient women and men, both of whom were embodiments of deity.

Perhaps the most interesting array of work is that related to gender in general, especially Suzanne Kessler and Wendy McKenna's *Gender: An Ethnomethodological Approach* (1978), Joyce McCarl Nielsen's *Sex and Gender in Society* (1990), and Judith Lorber and Susan A. Farrell's *The Social Construction of Gender* (1991). These books, among others, question accepted and assumed gender roles and definitions such that the entire category of gender is deconstructed and possibly no longer needed. Kessler and McKenna were particularly helpful in setting forth the theoretical groundwork for this project, which will be discussed in the next section.

The last resources that were necessary for this study were those on content analysis. Most such analysis is done with words, which are relatively easy to count. A bit more tricky is that done with themes, in which the researcher must identify motifs, somewhat subjectively. Even less work has been done with only pictures. One very helpful resource was Liesbet van Zoonen's *Feminist Media Studies* (1994) because media often deals with many different genres, including pictures. While doing the actual data gathering, I noticed the limits of content analysis. Her work confirmed my suspicions which then led to the qualitative section.

Gender Learning and the Sacred

Feminist scholars have recently called into question the entire category of gender. If the Women's Movement has proven that women and men are social equals, why must there be two distinct social statuses (Lorber, 1991)? With the sole exception of pregnancy and childbirth, experts in many fields (e.g. history, psychology, biology, sociology, theology) have determined that women and men are more alike on the average, than different (Murphy-Geiss, 1995). Perhaps true equality will follow the widespread acceptance of this notion. But is an acceptance of such a basic understanding of social life really possible?

Gender, as a category, is everywhere, from birth to death. Babies are dressed in pink or blue, children are raised with gender appropriate toys and activities, adults take on gender roles in families, work, friendships, etc. and even death rates are gendered. It is a basic unit of life. I suspect that to mistake someone's gender would be more embarrassing to most people that to forget someone's name. Examples are too numerous to list.

What do we know about gender? First, it is known that children have fixed gender identities by about age 3 (Money and Eerhardt, 1972). Much of that identity is learned through children observing parents, and parents reinforcing appropriate behaviors in children. At age 3, one's own gender is known, and gender typing of others is becoming evident, but by age 6, such typing is strong and extremely dichotomous. Men are one way and women another, and the two can neither change nor mix (Kessler and McKenna, 1978). It is during these crucial years of 3-6 that much of the basic social construction of gender is learned.

It is for this reason that Sunday School materials for Kindergarten and 1st grade are so important. These are the years during which children decide what women are like and what men are like. Because they learn what they see, I focused only on pictures. Text is not as noticed at that age (or maybe any age). Recently, the 5 year old son of a local clergywoman was shocked to see a visiting pastor who was a man. The child did not know men could be ministers, only having seen his mother. It was for this reason that I chose to look at this age group in particular.

Durkheim's analysis of the sacred and the profane is also important to this study. In *The Elementary Forms of the Religious Life* (1915), Durkheim follows the process by which mundane objects become sacred for people, taking on special qualities such as power and immutability. It is due to this sacred quality that gender roles learned in Church may have greater power than those learned elsewhere, and would be the slowest to change. If the Church is truly interested in gender equality (this may not be true, and would at least differ by denomination), can they continue to cling to traditional gender roles, suggesting, or overtly teaching that they are ordained by God?

Even though some churches talk of liberation and social change, it is more likely that Durkheim's analysis is correct: the Church, as the keeper of the sacred, is a powerful entity resistant to much change. One such area of tradition maintenance is gender roles. If the Church wants to maintain traditional gender roles, it would follow that they might contribute to gender learning through providing appropriate models for society. The 4 hypotheses for this study are based on these assumptions derived largely from both Kessler and McKenna, and Durkheim.

Method and Data Collection

Content analysis seemed the best way to begin to study written Sunday School materials. My goal was to determine what publishers seem to be trying to communicate. This does not account for teaching styles nor the perceptions of the children, so we cannot yet know if the communication intended is that which is received. Through content analysis, only the resources themselves are accessible. Also, we cannot know for sure if gender learning is an overt goal of the writers and editors. Limiting the research to the content of the materials permits us only to count what is evident, not motivations or intentions.

Because I am most familiar with United Methodist materials, I easily chose Cokesbury as a sampling unit. Because there is a great debate in many churches over the decision to use Cokesbury or David C. Cook resources, that was the next obvious choice. The format used by these two large publishers is identical, making for ease of comparison. Beyond these two, I wanted a selection of both liberal and conservative resources, so I went to the professional Christian Education Director at my church for a list of possibilities. I also visited Christian bookstores and a Seminary library to make sure I was covering all the biggest publishers. My list was consciously limited to Kindergarten and 1st grade materials so I could focus on early and non-readers by studying only pictures while disregarding the text. I assume many children do that very thing. I also chose to use only those made since 1991, focusing on the last 5 years. This was simply to make sure all resources were from the same period. I accidentally stumbled upon some Cokesbury materials from the 1960's - 1980's, so one from each decade was analyzed for the purpose of a small historical comparison. A third limitation was simply what was available. Some libraries and publishers keep back supplies of materials and others only what is current. Some publishers sell or donate single copies of their materials, while others require larger orders. Eventually, I was able to obtain those listed in Table 1. Because of all of these limitations, it is not a random sample, but I am certain that it represents all that is currently available.

Table 1: Titles of Curricula and Publishers

	Title/Publisher	Date	Age Level
1)	Christ in Our Life/Concordia	Spring 1995	Kindergarten
2)	Bible in Life/David C. Cook	Fall 1991	Primary
3)	Bible in Life/David C. Cook	Spring 1992	Primary
4)	Bible in Life/David C. Cook	Fall 1993	Primary
5)	Bible Time/Scripture Press	Fall 1994	4s & 5s
6)	Primary Days/Scripture Press	Spring 1994	Primary
7)	Jesus is Our Leader/Standard	Winter 1995	4s & 5s
8)	Jesus is Our Leader/Standard	Winter 1995	Primary
9)	Witness/Augsburg Fortress	Spring 1995	Kindergarten
10)	Witness/Augsburg Fortress	Spring 1995	Primary
11)	Invitation/Cokesbury	Winter 1993	5 - 6
12)	Invitation/Cokesbury	Spring 1993	5 - 6
13)	Invitation/Cokesbury	Summer 1993	5 - 6
14)	Invitation/Cokesbury	Fall 1993	5 - 6
15)	Invitation/Cokesbury	Spring 1994	5 - 6
16)	New Invitation/Cokesbury	Winter 1995	5 - 6
17)	Old Cokesbury	Fall 1981	Kindergarten
18)	Old Cokesbury	Fall 1971	Kindergarten
19)	Old Cokesbury	Fall 1961	Kindergarten
20)	Word Among Us/United Church	Fall 1994	Young Children
21)	Word Among Us/United Church	Winter 1995	Elementary

I grouped them into three major sets for ease of analysis. The materials from 1961, 1971, and 1981 made a group called "old" resources (#17-19). The others were divided based on publisher, philosophy, and theology, into "conservative" (#1-8) and "liberal" (#9-16, 20, 21). As it turned out, the mainline Churches published the "liberal" materials (United Methodist Church, Evangelical Lutheran Church in America, and United Church of Christ) and the other publishers the "conservative."

To define the first set of variables (hypotheses 1 & 2), I leafed through all of the resources, looking at the roles of men and women. Calling them "traditional" and "non-traditional" was not sufficient. I chose some of the sub-variables (e.g. nurturing children, cooking, clergy, soldier) at that time, and others surfaced later on. Overall, I was interested in the total numbers of people pictured and the percentages that were engaged in gender traditional and non-traditional behaviors. Attention to sub-variables helped to protect the reliability of the study, in that results were then easily checked against the findings of two research assistants.

It also became clear that two further specifications were necessary. The first was a distinction between Biblical scenes and modern scenes. Because one would expect more males in general, and more traditional gender roles in the Biblical scenes, I felt that the data would be clearer if these two were separated. Second was the division between adults and children. It became clear that children have unique gender roles that do not always match with those of adults. For example, more young boys are pictured doing household chores, such as helping with dinner than adult men. Similarly, young girls are pictured playing organized sports (along with boys), whereas among adults, I found only men. This distinction was made for clarity.

The other set of variables (hypotheses 3 & 4) involved looking at entire scenes. Scenes were noted if they were "family scenes" as opposed to any other possibility. Then, the families were further split into "traditional," "non-traditional," and "unknown." There were so few non-traditional and unknown that these were later combined, but it was good to discover that after the fact than to have to go back and divide them. The entire list of sub-variables with brief explanations is found in Table 2.

Although the sample is relatively small considering the amount of Christian Education curricula that is printed, the materials chosen provided quite a lot of pictures for analysis. There were 21 different resources used, each 12 weeks in length. 19 of the 21 resources were 4 pages in length for each week, and 2 resources had 2 pages each week. This made for 960 pages of curricula which depicted 1119 scenes and 3902 people. To begin to get a handle on the data, once counted, simple percentages were taken of each variable. Then, t-tests and ANOVAs were run for significance and variance.

Before moving to the quantitative results, let me say a bit about the qualitative method. In "counting heads" and trying to be completely objective, it became clear that some messages could not be counted. In fact, in some cases, counting may have actually created data that contradicted the purpose of the chosen variables.

Table 2: Sub-variables Defined

MT/FNT	*Male Traditional/Female Non-traditional*
MT/FNT 1	business/professional
MT/FNT 2	sports/boys toys
MT/FNT 3	tools/yard work
MT/FNT 4	heavy work/train or truck driver
MT/FNT 5	soldier/ruler/hunter (associated with weapons)
MT/FNT 6	farmer/fisher/shepherd
MT/FNT 7	clergy
MT/FNT 8	obvious family leadership with spouse present
MT/FNT 9	one gender learning groups
FT/MNT	*Female Traditional/Male Non-traditional*
FT/MNT 1	nurturing child (feeding or comforting; not just talking)
FT/MNT 2	food/water collection or preparation
FT/MNT 3	cleaning for family (not simply for self)
FT/MNT 4	crafts (sewing, knitting, etc.)
FT/MNT 5	teacher
FT/MNT 6	ballet/girls toys
FT/MNT 7	obvious deference to other gender
FT/MNT 8	crying (babies excluded)
FT/MNT 9	beauty concerns

For example, a female police officer was counted as a "professional woman," but it is interesting to note that she is pictured as a crossing guard for a group of children. Is she then breaking out into a non-traditional role for women, or is she maintaining the traditional role of caretaker for children? In the same way, a number of male clergy were pictured teaching children. Are they traditional male clergy, non-traditional male teachers, or non-traditional caretakers for children? Although the numbers are interesting, I couldn't help but notice, right from the start, weaknesses in the method of content analysis. Not only does it give precedence to manifest content, ignoring what is latent, it assumes that the chosen variables are good indicators of meaning (van Zoonen, 1994:73). To compensate, I kept a list of observations throughout so as to provide a kind of corrective to the statistics. In fact, in the long run, this may be a more valid method for analysis of Sunday School materials. Still, I think both are interesting, and probably necessary.

Quantitative Results

In identifying traditional and non-traditional roles, it became immediately clear that most people were doing non-gendered activities, that is neither traditional nor non-traditional. Of the 3902 people pictured in all sources, only 692 (5.6%) were involved in a gendered activity. This was not surprising, but it made for a relatively small sample overall.

To simplify matters, from here on, I will report only figures related to adults pictured. As mentioned, children were counted separately, but sharing those numbers as well would be too long for this paper. Because children's roles are more loosely defined and more fluid anyway, I will concentrate on adults whose roles are clearer.

Many more people were depicted as in traditional roles as opposed to non-traditional in all sources. Not including the old materials (because one would expect more traditional roles there) there were 465 (90%) adults depicted traditionally and only 54 (10%) depicted non-traditionally, a difference which is significant at the .05 level. This was true across the board. The resource with the most adults in non-traditional roles (16%) was #13 (Cokesbury, Summer '93) while at the other end, #7 (Standard, Winter '95) and #20 (United Church Press, Fall '94) had none. More specific breakdowns gave similar results. Biblical scenes depicted 31 (13%) non-traditional adults while modern scenes pictured 23 (14%). Men were shown in non-traditional roles in 38 cases (9%) and women in 16 (12%).

Table 3 lists the breakdown of raw data and percentages of the major variables, men and women in traditional and non-traditional roles. While much of it is interesting, because of the small sample mentioned earlier, only one variable shows a relationship of significance. In the modern pictures, there is a significant difference (at the .02 level) in the numbers of women depicted traditionally. 35% of the women pictured in conservative materials are in traditional roles, while this is true of only 12% in the liberal resources. Interestingly, the old materials fall in between at 21%. It may also be noteworthy that there were no people in non-traditional roles in the old materials while most of the recent publishers have shown at least one.

Tables 4 and 5 show the data for families and the breakdown of sub-variables, respectively. Once again, sample size prohibits statistical significance, but it was surprising that liberal resources depict more family scenes than conservative materials. On the other hand, of the family scenes pictured, conservative publishers are much more likely to portray traditional families overall. This was especially true of the Biblical scenes, which may carry more of a sacredness. In other words, modern families may be non-traditional, but God's intention, as known through the Bible is for traditional families. A larger sample will have to be pursued. The table which contains sub-variables is for information only.

After noticing the obvious lack of women clergy depicted in conservative materials (none) and the seemingly large number in the liberal materials (6 out of 16 clergy), Table 6 was conceived. Unfortunately, the sample afforded too few units for statistical support, but I suspect a larger sample would show figures consistent with

Table 3:
Percentages and (n)s for Adult Males & Females, Traditional & Non-traditional

	Conservative	Liberal	Old
Bible male adults	85% (689)	76% (577)	100% (61)
Bible female adults	15% (123)	24% (184)	0% (0)
Bible male traditional	25% (169)	25% (145)	20% (12)
Bible male non-traditional	1% (8)	3% (19)	0% (0)
Bible female traditional	19% (23)	15% (27)	0% (0)
Bible female non-traditional	2% (2)	1% (2)	0% (0)
Modern male adults	45% (94)	48% (121)	46% (70)
Modern female adults	55% (114)	52% (129)	54% (82)
Modern male traditional	22% (21)	20% (24)	26% (18)
Modern male non-traditional	5% (5)	5% (6)	0% (0)
Modern female traditional	35% (40)*	12% (16)*	21% (17)*
Modern female non-traditional	3% (3)	7% (9)	0% (0)

* $p < .05$

Table 4:
Percentages and (n)s for Family Scenes, Traditional and Not Traditional

	Conservative	Liberal	Old
Bible family scenes	3% (7)	10% (22)	0% (0)
Bible families - traditional	71% (5)	55% (12)	0% (0)
Bible families - not traditional	29% (2)	45% (10)	0% (0)
Modern family scenes	16% (43)	15% (38)	29% (36)
Modern families - traditional	49% (21)	50% (19)	47% (17)
Modern families - not traditional	51% (22)	50% (19)	53% (19)

these. Continuing to glance through additional conservative materials from David C. Cook, I still have found no clergywomen. What is also interesting is that the percentage of clergywomen depicted in the liberal resources (37.5%) is higher than the 11% found in the Church in the United States (*U.S. News & World Report* September 11, 1995). There seems to be a definite attempt to provide these models for children. Given these numbers, it is more likely that a child will see a clergywoman in his/her Sunday School materials than in the pulpit.

Table 5:
Raw Data for Male and Female Adults, Trad. and Non-trad. Sub-variables

	Conservative	Liberal	Old
total male traditional	21	24	18
male traditional 1	1	2	9
male traditional 2	3	1	0
male traditional 3	4	5	3
male traditional 4	5	2	1
male traditional 5	0	1	0
male traditional 6	2	2	1
male traditional 7	5	10	2
male traditional 8	1	1	2
total male non-traditional	5	6	0
male non-traditional 1	1	4	0
male non-traditional 2	1	1	0
male non-traditional 3	1	0	0
male non-traditional 5	2	1	0
total female traditional	40	15	17
female traditional 1	7	6	3
female traditional 2	7	4	8
female traditional 3	1	1	0
female traditional 4	1	0	0
female traditional 5	17	5	5
female traditional 7	1	0	1
female traditional 9	6	0	0
total female non-traditional	3	9	0
female non-traditional 1	2	2	0
female non-traditional 2	0	1	0
female non-traditional 3	1	0	0
female non-traditional 7	0	6	0

Table 6:
Percentages and (n)s for Modern Male and Female Clergy

	Conservative	Liberal
Male clergy	100% (5)	62.5% (10)
Female clergy	0% (0)	37.5% (6)

Qualitative Observations

In this section, I want to illustrate some examples of qualitative differences in the various resources that would lead me to accept or reject the hypotheses, in light of and in spite of the statistics. Most of these observations were made as I looked at the pictures and tried to fit them into my established code, seeing where things did not easily fit, or where presentations were different, even when numbers were not. Because of time constraints, I will share just a few examples.

First of all, it is not clear whether there are different standards for men and women in Biblical scenes versus modern scenes, regardless of the theological position of the curriculum. The Palm Sunday lesson of Augsburg-Fortress (#10) contains the only picture which included women in obviously covered and background positions. The women are pictured in Islamic veils, simply observing the procession. All participants are men and boys. Although this depiction may be realistic for the Biblical time and the culture, no other curriculum showed women in this way. On the other hand, Augsburg-Fortress also includes depictions of modern women include non-traditional roles, such as doctors.

Another scene from Augsburg-Fortress (9) depicts the very rare scene of a man alone caring for a baby, only found in the liberal materials. In a city park, the middle aged man is sitting on a park bench while holding on to a child's stroller. The only man caring for a child found in the conservative materials is from Concordia (1). A sick boy is laying on the sofa while a father figure is taking his temperature. Although non-traditional, he is not alone. The mother is standing by with a drink for the child and grandmother is on the phone. Still, both men were counted in the same category of MNT 1 (nurturing children) but qualitatively, there seems to be a difference.

As suspected, Mary usually holds Jesus, but in a few scenes, Joseph does hold the baby. In all of these scenes though, no matter what curriculum, Mary is close enough to intercede if necessary. She is so close that it is usually difficult to determine whether or not she is also holding the baby with him. No wonder my church's nativity scene looked unfamiliar!

Another aspect of Biblical scenes that was evident was the inclusion of women in traditionally male scenes. All resources tend to show the male disciples learning together with no women present, or just a few onlookers in the background. In a few cases, there seems to be an obvious attempt to include women where they are not usually assumed to have been. One scene from Invitation/Cokesbury (12) appears to depict disciples after the empty tomb is discovered. Women were likely to have been present according to the texts, but my analyses were based on visual reactions, excluding any text. The student may not know who is pictured. In fact, in a few discussions with 5 and 6 year olds, they often did not know if Jesus was in a picture or which person he was. So, in this case, although Jesus may be risen, one might think that Jesus is the man in the center (looks like the typical depiction: leader, youngish and bearded) and that he prayed with both the men and women who surround him. The problem for the quantitative section is that in this scene, no one was counted as non-traditional. That is to say, women disciples praying with Jesus were considered traditional. Overall, women in pray is not atypical, but pictured with Jesus as disciples may be worth noting. Perhaps in the future, Biblical scenes will require a different code than modern ones. Similarly, a man sewing in a modern scene is non-traditional, but in a Biblical scene, he is a traditional professional tentmaker.

Another scene shows a traditional church scene from a conservative publisher (#1 Concordia). Not only is the pastor male, but so are the ushers, and the organist is female. I would consider all of these traditional roles, but I counted only the pastor, according to my original plan. Cokesbury, a more liberal resource, included three scenes in explanation of baptism. One of those pictured is a clergywoman. It seems that an obvious attempt is made to show women clergy by picturing both men and women. Still this scene would have been counted as one female non-traditional and two male traditionals when clearly, the non-traditional character of the picture is predominant, especially when compared to the conservative resources which showed no female clergy at all.

An example from David C. Cook (#2) illustrates another possible confusion. It appears that a man and woman are working together at a tool bench in the garage or basement while a young boy looks on. Hence, the woman was counted as non-traditional. After reading the text though, one learns that the woman is simply helping to look for her husband's tools which the child has misplaced. To the child, this scene may appear non-traditional, but it may be unfair to judge the intentions of the publishers if not also reading the texts for clarification. The attempt to be objective and stick by a predetermined code may lead to confusing results in cases such as this.

Another example may also be understood in numerous ways. A busy street corner is depicted in David C. Cook, #4. At first, one notices the woman police officer who is stopping the traffic so that a group of children can cross the street. Upon looking further, one notices that the children are accompanied by a woman (traditional), that a man is walking beside a woman who is pushing a baby stroller (traditional), and that in a window, a man is leading a family in studying a book, presumably the Bible (again, traditional). While the woman is a police officer, her assignment is to cross children. Is she really a crossing guard? Also, note that in the same scene, three highly traditional groups are depicted. But this woman officer became one of only two professional women in the conservative materials. Perhaps judging entire scenes as traditional or non-traditional using a scale would afford more telling results. Unfortunately, this would be open to greater subjectivity as well.

Another helpful technique was to make a comparison between a conservative resource (David C. Cook, 1995) and a liberal resource (Cokesbury, 1995) in their depiction of the same lectionary text. (These particular resources were not tabulated with the quantitative data because they were discovered too late. Still, the illustration is pertinent). The Biblical story is about a woman healed by Jesus. The two figures represent the large, summary picture for the lesson in each case. The conservative materials show the healed woman, cooking a meal for Jesus, stressing the "happy dinner" after the healing and her role in cooking it. The liberal resource emphasizes the actual healing itself, showing the woman on a bed and Jesus touching her hand. Is it different to stress women as recipients of Jesus' ministry or as cooks? I believe it is, so comparing the exact same sets of curriculum which depict the same Scripture lessons can also be illuminating in terms of gender. Unfortunately, many sources don't use the lectionary, limiting the sample to those that do.

The next example shows only a personal opinion, but maybe it is more widely held. David C. Cook (#2) shows Adam and Eve, apparently awed by the creation. In my opinion, Eve looks like an idiot (cross-eyed at a butterfly), while Adam looks like a strong, powerful man, standing among the trees with larger animals such as mountain lions and zebras. How can these kinds of personal feelings be counted or studied objectively?

The final example is of a woman holding a child from both of the United Church Press resources (#20 & #21). Considering only the picture, it appears to be a traditional woman, nurturing a child, but the text compares her to God and Her comfort of Her children. Again, a confusing scene to count. Female divinity is about as non-traditional as it gets, but because I had not expected it, I had developed no way to measure it. Unfortunately, this particular scene represented a traditional woman according to my code. The distinction had to be picked out within qualitative analysis.

Conclusion

Hypothesis #1 is found to be correct. All Sunday School materials depict people in largely traditional gender roles, but only as opposed to non-traditional roles. Indeed, the greatest majority of people are depicted in non-gendered roles.

Hypothesis #2 is supported only for depictions of modern women. More conservative publishers depict more women in traditional roles than do liberal publishers, and even in greater numbers than the older liberal materials.

Hypothesis #3 is not supported. There are very few family scenes in any of the resources, both Biblical and modern. In addition, traditional family scenes only make up about half of those few family scenes overall (with conservative Bible families making up the high of 71%), but with such a small sample, nothing definitive can be said.

Hypothesis #4 is also insupportable. Although conservative materials depict almost 3/4ths of families as traditional, the overall numbers are too small to provide statistical confirmation.

More research is needed. In the future, I would suggest looking not only at pictures, but at text. The intentions of the publishers cannot be known otherwise.

Another interesting piece would be interviews with children to ascertain their perceptions of these materials. It would also be intriguing to watch the figures change over time. The few older materials which I happened upon should be expanded to include other publishers and many more years. Still, I would consider this study a first step, an attempt to create a code for content analysis that can now be improved upon as well as an indication that overall, (1) the Church does little toward the eradication of traditional gender roles in their Sunday School materials and that specifically, (2) women especially, are depicted traditionally, particularly in conservative resources.

References

Bible in life (Primary). Fall 1991. Elgin, IL: David C. Cook Pub. Co.

Bible in life (Primary). Spring 1992. Elgin, IL: David C. Cook Pub. Co.

Bible in life (Primary). Fall 1993. Elgin, IL: David C. Cook Pub. Co.

Bible in life: Stories (ages 4 & 5). 1995. Elgin, IL: David C. Cook Pub. Co.

Bible Time (4s & 5s). Fall 1994. Glen Ellyn, IL: Scripture Press.

Borrowdale, Anne. 1989. *A woman's work: Changing Christian attitudes.* London: SPCK.

Boslooper, Thomas. 1980. *The image of woman.* Barrytown, NY: Unification Theological Seminary.

Boulding, Elise. 1976. *The underside of history: A view of women through time.* Boulder, CO: Westview Press.

Cameron, Averil, and Amélie Kuhrt, eds. 1983. *Image of women in antiquity.* Detroit: Wayne State Univ. Press.

Christ in our life (Kindergarten). Spring 1995. St. Louis, MO: Concordia Pub. House.

Christ, Carol P., and Judith Plaskow, eds. 1979. *Womanspirit rising.* San Francisco: Harper & Row.

Daly, Mary. 1973. *Beyond God the father: Toward a philosophy of women's liberation.* Boston: Beacon Press.

Durkheim, Émile. 1915. *The elementary forms of the religious life: A study in religious sociology.* London: George Allen & Unwin, Ltd.

Fiorenza, Elizabeth Schüssler. 1984. *Bread not stone: The challenge of feminist biblical interpretation.* Boston: Beacon Press.

Holsti, Ole R. 1969. *Content analysis for the social science and humanities.* Reading, MA: Addison-Wesley Pub. Co.

Invitation (5-6). Winter 1993. Nashville, TN: Cokesbury.

Invitation (5-6). Spring 1993. Nashville, TN: Cokesbury.

Invitation (5-6). Summer 1993. Nashville, TN: Cokesbury.

Invitation (5-6). Fall 1993. Nashville, TN: Cokesbury.

Invitation (5-6). Spring 1994. Nashville, TN: Cokesbury.

Jesus is our leader (4s & 5s). Winter 1995. Cincinnati, OH: Standard Press.

Jesus is our leader (Primary). Winter 1995. Cincinnati, OH: Standard Press.

Kessler, Suzanne J., and Wendy McKenna. 1978. *Gender: An ethnomethodological approach.* Chicago: The Univ. of Chicago Press.

Lorber, Judith. 1991. Dismantling Noah's ark. In *The Social Construction of Gender,* ed. Judith Lorber and Susan A. Farrell, 355-369. Newbury Park, CA: Sage Publications, Inc.

Lorber, Judith, and Susan A. Farrell, eds. 1991. *The Social Construction of Gender.* Newbury Park, CA: Sage Publications, Inc.

McFague, Sallie. 1987. *Models of God: Theology for an ecological, nuclear age.* Philadelphia: Fortress Press.

Michel, Andrée. 1986. *Down with stereotypes! Eliminating sexism from children's literature and school textbooks.* Paris: UNESCO.

Money, J., and A. Eerhardt. 1972. *Man and woman/boy and girl.* Baltimore: Johns Hopkins Press

Murphy-Geiss, Gail E. 1995. Degendering motherhood. Paper read at 90th Annual Meeting of the American Sociological Association, 19-23 August, at Washington Hilton and Towers, Washington, D.C.

New Invitation (5-6). Winter 1995. Nashville, TN: Cokesbury.

New Invitation (5-6). 1995. Nashville, TN: Cokesbury.

Nielsen, Joyce McCarl. 1990. *Sex and gender in society: Perspectives on stratification.* Prospect Heights, IL: Waveland Press.

O'Faolain, Julia, and Lauro Martines. 1973. *Not in God's image.* NY: Harper & Row, Publishers, Inc.

Old Cokesbury (Kindergarten). Fall 1981. Nashville, TN: Cokesbury.

Old Cokesbury (Kindergarten). Fall 1971. Nashville, TN: Cokesbury.

Old Cokesbury (Kindergarten). Fall 1961. Nashville, TN: Cokesbury.

Primary Days (Primary). Spring 1994. Glen Ellyn, IL: Scripture Press.

Ruether, Rosemary Radford. 1983. *Sexism and God-talk: Toward a feminist theology.* Boston: Beacon Press.

Russell, Letty M. ed. 1985. *Feminist interpretation of the Bible.* Philadelphia: Westminster Press.

Scrase, Timlthy J. 1993. *Image, ideology and inequality: Cultural domination, hegemony and schooling in India.* New Delhi: Sage Publications.

Stacey, J., S. Béreaud, and J. Daniels. eds. 1974. *And Jill came tumbling after: Sexism in American education.* NY: Dell.

Trible, Phyllis. 1978. *God and the rhetoric of sexuality.* Philadelphia: Fortress Press.

U.S. News and World Report Outlook. September 11, 1995. *U.S. news and world report.* Washington, D.C.: U.S. News and World Report Inc.

van Zoonen, Liesbet. 1994. *Feminist media studies.* London: Sage Publications.

Van Leeuwen, Mary Stewart, Annelies Knoppers, Margaret L. Koch, Douglas J. Schuurman, and Helen M. Sterk. 1993. *After Eden: Facing the challenge of gender reconciliation.* Grand Rapids, MI: Wm. B. Eerdmans Pub. Co.

Weber, Robert Philip. 1985. *Basic content analysis.* Beverly Hills, CA: Sage Publications.

Weitzman, L., D. Eifler, E. Hokada, and C. Ross. 1972. Sex-role socialization in picture books for pre-school children. *American Journal of Sociology* 77/6 (May): 1125-1150.

Witness (Kindergarten). Spring 1995. Minneapolis, MN: Augsburg Fortress.

Witness (Primary). Spring 1995. Minneapolis, MN: Augsburg Fortress.

Women on Words and Images (WOWI). 1972. *Dick and Jane as vicitms: Sex stereotyping in children's readers.* Princeton: WOWI.

Word among us (Young Children). Fall 1994. Cleveland, OH: United Church Press.

Word among us (Elementary). Winter 1995. Cleveland, OH: United Church Press.

I AM WOMAN—"SPEAK LORD"

Margaret Roberts Wynne S.F.O.

Women in Religion

Considering the proposition of "Women and Religion," women are religion.

In Pagan times, early Greece, Rome, Third World Cultures—women were Goddesses of Love, Fertility, Agriculture, were sacrificial victims at altars of lust, fear, appeasement. Mono-theistic Religion defines her and defends her, and she defends it.

Hebrew women, honored and revered, impart to their children the practice of Judaism in domestic tradition and ritual feasts, despite constant threat, persecution, the victims of blind hate, through time and many cultures.

African mothers kept Faith through the devastation of hundreds of years of slavery, walking with Jesus, knowing that God was "Comin' for to carry me home." Spirituals, unique in the Afro-style, became the religious teaching tool of mammies.

Ireland's mothers involved her families in special devotions, the Rosary beads, Novenas, the Angelus, Grace at meals, prayer for the endangered or the dead, as well as faithful weekly Mass attendance, infant Baptism, the Eucharist, Confirmation in young adulthood, proper sacramental Matrimony—a life cycle of rituals and Sacraments, ever-consciously teaching Christ's lessons of Eternal Life.

Pioneer American women used small home pipe organs to keep alive the tradition of singing hymns and daily reading of the scriptures in the family.

But man, with his natural attributes as hunter-provider has often been absent or distant, remote from the family and community, despite the need for prompt, earnest, response to urgent needs both practical and spiritual.

Woman, therefore, as companion and assistant in a society made of, and for, men has been the constant, stable, if often invisible, parent-teacher-priestess. In partnership with God, parents produce and succor a domestic faith-community according to abilities, conviction and of opportunity.

This has been the classic model for Family and Faith through generations, but imperatives and social attitudes of today have altered Society values and practice.

Women's Place

For the 2000 year history of women in the church, her role was similar in religion to her lay role—subservient.

In religion, Women consecrated their lives to God, in adoration, evangelization, and works of charity, but under obedience to Pope and local bishop.

To be scientific, is to return to origin. God's purpose for Woman is to be companion and helpmate of Man. The original offense of humanity was Eve's ambition and her temptation of Adam to be "as God." Thus, women's place in religion is, at best, sensitive and delicate. When woman fulfills her God-given purpose she is His magnificent creation, but God's Will is the primary Plan.

When you realize that Christ chose his priesthood from ordinary working men of the everyday world, you know that he was "making a Statement" about the protection of the Home, Family and Faith, in the traditional hands of women. The women in his earthly entourage were His Blessed mother, relatives of His apostles, the converted sinner, Mary Magdalene.

Today, women have properly assumed leadership in Law, Government, Arts and Sciences, Education and Industry. Centuries of repression and social slavery, have been denounced and rejected by themselves and an enlightened humanity.

But in the enthusiasm and determination to correct ancient wrongs, a bogus effort to trade-off male and female characteristics and responsibilities has destroyed family and the Judeo-Christian Civilization. This cultural winter now envelopes every aspect of society: Infancy, Age, Government, Education, Medicine, Religion.

In its demise, "Woman's work" is shown to be as vital and sacred as Man's priesthood.

Female Priesthood

The term "Woman Priest" is an oxymoron, not limited to gender reference, but in the sense that Woman has always been in religious ministry, by gender-design, The only missing elements have been self-esteem and public recognition.

The depraved and pathetic condition of society today and the irrelevancy of Religion plainly demonstrate that Homemaking and Childcare is Ministry. (For want of a mother a child is lost; for want of a child, family is lost, for want of families the Church is lost.) The natural Woman *is* Religion.

If marriage, thus maternity, is her choice, it is the challenge of Today's Woman to match the inspired model of moral leadership in preserving the Faith bequeathed to her by her maternal ancestors, despite Reformation, Famine, Slavery, Holocaust, Depression or Disparity of Cult.

Great Women in Religion

Our earliest religious history—the Old Testament presents Woman in a secondary light—spouse, mother, temple maiden.

But, Anno Domini (A. D.,) God has honored Woman consistently through the centuries. Starting with his spouse/mother, Mary, of Nazareth, "our tainted Nature's solitary boost," final Holy Woman of the Old Testament, First Woman of the New Testament—the new Eve. She was created and pre-ordained by the Holy Trinity to represent humanity in the incarnation of Jesus. Her Fiat embraced the mundane and the glorious, joys and sorrows, Crucifixion of her God, her child, herself. She has shown Woman the meaning and cost of religious ministry.

Among the first Christians, women, often and usually, went to their death for witnessing and ministering the Faith to their families. It was said that the blood of such martyrs watered the seed of Christianity. Woman has always been at the heart of Religion.

Religious women formed communities from early Christianity. This consecrated Sisterhood dedicated their lives in Religion to nurture neglected people, body and soul, medically, educationally, and spiritually, without personal gain or honors—a civilizing, Peace-presence midst, hunger, ignorance and illness. This selfless devotion to God's work prepared a people for the Word of God and preservation of the Christian faith through generations.

In lay life, orphaned and rejected children have been lovingly cared for and trained by unlettered grandmothers, maiden aunts, older sisters, nannies, housekeepers—perhaps a single light and link to Faith, often in a dearth of clergy. Only in recent times has religion taken on the aspect of "higher learning."

In practice , if not in theory, Woman has brought boys to priesthood and the Episcopacy, Cardinalate, Papacy—Sainthood. Christianity honors women in Religion throughout its 2000 year history, as Saints, models and teachers of Faith.

ST. HELENA 250-330 A. D. Mother of the Emperor Constantine of the Holy Roman Empire. She was born a pagan, converted her family as Christian; at the age of 80, found the True Cross of Jesus in the Holy Land, built basilicas on the Mount of Olives and Bethlehem; aided the poor, prisoners and soldiers.

ST. MONICA 331-87 A. D. mother of St. Augustine, converted her husband and prayed for 30 years to influence her son, Augustine's conversion. He has been a pillar of the church through the ages, as a result of her example and efforts.

ST. CATHERINE OF SIENA 1337-80 A. D. She was born of a well-to-do family— 24th child—resisted parent's wish for her marriage. Entered religious life as result of very early mystical experience; endured diabolical attacks and dry spiritual periods; was a hospital Nurse in cancer and leprosy cases. She advised Pope Gregory to return the Papacy to Rome from Avignon, France. In 1970, Pope Paul VI declared her a Doctor of the church.

ST. TERESA OF AVILA 1515-82 A. D. She was the first woman to be declared Doctor of the Church, in 1970 by Pope Paul VI. She was a Carmelite Order nun who reformed and restructured women's life in religion, against strong opposition. She authored books and treatises which are as important today as at her time.

ST. JOAN OF ARC 1412-31 A.D. Religious Patroness of France.She literally took up arms at 14 years old leading a war for restoration of Peace and Justice for her country, led by her inner "voice." At only 19, she was burned at the stake, falsely accused of heresy and witchcraft; 25 years later she was cleared of the charges.

QUEEN ISABELLA of the 15th Century Spain has not been called a saint, but her Faith inspired her to commission Christopher Columbus to explore and push the outer limits of Religious evangelism to the New World—North and South America.
Woman, in her own time and place, has inestimable power to influence future Religion/Church.

GOLDA MEIR as Prime Minister of the new state of Israel placed priority on politics, in which case Religion is Politics.

QUEEN ELIZABETH II, of present day England and therefore, head of state Religion, the Episcopal Church, is titular leader only; her religious leadership seems confined to personal example—a witness for millions of faithful followers, nonetheless.

INDIRA GANDHI, esteemed daughter of the great Indian religious leader, Mahatma Gandhi, ruled as prime minister and religious leader, finally paying the price: assassination.

Today the humble nun, *MOTHER TERESA* of Calcutta, India, performs the miracle of nourishing hordes of rejected humans, around the world, where church and government failed or cowered. She says that "feeding their souls" is a greater need than food, which she supplies along with medicine and shelter. Love is the real hunger.
And, reaching the zenith of Evangelization, is *MOTHER ANGELICA*, out of the cloister, to feed the souls of mankind, via TV cable and radio, on her E.W.T.N. (Eternal Word Television Network),transmitting Religion to millions, via satellite. No man founded or funded this pioneering thrust into religious cyberspace. God inspires Woman to her full potential in his creative plan. There is no greater glory.
Priesthood is *God's* plan for spiritual *Fatherhood*——in His image and likeness, like Adam.

Each of you is a son of God because of your faith in Christ Jesus. All of you who have been baptized in Christ have clothed yourselves with him. *There does not exist among you* Jew or Greek, slave or freeman, *male or female.* All are one in Christ Jesus. Further more, *if you belong to Christ* you are descendants of Abraham, which *means you inherit all* that was promised.

(Galatians. 3:26-29)

In conclusion, there is no question concerning Woman in Religion. God himself has *pre*-ordained Woman for his highest, holiest work; sustenance and evangelization of mankind. Woman's response must be Samuel's : "Speak Lord, your servant is listening."

* * * * *

Afterthought

Not everyone can be First born and each person in a family has individual importance, purpose, advantage. With caring parents, no family position is prime for Love.

The older, stronger child has only more responsibility—accountability. Succeeding children have the duty of cooperation and constructive help, each according to ability. So, with Adam and Eve—male and female—First born prototype and new-and-improved Second born.

Most women, even the "average" woman, admires and loves her God, her father, her brother, her husband, her spiritual leader—rabbi, minister, priest. As a result the average woman prefers and expects male leadership.

It would be an emasculated, destitute Church without God-given, inspired male priesthood. There is no question of Woman's ability, inspiration, desire. *Her* mandate is to *Mother*: nourish, teach, cooperate, in the real world and the Church.

June 28, 1995

References .

Religion: Doctrine and Practice—Francis B. Cassidy, S.J. 1934
Good News Bible—Study Edition 1979 New Testament of The Jerusalem Bible 1967.
Religions of the World Made Simple—John Lewis, BSO. Ph.D. Marley College, Oxford University, England 1958.
Dictionary of Saints-Abridged Edition—John J. Delaney 1983.

ABOUT THE AUTHORS

RÉGINE AZRIA is a researcher at the Centre National de la Recherche Scientifique in Paris and teaches classes in the Sociology of Judaism at the Institut catholique de Paris and at the University of Lausanne. She is a member of the *Centre d'Etudes Interdisciplinaires des Faits Réligieux* and co-editor of the *Archives de Sciences Sociales des Réligions* (Paris). The author of numerous articles on contemporary Jewry and Judaism, her new book is called *Le judaisme*. Paris, ed. la Decouverte (coll. Reperes). Her work is also published in *Identites réligieuses en Europe*, sous la direction de Grace Davie and Daniele Hervieu-Leger, Paris, ed. la Decouverte, 1996 (coll. Recherches) and *Les nouvelles manieres de croire*, sous la direction de Leila Babes, Paris, les editions de l'Atelier, 1996.

STUART Z. CHARMÉ, Ph.D., is Associate Professor of Religion at Rutgers University (Camden). He was trained in "Religion and Psychological Studies" at the University of Chicago Divinity School. He has written two books on identity and the construction of self and another based on the work of Jean-Paul Sartre. His present research deals with the impact of gender and multiculturalism on questions of religious and ethnic identity in children, with special attention to the area of Jewish identity.

TERESA DONATI received her BA from Barnard College, her MA and Ph.D. from Columbia University. She is Professor of Sociology at Fairleigh Dickinson University, Teaneck campus. Her courses include: Sociology of Religion, Jewish-American Ethnicity, Ecology and Society (which has a strong philosophical/religious literature component). Her previous work includes "Hiding the Priest," a study of women who marry or have relationships with Roman Catholic priests and "Phantom Triads," a study of spousal differences in Jewish observance and the consequences, after divorce, on Bar and Bat Mitzvah.

SUSAN A. FARRELL is Assistant Professor of Sociology in the Behavioral Sciences and Human Services Department of Kingsborough Community College, CUNY, in Brooklyn, NY. Her work on Women-Church grows out of a wider research question on the interconnections between religion, gender, sexuality, and ethics which formed the basis for her dissertation *Sexuality, Gender, and Ethics: The Social Construction of Feminist Ethics in the Roman Catholic Church* (Ann Arbor, MI: University Microfilms International, 1992). She is the co-editor with Judith Lorber of *The Social Construction of Gender* (Newbury Park, CA: Sage) in which she has an essay "'It's Our Church, Too!' Women's Position in the Roman Catholic Church Today." She is currently at work on a book on *Women-Church* a multi-organizational group working for change in the Roman Catholic Church.

RICHARD FLORY is Assistant Professor of Sociology at Biola University. His research interests include religion and social change in the United States, in particular, Fundamentalism and Evangelicalism. His current research examines the relationship between the industrialization of the Pacific Coast of the United States and the rise of Protestant Fundamentalism in Southern California.

DON HUFFORD is an Associate Professor of Education at Kansas Newman College, Wichita, KS. He has a Ph.D. in Foundations of Education with a minor concentration in Religion from the University of Kansas. He also studied at the graduate level at Southern Methodist University, Boston University School of Theology, and McCormick Seminary in Chicago. Prior to becoming a college teacher, he was an administrator for residential treatment programs for children and adolescents in Illinois and Kansas and the director of a Settlement House in Boston.

ANNA KARPATHAKIS is an Assistant Professor of Sociology at Nebraska Wesleyan University in Lincoln, NB. Her research focuses on the Greek American population in the New York City area. She also studies recently arrived Greek immigrants. She's currently editing a book on religion in New York City with Tony Carnes. In addition, she's editing a collection of papers from a conference on the Greek American Family. With Jean Belhkier, she is co-editing a Race, Class, and Gender text-reader.

J. SHAWN LANDRES is a doctoral student and Regents Special Fellow in the Department of Religious Studies, University of California, Santa Barbara, writing his dissertation on authenticity and responsibility as theoretical problems for the sociology of religion. From October, 1996, he is the Keith Murray Senior Scholar at Lincoln College, University of Oxford, in Social Anthropology. He has published widely for both academic and general readers, including another article on gender and religion, "Symbolic Subject, Subjected Symbol: Mizuko Kuyo, Gender, and the Social Order in Japan" which appeared in 1996 in the *Journal of Contemporary Religion*. An expanded version of the chapter in this volume will appear in Randall Balmer and J. Shawn Landres, eds., *Evangelicalism, Gender, and Sexuality* (forthcoming, 1997).

ADAIR LUMMIS (Ph.D. Columbia University, 1979) is a Faculty Research Associate at the Center for Social and Religious Research, Hartford Seminary, Hartford, Connecticut. She is a coauthor of three books: with Jackson Carroll and Barbara Hargrove, *Women of the Cloth: New Opportunities for Churches*. Harper and Row, 1983; with Yvonne Haddad, *Islamic Values in American Life*. Oxford University

Press, 1987; with Miriam Therese Winter and Allison Stokes, *Defecting in Place: Women Claiming Responsibility for Their Own Spiritual Lives.* Crossroad, 1994. Her paper in this volume is based on a portion of the data collected for a large study of clergy women and men in fifteen denominations. A book on the whole study will be published under the following authorship and title: Barbara Brown Zikmund, Adair T. Lummis and Patricia M.Y. Chang, *An Uphill Calling: Clergy Women and Men in the Contemporary Protestant Church.* (forthcoming 1997, John Knox/Westminster).

GAIL MURPHY-GEISS is a PhD candidate in Religion and Social Change in the Joint program at the University of Denver and Iliff School of Theology. Her main research interest is religion, gender and "family values." Gail is an ordained United Methodist clergywoman who served 7 years in college chaplaincy before entering academia full-time.

MARGARET ROBERTS WYNNE was born in Cleveland, Ohio January 3,1923 to parents: George H. Roberts and Margaret Devine. She is called 'Margie" by family and closest friends. Educated in Cleveland Catholic Schools, she graduated Lourdes Academy where her favorite subjects were religion, history, English, art and music. She and her family experienced first hand the Great Depression and World War II. Her major employment was as a secretary in the civil service including the War Department, Cleveland Ordnance District and the Veterans Administration. Margaret was inspired by the distinguished career of her paternal grandaunt, Agnes Chute King of Cleveland, Buffalo and Ironton, Ohio, an eminent educator and lecturer, a pioneer Irish American writer and columnist in the IRISH WORLD in the 1920's-30s. Much of her work encompassed religious and cultural topics as well as novels. In 1946 Margaret married William A. Wynne. Within six years four daughters and two sons were born to them. Their family was completed by 1964 with two more sons and a daughter, nine in all: Joanne, Bill, Susan, Marcia, Rob, Donna, Patrick, Meg and Jay. Before marriage Margaret entered the Franciscan Third Order (now Secular Franciscan Order) for lay people living the gospel life in the world as St. Francis did. For a number of years she was Novice Director in the Blessed Giles Fraternity, Parma, Ohio. In 1969 Margaret's patriotic 100 word essay "What It Means To Be An American" took Grand Prize in a Cleveland radio contest. The Wynne clan now includes 22 grandchildren, Future-church of the third millennium.